THE ANCESTRAL PHILOSOPHY
Hellenistic Philosophy in
Second Temple Judaism

Essays of David Winston

edited by
Gregory E. Sterling

Brown Judaic Studies
Providence

THE ANCESTRAL PHILOSOPHY
Hellenistic Philosophy in Second Temple Judaism

Essays of David Winston

edited by
Gregory E. Sterling

Library of Congress Cataloging-in-Publication Data
Winston, David, 1927–
    The ancestral philosophy : Hellenistic philosophy in Second Temple Judaism /
essays of David Winston ; edited by Gregory E. Sterling.
       p. cm.— (Brown Judaic studies ; no. 331) (Brown Judaic studies. Studia Philonica
monographs ; 4)
    Includes bibliographical references and index.
    ISBN 1-930675-08-9 (cloth : alk. paper)
    1. Judaism—History—Post-exilic period, 586 B.C.–210 A.D. 2. Jews—Civilization—
Greek influences. 3. Philosophy, Ancient. 4. Hellenism. 5. Bible. O.T. Apocrypha. Wisdom
of Solomon—Criticism, interpretation, etc. 6. Philo, of Alexandria. I. Sterling, Gregory E.
II. Title. III. Series. IV. Series: Brown Judaic studies. Studia Philonica monographs ; 4

BM176.W56 2001
181'06—dc21   2001043435

08 07 06 05 04 03 02 01   5 4 3 2 1

Printed in the United States of America
on acid-free paper

THE ANCESTRAL PHILOSOPHY
Hellenistic Philosophy in
Second Temple Judaism

Essays of David Winston

Program in Judaic Studies
Brown University
Box 1826
Providence, RI 02912

BROWN JUDAIC STUDIES

Series Editors 2001–
David C. Jacobson
Ross S. Kraemer
Saul M. Olyan

Series Editor 1991–2001
Shaye J. D. Cohen

Number 331
Studia Philonica Monographs 4

THE ANCESTRAL PHILOSOPHY
*Hellenistic Philosophy in
Second Temple Judaism*

Essays of David Winston

edited by
Gregory E. Sterling

STUDIA PHILONICA MONOGRAPHS

STUDIES IN HELLENISTIC JUDAISM

The Studia Philonica Monographs series accepts monographs in the area of Hellenistic Judaism, with special emphasis on Philo and his *Umwelt*. Proposals for books to be published in the Monographs series should be sent to Prof. David M. Hay, Coe College, Cedar Rapids, IA 52402, U.S.A.

Article-length contributions should be sent to Prof. Gregory E. Sterling, Co-Editor, The Studia Philonica Annual, 137 O'Shaughnessy, University of Notre Dame, Notre Dame, IN 46556. Books for review in the Annual should be sent to Alan Mendelson, Book Review Editor, Department of Religious Studies, McMaster University, Hamilton, Ontario, L8S 4K1, CANADA.

Contributors are requested to observe the "Instructions to Contributors" located at the end of the volume. These can also be consulted on the Annual's website: http://www.leidenuniv.nl/philosophy/studia_philonica/. Articles which do not conform to these instructions cannot be accepted for inclusion.

CONTENTS

Preface

It is well known that when Greeks first encountered Jews they compared them to philosophers. This was particularly true of Greeks who were themselves philosophers. Theophrastus, the successor of Aristotle at the Lyceum, was the first to make such a comparison. In his work *On Piety*, he described Jewish practices through the categories of natural theology: "since they are philosophers by race, they speak to one another about God and at night make a study of the stars."[1] The Peripatetic's interest in Jewish theism suggests that he found something intriguing about their beliefs; perhaps he knew that the Jews were aniconic monotheists.[2] The same perception probably lies behind the statement of Megasthenes, the philosopher-ambassador of Seleucus Nicator, who thought that the speculations about nature by the Brahmans and Jews proved that there were philosophers outside of Greece.[3] Clearchus of Soli also associated the Jews with India.[4] In an anecdote that he attributed to Aristotle, Clearchus claimed that the Jews descended from Indian philosophers. The basis for this view was a chance encounter in Asia between Aristotle and a certain Jew who "was a Hellene not only in speech but in his soul." The proof of this was in the content of his speech. Clearchus did not specify what this was, but according to Josephus who preserved the fragment, he went on to describe the "endurance" (καρτερία) and "moderation" (σωφροσύνη) of the man.[5] The inclusion of two of the four cardinal virtues suggests that his interest in Jewish views extended beyond metaphysics to include ethics. All three

---

[1] Theophrastus, *De pietate* in Porphyry, *Abst.* 2.26 in M. Stern, *Greek and Latin Authors on Jews and Judaism* (3 vols.; Jerualem: Israel Academy of Sciences and Humanities, 1974) 4 (1:10-12), hereafter abbreviated *GLAJJ*.

[2] So W. Jaeger, "Greeks and Jews: The First Greek Records of Jewish Religion and Civilization," *JR* 18 (1938) 133. Jaeger argued that Theophrastus knew the work of Hecataeus of Abdera (pp. 134-43), who did discuss the Jewish understanding of God (Diodorus Siculus 40.3.4 [*GLAJJ* 11 {1:26-35}]). On the issue of Theophrastus' source see the discussion and bibliography in G. E. Sterling, *Historiography and Self-definition: Josephos, Luke-Acts and Apologetic Historiography* (NovTSup 64; Leiden: E. J. Brill, 1992) 77-78.

[3] Megasthenes in Clement, *Strom.* 1.15.72.5 (*GLAJJ* 14 [1:45-46]).

[4] Jaeger, "Greeks and Jews," 132 n. 14, argued that Clearchus was dependent on Megasthenes. Stern, *GLAJJ*, 1:45, rejected this source identification since Megasthenes mentioned the Brahmans and Clearchus the Calani. It is probable that Clearchus is independent and that both reflect the interest of Peripatetics in Eastern theology.

[5] Clearchus of Soli, *De somno* 1 in Josephus, *C. Ap.* 1.176-83 (*GLAJJ* 15 [1:47-52]).

Greek authors reflect the interest that Greek philosophers had in Eastern religions and the conviction that there was an affinity between Hellenistic philosophy and Jewish religion.

Jewish authors made the same point, although the majority of the evidence we have is from the Roman period. Philo spoke of his "ancestral philosophy"[6] and presented Jewish groups such as the Therapeutae and Essenes as philosophers.[7] Josephus similarly spoke of an "ancestral philosophy"[8] and presented the Pharisees, Sadducees, and Essenes as the three philosophical traditions of Judaism.[9] The author of 4 Maccabees likewise called Judaism a philosophy.[10]

Were such identifications and presentations merely rhetorical devices that were designed to make one of the peoples of the East intelligible to the larger Graeco-Roman world or were there real similarities between Hellenistic philosophy and Judaism that created a dynamic between pagans and Jews? I am convinced that the latter is the case. On the one hand, there is a good deal of evidence that suggests a number of pagans found Jewish ethical monotheism attractive.[11] On the other hand, a number of Jews became so thoroughly steeped in Hellenistic philosophy that they were identified with specific schools–although the specific identifications are often problematic, e.g., Aristobulus was frequently called a Peripatetic;[12] Philo was labeled a Pythagorean in some texts[13] and a Platonist in the famous aphorism, "Either Plato philonizes or Philo platonizes."[14] The influence of Hellenistic philosophy on Judaism was, however, far more

---

6 *Somn.* 2.127; *Mos.* 2.216; *Contempl.* 28; *Legat.* 156. Cf. also *Legat.* 245, where it is labelled ἡ Ἰουδαϊκὴ φιλοσοφία.

7 *Contempl.* 26, 28, 67, 69, 89 and *Prob.* 88 respectively.

8 Josephus, *C. Ap.* 2.47; cf. also 1.54.

9 Josephus, *B.J.* 2.119-66; *A.J.* 18.11-25. On Josephus' use of philosophy to present Judaism see S. Mason, "'Should any wish to enquire further' (*Ant.* 1.28): The Aim and Audience of Josephus's *Judean Antiquities/Life*," in *Understanding Josephus: Seven Perspectives* (ed. S. Mason; JSPSup 32; Sheffield: Sheffield Academic Press, 1998), 87-95.

10 4 Macc 5:22.

11 L. Feldman, *Jew and Gentile in the Ancient World: Attitudes and Interactions from Alexander to Justinian* (Princeton: Princeton University Press, 1993), 177-415, has emphasized this more than any other recent scholar.

12 TT 2, 4, 8, 8a, 8b, 12, 13, 14, 14a, 15. Cf. also T 8c, where he is called *philosophus*. I have used the edition of C. R. Holladay, *Fragments from Hellenistic Jewish Authors, Volume 3: Aristobulus* (SBLTS 39; Atlanta; Scholars Press, 1995).

13 Clement, *Strom.* 1.360 (PCW 1.lxxxxv); 2.482P (PCW 1.lxxxxvi); Sozomon, *Hist. Eccl.* 1.12.9 (PCW 1.cvi). On this see D. T. Runia, "Why does Clement of Alexandria call Philo 'the Pythagorean'?" *VC* 49 (1995): 1-22.

14 This is first attested in Jerome, *Vir. ill.* 11 (PCW 1.ciii). For a complete list and discussion see D. T. Runia, "Philonic Nomenclature," *SPhA* 6 (1994): 1-27.

pervasive than these specific examples, it touched a significant number of Jewish thinkers in the Second Temple period and shaped a number of fundamental concepts within Judaism.

How pervasive was it? A person would think that given the fact that ancient authors drew the comparison between Judaism and Hellenistic philosophy that we would have a full scale study that explores this issue. We do not. This collection of essays is an attempt to begin the process of filling this lacuna. No one in the second half of the twentieth century contributed more to this field of inquiry than David Winston. However, his essays have appeared in a wide range of works–some of which are relatively obscure– over a significant period of time. The cumulative impact of his research is therefore known only to specialists within the field. This collection is an attempt to bring a selection of his essays together so that the reader can appreciate both the importance of the issues that are at stake and the intricacies involved in comparative analyses.

The hermeneutic is demanding. It requires competence in both Hellenistic philosophy and Second Temple Judaism. Typically scholars are proficient in one of the areas but not both. David Winston is one of the few people who controls both: he is fully at home with Second Temple Jewish material and with Hellenistic philosophy. His rabbinic training has given him a third area of expertise. These three fields are his areas of specialization. At the same time, he has always worked within the framework of the history of ideas. The essays repeatedly demonstrate the breadth of his interests as they extend to Persian, Islamic, and the modern periods. His expertise in the ancient material means that the essays are historically focused; his interest in the history of ideas gives them a constructive dimension.

The collection is selective. I have not included some of his best known and most easily accessible essays.[15] This material will be reworked and appear in his forthcoming *The Mind of Philo of Alexandria.* I have included the essays that help to cover the range of relevant texts, enable the reader to compare treatments of the same topics by different authors, or are difficult to find. The essays begin with an overview and proceed in the

---

[15] A bibliography of his works can be found in *SPhA* 9 (1997): xvii-xxiii. To this now add the following. Review of L. Grabbe, *Etymology in Early Jewish Interpretation: The Hebrew Names in Philo, JQR* 84 (1993-94): 386-87; Review of D. Sly, *Philo's Alexandria, Ancient Philosophy* 17 (1997): 489-90; Review of T. Seland, *Establishment Violence in Philo and Luke, JQR* 88 (1998): 372-74; "Philo and the Wisdom of Solomon on Creation, Revelation, and Providence," in *Shem in the Tents of Japhet* (ed. J. L. Kugel; forthcoming); and "Philo of Alexandria on the Rational and Irrational Emotions," in a forthcoming work edited by J. T. Fitzgerald.

chronological order of the ancient Jewish authors. I have arranged them in four major groups: Hellenistic Philosophy in Second Temple Judaism, Ben Sira, the Wisdom of Solomon, and Philo of Alexandria. Pseudo-Aristeas, Aristobulus and 4 Maccabees are covered within the essays although there are no specific essays devoted to them. The reason for this is simple: Professor Winston did not write essays dealing exclusively with them. Within each of the four main parts I have attempted to arrange the essays in a similar order so that a reader can quickly compare analyses of different authors on a similar topic. I have also tried to arrange them so that conceptually they move in a systematic fashion. The basic themes include creation, theodicy, freedom of the will, the role of the sage, and mysticism.

All of the essays have been modified from the form in which they were originally published. Professor Winston kindly read through them and made a number of minor adjustments. Most of these involve the addition of bibliographical references (ancient and modern), although a few involve some conceptual additions. I have reset all of the essays into a uniform style sheet. Two doctoral students assisted with the process: Deborah Prince and Ronald Cox. They, especially the latter, converted the essays into the style form of *The SBL Handbook of Style*. All abbreviations follow the guidelines of that style sheet. I hope that this improves the experience of reading the book. Some of these essays were written at a time when inclusive language was not common. I have tried to make the language more inclusive. I have not altered the translations of ancient texts. Nor have I completely recast the language to reflect the contemporary idiom when this would involve the rewriting of a sentence. Within these guidelines I have tried to remove as much of the exclusive gender language as possible.

There are a number of people who deserve a word of gratitude for this collection. Margaret Jasiewicz of the University of Notre Dame entered the essays in electronic form. Gonni Runia typeset the essays with her usual but not so common professional skill. David Runia offered a number of helpful suggestions. Steven Schweitzer, a doctoral student at Notre Dame, prepared the indices. Each of the publishers graciously granted the right to reprint the essay(s) which they had originally published. I am grateful to them for their partnership in scholarship. The original publication information is listed on accompanying pages. David Hay, the editor of the Studia Philonica Monograph series, has been enthusiastic about the project from its inception. It is appropriate to publish these essays in this series since David Winston has been affiliated with it from its inception to the present. The Institute for Advanced Study at the Hebrew University of Jerusalem gave me the time to finish this project. I deeply appreciate the reprieve from administrative and teaching responsibilities that they extended. Finally, I want to thank David Winston. He has been and remains both a mentor and a friend.

I hope that this volume will serve to stimulate research into the field that David Winston spent his scholarly career investigating. Sitting in Jerusalem, I am reminded that the contents of this collection are important for more than academic reasons. Jewish appropriations of Hellenistic philosophy in the Second Temple period represent ancient attempts to forge a sense of Jewish identity within the context of the Graeco-Roman world. Ancient Jewish authors looked for common ground with the larger world, but did not surrender their own distinctive identity. Their attempts to find a common set of values that appreciated the other without abolishing the self are what make such texts important reading in the twenty-first century.

Gregory E. Sterling
Institute for Advanced Studies
Hebrew University
Jerusalem

Previous Publications

Chapter One
"Hellenistic Jewish Philosophy." *Routledge History of World Philosophies* 2 (1997): 38-61.

Chapter Two
"Theodicy in Ben Sira and Stoic Philosophy." Pages 239-49 in *Of Scholars, Savants, and their Texts: Studies in Philosophy and Religious Thought (Essays in Honor of Arthur Hyman.)*. Edited by R. Link-Salinger. New York: Peter Lang, 1989.

Chapter Three
"Freedom and Determinism in Greek Philosophy and Jewish Hellenistic Wisdom." *SPh* 2 (1974): 40-50.

Chapter Four
"The Book of Wisdom's Theory of Cosmogony." *HR* 11 (1971): 185-202.

Chapter Five
"Creation ex nihilo Revisited: A Reply to Jonathan Goldstein." *JJS* 37 (1986): 88-91.

Chapter Six
"Wisdom in the Wisdom of Solomon." Pages 149-64 in *In Search of Wisdom: Essays in Memory of John G. Gammie*. Edited by L. G. Perdue, B. B. Scott, and W. J. Wiseman. Louisville: Westminster/John Knox, 1993.

Chapter Seven
"The Sage as Mystic in The Wisdom of Solomon." Pages 383-97 in *The Sage in Ancient Israel and the Ancient Near East*. Edited by J. G. Gammie and L. G. Perdue. Winona Lake, IN: Eisenbrauns, 1990.

Chapter Eight
"Philo's Theory of Eternal Creation." 2:593-606 in *American Academy for Jewish Research Jubilee Volume*. Edited by S. Baron and I. E. Barzilay. 2 vols. Jerusalem: American Academy for Jewish Research, 1980. Repr. "Creation Temporal or Eternal." Pages 13-21 in *Philo of*

Alexandria, The Contemplative Life, The Giants, and Selections. New York: Paulist Press, 1981.

Chapter Nine

"Theodicy and the Creation of Man." Pages 105-11 in *Hellenica et Judaica: Hommage à Valentin Nikiprowetzky.* Edited by A. Caquot, M. Hadas-Lebel et J. Riaud. Leuven/Paris: Peeters, 1986.

Chapter Ten

"Freedom and Determinism in Philo of Alexandria." *SPh* 3 (1974-75): 47-70. Repr. *Colloquy 20 of the Center for Hermeneutical Studies in Hellenistic and Modern Culture* 20 (Berkeley: Center for Hermeneutical Studies in Hellenistic Culture, 1976): 1-15. Repr. "Philo's Doctrine of Free Will." Pages 181-95 in *Two Treatises of Philo: A Commentary on* De gigantibus *and* Quod Deus immutabilis sit. BJS 25. Chico, CA: Scholars Press, 1983.

Chapter Eleven

"Was Philo a Mystic?" *SBLSP* 13 (1978): 1.161-80. Repr. pages 15-39 in *Studies in Jewish Mysticism: Proceedings of Regional Conferences held at the Univesity of California, Los Angeles, and McGill University in April, 1978.* Cambridge: American Association of Jewish Studies, 1982. Repr. "Philo's Mysticism." Pages 21-35 in *Philo of Alexandria, The Contemplative, The Giants, and Selections.* New York: Paulist Press, 1981.

Chapter Twelve

"Sage and Supersage in Philo of Alexandria." Pages 815-24 in *Pomegranates and Golden Bells: Studies in Jewish and Near Eastern Ritual, Law, & Literature in Honor of Jacob Milgrom.* Edited by D. P. Wright, D. N. Freedman, and A. Hurvitz. Winona Lake, IN: Eisenbrauns, 1995.

Chapter Thirteen

"Judaism and Hellenism: Hidden Tensions in Philo's Thought." *SPhA* 2 (1990): 1-19.

Chapter Fourteen

"Philo and the Rabbis on Sex and the Body." *Poetics Today* 19:1 (Spring 1998): 41-62.

PART ONE

HELLENISTIC PHILOSOPHY AND
SECOND TEMPLE JUDAISM

CHAPTER ONE

Hellenistic Jewish Philosophy

1. *Introduction*

Early Greek references to the Jews included the notion that they were a race of philosophers or descendents of the philosophers of India, and it is even argued that Moses had arrived at his non-anthropomorphic conception of God through astrophysical speculation.[1] Moreover, the Greek inclination to idealize Eastern wisdom led to the assertion that Pythagoras was dependent on the doctrines of the Jews and Thracians, and is exemplified by the anecdote that Aristotle learned more from a certain Jew of Coele-Syria, who had sought him out while he was in Asia Minor, than the latter had learned from him.[2] A reflection of this Greek tendency is found in various Hellenistic Jewish writings and culminates in Philo's statements that pagan lawgivers borrowed from Moses, and that Heraclitus and Zeno also derived some of their teachings from the great Jewish prophet.[3] The

---

[1] Theophrastus, Megasthenes, Clearchus of Soli, Hecataeus of Abdera (M. Stern, *Greek and Latin Authors on Jews and Judaism* [3 vols.; Jerusalem: Israel Academy of Sciences and Humanities, 1976], 1.10, 46, 50, 28). Cf. Herodotus, *Hist.* 1.131; Strabo, *Geogr.* 16.35.

[2] Hermippus of Smyrna, Clearchus of Soli (Stern, *Greek and Latin Authors*, 1.50, 95); Origen, *Cels.* 1.15. The high point of this admiration for Eastern wisdom is reached in the well known statement of the Neopythagorean Numenius of Apamea (2nd cent CE), "What is Plato, but Moses speaking Attic Greek?" (ibid., 2.209).

[3] *Spec.* 4.61; *QG* 3.5; 4.152, 167; *Leg.* 1.108; *Prob.* 57; *Deo* 6-7: Moses spoke of the 'designing fire' (πῦρ τεχνικόν) that informs the world long before the Stoics did, and much more clearly (F. Siegert, *Philon von Alexandrien: Über die Gottesbezeichnung "wohltätig verzehrendes Feuer" [De Deo]. Rückübersetzung des Fragments aus dem Armenischen, deutsche Übersetzung und Kommentar* [Tübingen: J. C. B. Mohr, 1988], 27-28). Significantly, Philo leaves the question of dependence open with regard to Socrates (*QG* 2.6: "whether taught by Moses or moved by the things themselves") and never mentions it with regard to his revered Plato, whom he characterizes as 'most holy' and 'great' (*Prob.* 13; *Aet.* 52). In *Prov.* 1.22, he merely states that Moses had anticipated Plato in saying that there was water, darkness, and chaos before the world came into existence, just as in *Aet.* 19 he similarly states that Moses had anticipated Hesiod in saying that the world was created and imperishable. Cf. Aristobulus, who asserts that Plato, Pythagoras, and Socrates, as well as Orpheus, Linus, Hesiod, Homer and even Aratus, borrowed from Moses, whose books had been translated into Greek long before the Septuagint (frags. 2 and 4, J. Charlesworth, *Old Testament Pseudepigrapha* [2 vols.; Garden City, N.Y.; Doubleday, 1985], 2:839-41). Eupolemus (1st cent. BCE), by claiming that Moses was the first wise man, contends that wisdom originated

reality, of course, was just the reverse. It was the Greek philosophical tradition that had inseminated the Jewish mind in an encounter that largely took place in the Diaspora, since the sages of the land of Israel were essentially indifferent to philosophical speculation, though in a general way even they were not completely untouched by it.

The initial penetration of Greek philosophical thought seems to have occurred in the writings of the Jewish wisdom tradition, inasmuch as the wisdom schools had international connections and its members were frequently recruited for foreign service, some even serving in the courts of foreign kings (Isa 22:15). It has been demonstrated, for example, that Prov 22:17-23:12 is dependent on the Egyptian *Instruction of Amenemope*, while the 'Sayings of Agur' (Prov 30:1-14) and the 'Sayings of Lemuel' (Prov 31:19) "appear to be borrowed from Transjordanian, probably Aramaic, wisdom collections."[4] We shall accordingly begin our account of Hellenistic Jewish philosophy with the biblical text of Qohelet, and the extra-canonical Wisdom of Ben Sira, and Wisdom of Solomon.

2. *Qohelet*

The first glimmer of Jewish contact with the philosophical genius of the Hellenic mind appears to involve an interaction that is largely contextual and reflects a broad level of Greek conceptuality and mood rather than specific schools of thought or technical doctrines. Qohelet is concerned above all with the individual, and his basic approach is rooted in personal experience and observation, self-consciously described and emphasized by the frequent redundant first person pronoun and the twelve-fold reference to his heart in 1:12-2:26 [5] Fox has noted that the importance Qohelet gives to the validation of his thought is unique in Jewish wisdom literature, since the wisdom teachers do not offer their experience as a source of new knowledge and rarely invoke experiential arguments. When they do, it is for the most part a rhetorical strategy, used to engage the pupil's attention.[6] Moreover, Qohelet's highly introspective reporting, which constantly

---

among the Jews, and thus implies that Greek philosophy is ultimately dependent on Moses (see frg. 1).

[4] A. Lemaire, "The Sage in School and Temple" in *The Sage in Israel and the Ancient East* (ed. J. G. Gammie and L. G. Perdue; Winona Lake: Eisenbrauns, 1990), 173. See also M. Lichtheim, *Late Egyptian Wisdom Literature in the International Context* (Freiburg: Universitatsverlag; Göttingen: Vandenhoeck & Ruprecht, 1983).

[5] Plato defined thought as a silent inner conversation of the soul with itself (*Soph.* 263e).

[6] See M. V. Fox, *Qohelet and His Contradictions* (Decatur; Almond Press, 1989), 86-100. Fox notes that, unlike the other wisdom teachers, Qohelet's favorite verb of perception is

draws attention to his personal reactions to various situations in an apparent effort to persuade by empathy (2:2, 17; 7:26), has no close parallels in other wisdom literature, and is clearly reminiscent of Socratic dialogue. Indeed, Socrates' relentless probing, which in Plato's early dialogues invariably ends in utter perplexity and puzzlement, is closely analogous to Qohelet's endless questioning and his firm conviction that the true nature of the divine plan for humanity constitutes an impenetrable mystery (3:11; 7:23-24; 8:17).[7]

It has been observed that Qohelet has a strong preference for the word כול, all, which is exhibited in his frequent attempts to characterize and evaluate various physical and psychological manifestations, and that this

---

'seeing', not 'hearing' (p. 98). This too is characteristically Greek and is a notion that is highly prominent in Philo's writings (*Abr.* 57; *Deus* 45; *Spec.* 4.60-61; cf. Heraclitus, fr. 101a, in H. Diels and W. Kranz, eds. *Die Fragmente der Vorsokratiker* (3 vols.; 8th ed.; Berlin: Weidmannsche Verlagsbuchhandlung, 1956), 1:173). Fox also points out that although Qohelet is painfully aware that human knowledge is severely limited by God, it is nonetheless his view that "through wisdom we may rise above our helplessness, look at the world and at God from a certain distance, and judge both" (*Qohelet and His Contradictions*, 119). "My father related to me," writes R. Joseph B. Soloveitchik (*Halakhic Man* [Philadelphia: The Jewish Publication Society of America, 1983], 73-74), "that when the fear of death would seize hold of R. Chayyim [Joseph's grandfather, founder of the Brisker method of conceptual analysis of talmudic law], he would throw himself, with his entire heart and mind, into the study of the law of tents and corpse defilement ... When halakhic man fears death, his sole method wherewith to fight this terrible dread is the eternal law of the Halakhah ... It is through cognition that he 'acquires' the object that strikes such alarm into him." Cf. also Martha Nussbaum's remark: "It occurred to me to ask myself whether the act of writing about the beauty of human vulnerability is not, paradoxically, a way of rendering oneself less vulnerable and more in control of the uncontrolled elements of life" (*The Fragility of Goodness* [Cambridge: University Press, 1986] xv).

[7] See I. von Loewenclau, "Kohelet und Sokrates," *ZAW* 98 (1986): 327-38. She notes that Spinoza designates Qohelet as *philosophus* in his *Tractatus* 6 (in B. Spinoza, *Opera* [C. Gebhardt, ed.; 4 vols; Heidelberg: Carl Winter, 1972]), 3.95, line 19. She also compares Qoh 12:11, "The sayings of the wise are like goads, like nails fixed in prodding sticks," with Plato, *Apology* 30e, where Socrates describes himself as one who attaches himself to the city "as a gadfly to a horse that is sluggish on account of its size and needs to be aroused by stinging." "Qohelet and his circle have a new goal: the sage's task is not only to give counsel, but to rouse people from their certainties. Such an accentuation fits the Hellenistic period with its multifaceted intellectual and political upheavals." Significantly, Qohelet describes his activity not as teaching but as 'studying and probing' (1: 1 3; 7:25). Of the 227 verses of Qohelet, we find only 27 to be admonitory. Socrates similarly says, "I was never any one's teacher" (*Apol.* 33a), and "I know that I do not know" (*Apol.* 21d; cf. *Charm.* 165b). Finally, she draws a parallel between the complaint that Socrates "keeps repeating the same thing" (*Gorg.* 490e), and the fact that Qohelet's mind is similarly fixed on one basic theme, הבל, a word that recurs no less than 32 times, in addition to the recurrence of other key words to which he is addicted, such as מקרה, עמל, יתרון, and עת.

form of expression is not found elsewhere in Scripture, though it is very common in Greek philosophical literature.[8] Qohelet indeed opens with just such an evaluation, declaring that all is הבל, a word that is variously translated as vanity, futility, or absurdity. Levy and Amir have noted the resemblance between this recurrent judgment of Qohelet and the aphorism attributed to the Cynic Monimus of Syracuse (4th cent. BCE) declaring all human supposition to be illusion (הבל, literally smoke).[9]

Hengel cites a series of Greek texts that reflect popular Greek philosophy and provide close parallels to Qohelet. The problems raised by the doctrine of divine retribution,[10] which inform Qohelet's running critique, are similarly taken up by a Greek contemporary, Cercidas of Megalopolis (ca. 290-220 BCE), a politician and poet influenced by the Cynics. "Is the eye of justice," he writes, "as blind as a mole? ... Does a mist dim the eye of Themis the bright?" In Babrius's Fable 127, the old view that Zeus records human actions is satirized with the remark that he orders Hermes to write down their misdeeds severally on shards and piles them up in a chest close by himself, but since the shards lie heaped up one upon another awaiting the time he can examine them, some are late to fall into his hands (cf. Qoh 8:10-14). Somewhat analogously, according to Rabba, the famed 3rd generation Babylonian Amora, Job blasphemed by saying to God, "Perhaps a tempest has passed before you, and caused you to confuse איוב [Job] and איב [enemy] (b. B. Bat. 16a). Qohelet's obsession with the incalculability of

---

[8] See Y. Amir, "On the Question of the Relationship Between Qohelet and Greek Wisdom," *Bet Miqra* 22 (1964-65): 36-38. Ben Sira has a similar predilection for the abstract concept of the 'all' (הכול).

[9] Diogenes Laertius 6.83; Sextus Empiricus, *Math.* 7.88 (Bury, LCL): "Anaxarchus and Monimus [abolished the criterion] because they likened existing things to a scene-painting (σκηνογραφία: cf. Wis 15:4 and my comment *ad loc.* in D. Winston, *Wisdom of Solomon* [AB 43; Garden City, N. Y.: Doubleday, 1979]) and supposed them to resemble the impressions experienced in sleep or madness;" M. Aurelius 2.15. See L. Levy, *Das Buch Qohelet* (Leipzig: J. C. Hinrichs, 1912), 12; Amir, "Qohelet and Greek Wisdom," 38-39; R. Braun, *Kohelet und die frühhellenistische Popularphilosophie* (Berlin: De Gruyter, 1973), 45-46.

[10] M. Hengel (*Judaism and Hellenism* [2 vols.; trans. J. Bowden; Philadelphia: Fortress, 1974], 1:121) speaks of the 'break' with the doctrine of retribution, but Fox (*Qohelet and His Contradictions,* 121) has argued convincingly that "Qohelet both affirms divine justice and complains of the injustices that God allows. The contradiction is most blatant in 8:10-14, where Qohelet says that the righteous live long and the wicked die young, *and* that the opposite sometimes occurs. Qohelet recognizes it, bemoans it, but does not resolve it" (ibid., 121). "The book concludes with the affirmation of the certainty of divine judgment (12:14). Whether written by an editor or the author, it does not conflict with anything in the body of the book. The difference between the epilogue and the rest of the book is that the epilogue emphasizes God's judgment without raising the problem of the delay in judgment" (p. 128).

death, which renders us like animals trapped in a snare (9:12), is paralleled in a Greek epitaph from the third century BCE: "Truly the gods take no account of mortals; no, like animals we are pulled hither and thither by chance (αὐτομάτῳ; cf. Qohelet's use of מקרה in 3:19), in life as in death." Finally, Qohelet's advice to 'seize the day' (9:7-10), paralleled in the Babylonian epic of Gilgamesh and the Egyptian Song of the Harper, is also a popular theme in Greek tradition: "Remembering that the same end awaits all mortals, enjoy life as long as you live ... For know this well: once you have descended to the drink of Lethe, you will see no more of those things that are above." Similar advice is given in the Greek graffiti from the tomb of Jason in Jerusalem, dating from the time of Alexander Jannaeus (1st cent. BCE). Hengel concludes that the crisis in religion reflected in the above citations, which reached its climax about the third century BCE, "presumably did not fail to make a mark on the thought of Qohelet, and was apparently communicated to him by Ptolemaic officials, merchants and soldiers, who were not lacking even in Jerusalem."[11]

Fox correctly remarks that "underlying Qohelet's הבל judgments is an assumption that the system should be rational, i.e. that actions should invariably produce appropriate consequences."[12] The injustices that God allows to mar his creation render it for Qohelet contradictory and absurd, and this offends the inviolable criterion that anchors his entire intellectual existence, casting a pall over his life's work. This demand for rationality constitutes the heart of the mainstream tradition in Greek philosophy. For a philosopher like Nietzsche, "the fanaticism with which all Greek reflection throws itself upon rationality betrays a desperate situation," and is "pathologically conditioned."[13] In any case, it is this fundamental drive for rationality that prevents Qohelet from ignoring the ineluctable absurdity that characterizes the human enterprise as a whole and thus sharply distinguishes his approach from that of the Jewish wisdom tradition.

---

[11] Hengel, *Judaism and Hellenism*, 1:115-28. For texts and translations of the above citations, see Cercidas, *Meliambs. Fragments. and Cercidea* (ed. and trans. A. D. Knox; LCL; Cambridge: Harvard University Press, 1961), 197 (translation cited by us is that found in Hengel); Babrius, *Aesopic Fables in Iambic Verse* (ed. and trans. B. E. Perry; LCL; Cambridge: Harvard University Press, 1965), 165; W. Peek, *Griechische Grabgedichte* (Berlin: Akademie-Verlag, 1960), nos. 308 and 371; P. Benoit, "L'Inscription grecque du tombeau de Jason," *IEJ* 17 (1967): 112-13 ; B. Lifshitz, "Notes d'Épigraphie Palestinienne," *RB* 73 (1966): 248-55.

[12] Fox, *Qohelet and His Contradictions*, 47

[13] *The Twilight of the Idols: The Problem of Socrates* 10 (translation from W. Kaufmann, *The Portable Nietzsche* [New York: Viking Press, 1954], 478).

3. *The Wisdom of Ben Sira*

There can be little doubt that Ben Sira's opus (ca. 180 BCE) is marked by a consistent effort to effect a new synthesis of ideas. In an age when Hellenistic wisdom dominated the civilized world, he did his best to broaden the bounds of the Mosaic Law so that it would encompass universal wisdom. As Collins has remarked, Ben Sira's so-called nationalization of wisdom constituted in reality the universalization of the Torah.[14] The Torah is refracted for Sirach through the lens of wisdom, and the case for its legitimacy is made in wisdom's terms: "The whole of wisdom is fear of the Lord; complete wisdom is the fulfillment of the Law."[15]

It is especially, however, in his confrontation with the problem of evil that Ben Sira moves beyond the earlier wisdom tradition and is actively engaged in adapting Stoic arguments for the formulation of his main solution to this puzzling paradox, namely, that nature is to be seen as a harmony of opposites. Although Platonism did not arrive in Alexandria before the first century BCE, some knowledge of Stoic philosophy does appear to have penetrated the Alexandrian intellectual scene already in the third century BCE, for we are told that when Cleanthes, scholiarch of the Stoic School from 263 to 232, refused the invitation of Ptolemy Philadelphus, he sent his pupil Sphaerus there instead.[16] The visit of an isolated Stoic philosopher does not constitute a major presence and it is therefore unlikely that in the absence of a flourishing Stoic center such as those found in Rhodes and in Tarsus, Sirach would have possessed a detailed and technical knowledge of the Stoic philosophy, but its broad outlines were probably well known to him. Although he does not speak explicitly of the harmony of the universal order, his words clearly imply it. In Sir 33:7-14, he seeks to reconcile the unity of creation with a divine plan that consistently discriminates between pairs of opposites: good and evil, life and death, the sinner and the godly. In his effort to explicate the dietary laws, Pseudo-Aristeas had likewise noted the paradox that, in spite of the fact that creation was one, some things are regarded by the Torah as unclean for food, and in the course of his explanation of this surprising fact he noted that although all things are to the natural reason similarly

---

[14] J. J. Collins, "The Bibilical Precedent for Natural Theology," *JAAR* 45 Supplement B (1977): 53. See also Winston, *Wisdom of Solomon*, 36.

[15] Sir 19:20; cf. 1:27. See G. von Rad, *Wisdom in Israel* (trans. D. Martin; Nashville: Abingdon, 1972), 245-47. All translations from Sirach are from P. W. Skehan and A. di Lella, *The Wisdom of Ben Sira* (AB 39; Garden City: Doubleday, 1987).

[16] Diogenes Laertius 7.185. See P. M. Fraser, *Ptolemaic Alexandria* (3 vols.; Oxford: Clarendon, 1972), 1:481; 2:695, n. 17; R. Pautrel, "Ben Sira et le Stoicisme," *RSR* 51 (1963): 535-49.

constituted, being all administered by a single power, in every case there is a profound logic for our abstinence from some and our use of others (*Let. Aris.* 129, 143). Ben Sira similarly indicates that although every day has its light from the sun, certain days were by the Lord's decision distinguished and made holy, and though all humans were created out of the earth, some, in God's great wisdom, were hallowed and brought near to him, while others were cursed and removed from their place: "See now all the works of the Most High: they come in pairs, the one the opposite of the other" (Sir 33:15). All this evidently implies that the universe consists of a harmony of opposites in accordance with a mysterious divine design.[17]

The Stoics taught a similar doctrine. First, like Sirach, they declared that divine providence is "chiefly directed and concentrated upon three objects: to secure for the world the structure best suited for survival, absolute completeness, and above all consummate beauty and embellishment of every kind."[18] Then, too, like Sirach, they taught that this is the best possible world that could be produced, and that notwithstanding apparent imperfections here and there, Nature so organized each part that harmony is present in the whole.[19] As for the evil of natural disasters, "it has a rationale peculiar to itself ... and is not without usefulness in relation to the whole, for without it there could be no good."[20] Ben Sira's attitude is similar: "No cause then to say: What is the purpose of this? Everything is chosen to satisfy a need" (Sir 39:21). Indeed, the very elements that are good for the godfearing turn to evil for sinners (39:28-31; cf. Wis 16:24).

Another aspect of the theodicy issue in regard to which Ben Sira seems to have followed the Stoic lead is in his formulation of the paradox of freedom and determinism. The older wisdom literature did not feel this contradiction too keenly, and was content to assert that all was determined by the gods in advance, and yet at the same time to insist that success and failure, punishment and reward, were conditioned by human behavior. In the Egyptian *Instruction of Ptahhotep* (Old Kingdom period) we read: "His guilt was fated in the womb; He whom they guide cannot go wrong, whom they make boatless cannot cross."[21]

---

[17] Cf. Qoh 7:14; *T. Naph.* 2.7; *T. Ash.* 1.4-5; Philo, *Opif.* 33.

[18] Cicero, *Nat. d.* 2.58 (Rackham, LCL). Cf. Sir 42:17, 22-24; 43:1, 9, 11; Philo, *Spec.* 3.189; H. von Arnim, *Stoicorum veterum fragmenta* (4 vols.; Leipzig: Teubner, 1904-1924), 2.1009; Xenophon, *Cyr.* 8.7.22; Cicero, *Nat. d.* 2.93.

[19] Cicero, *Nat. d.* 2.87; Epictetus, *Diatr.* 1.12.16; Seneca, *Nat.* 7.27.4. See Hengel, *Judaism and Hellenism,* 1:147-49, and Y. Gutman, *The Beginnings of Jewish Hellenistic Literature* (2 vols.; Jerusalem: Mosad Bialk, 1958), 1:171-85 (Hebrew).

[20] Chrysippus, in Plutarch, *Mor.* 1065b (Cherniss, LCL); cf. M. Aurelius 10.6.

[21] See M. Lichtheim, *Ancient Egyptian Literature* (3 vols.; Berkeley: University of California Press, 1973), 1:67; S. Morenz, *Egyptian Religion* (trans. A. E. Kepp; London: Methuen,

It has been pointed out that the Demotic wisdom Instruction known as *Papyrus Insinger* was the first such Egyptian writing to deal consciously and explicitly with the freedom/determinism dilemma. What we find here is very much like the paradoxical Stoic formulation that all is in accord with Heimarmene, yet our actions are in our power. In light of the many Hellenistic elements in *Papyrus Insinger*, Lichtheim has concluded that it is very likely that in this case too we are dealing with such an influence. In view of the striking similarities between *Papyrus Insinger* and Ben Sira, it is reasonable to assume that their similar formulations of the freedom/determinism paradox were the result of their common use of Stoic sources.[22] Although a palpably determinist strain does run through the book of Proverbs, it nevertheless lacks an explicit and conscious expression of the paradox under discussion. Thus the author of Proverbs teaches that the sage will acquire wisdom, while the fool will hold it in contempt, thereby implying that their life courses are fixed in advance.[23] There is even a verse that asserts that God has created all, including the fool, for a special purpose (16:4). Nowhere, however, does the book of Proverbs declare unequivocally, as does Sirach, that God has determined a person's character even before his birth (Sir 1:14-15), or that a person was fashioned by God as clay in the power of the potter, so that in accordance with an eternal cosmic plan, the godly or blessed stand over against the sinner or the cursed (Sir 33:10-15). Moreover, Ben Sira includes, along with his starkly predestinarian passages, emphatic statements concerning one's freedom to choose one's life-path accompanied by an explicit warning against blaming God for causing human sin.[24]

4. *Wisdom of Solomon*

In the Wisdom of Solomon, the Hellenistic Jewish wisdom tradition so palpably verges on the philosophical that we can readily identify this book's Middle Platonist affinities and its considerable use of Greek philosophical terminology.[25] An exhortatory discourse featuring a highly enthusiastic and eulogistic invocation of Wisdom, it was written in Greek by a profoundly hellenized Jew of Alexandria, after that city's conquest by Rome in 30 BCE, when the earlier optimism of the Alexandrian Jewish

---

1973), 66-68.

[22] Lichtheim, *Late Egyptian Wisdom,* 107-96.

[23] Prov 14:6; 9:7; 13:19; 20:12.

[24] Winston, "Theodicy in Ben Sira" (in this volume) and idem, *Wisdom of Solomon,* 46-58.

[25] Idem, *Wisdom of Solomon,* 13, and 16, n. 14.

community for a rapprochement with the Greeks and for social and cultural acceptance by them, had been replaced by a mounting sense of disillusionment and disappointment. The centrality of its Platonic teaching of the immortality of the soul represents a new emphasis in Jewish tradition, while its concept of the preexistent soul (8:19), although it is only hinted at, may be the earliest attestation of this notion in Jewish literature. Even more significant, however, is the fact that Plato's doctrine of the adverse influence of body on soul (*Phaed.* 66b; *Resp.* 611c; *Tim.* 43b-c) and the superior state of soul pregnancy over its bodily form (*Symp.* 208e) is faithfully echoed in Wis 4:1, where it is said that it is better to be childless, provided one is virtuous, and in 9:15, where, in a verse replete with Platonic phraseology, the author speaks of "a perishable body weighing down the soul and a tent of clay encumbering a mind full of cares" (cf. Plato, *Phaed.* 81c; *Phaedr.* 247b).

In sketching his own spiritual odyssey, the author confesses to a passion for Woman Wisdom that had gripped him from early youth and had led him to cast his lot with her forever. This unbridled love for Wisdom is vividly reflected in his magnificent fivefold description of her, in which she is conceived as an eternal emanation of God's power and glory (7:25-26, 29-30), a Neopythagorean notion that even the more philosophically ambitious Philo was reluctant to express explicitly, preferring instead to use locutions that only implied it.[26] Unlike Ben Sira (1:4; 24:9), who asserts that God has created Wisdom, he says not a word about her creation, describing her instead in the present tense as a divine effulgence, of which one would have to say more precisely that she is "ever being produced and in a state of having been produced," to use a formulation later employed by the fifth century Neoplatonist Proclus.[27] As for the creation of the world, he adopts the Platonic notion that it was created "out of formless matter" (Wis 11:17), a view not inconsonant with that of the rabbis.[28]

In Wis 7:22-24 the author describes Wisdom by a series of twenty-one epithets (such as intelligent, subtle, agile, unsullied, unhindered, steadfast), borrowed largely from Greek philosophy, especially that of the Stoa. Posidonius, for example, had defined God as "intelligent breath (πνεῦμα νοερόν) pervading the whole of substance" (F100)[29] and Stoics had defined

---

[26] Ibid., 38, 185-86

[27] Proclus, *Commentaire sur le "Timée"* (ed. A. J. Festugière; 5 vols.; Paris: J. Vrin, 1966), 2:141.

[28] Winston, *Wisdom of Solomon*, 38; idem, "The Book of Wisdom's Theory of Cosmogony," *HR* 11 (1971): 185-202 (in this volume); idem, "Creation Ex Nihilo Revisited: A Reply to Jonathan Goldstein", 88-91 (pp. 78-82).

[29] Translation of Posidonius fragments are from L. Edelstein and I. G. Kidd, eds.,

the soul as a "subtle (λεπτομερές), self-moving body" (*SVF* 2.780). More-over, according to Chrysippus, "since the universal nature extends to all things, everything that comes about in anyway whatever in the whole universe ... will necessarily have come about conformably with that nature and its reason in due and unimpeded sequence (ἀκωλύτως)" (*SVF* 2.137). What characterizes the Stoic πνεῦμα above all, however, is that it pervades (διήκω) and permeates (χωρέω) all things (*SFV* 2.416, 1021, 1033). According to Stoic cosmology, an active principle, the Divine Logos, totally pervaded a passive principle, qualityless matter, as the passage of body through body. The pneuma's extension through matter is described as tensional motion (τονικὴ κίνησις), characterized as a form of oscillation, a simultaneous motion in opposite directions.[30] This scientific theory appealed so strongly both to Philo and the author of Wisdom, that they were willing to take up this stark corporealism and adapt it to their own Platonist way of thinking, no doubt made possible by their transposing the materialist Stoic terminology into literary metaphor.

In a fine ode to Wisdom's saving power in history (Wis 10:1-21), the author assimilates the old covenantal salvation history with its miraculous and sudden divine irruptions to the immanent divine ordering of human events as mediated by the continuous activity of Wisdom. It is her genera-tion by generation election of holy servants (7:27) that structures the life of Israel. As the Divine Mind immanent within the universe and guiding and controlling all its dynamic operations, Wisdom represents the entire range of the natural sciences (7:17-21), is the teacher of all human arts and crafts, skilled in ontology, logic, and rhetoric, and the source of all moral knowledge (8:7 enumerates the four cardinal virtues, emphasized by Plato, Aristotle, and the Stoics). It is undoubtedly significant that the author, unlike Ben Sira, nowhere explicitly identifies Wisdom with Torah. His statement that "love of Wisdom means the keeping of her laws" (6:18) is ambiguous, and probably refers to the statutes of natural law. All we have from him in this regard is but a passing allusion to Israel's mission of bringing the imperishable light of the Law to the world (18:4). Very likely he believed with Philo that the teachings of the Torah were tokens of the Divine Wisdom, and that they were in harmony with the law of the universe and as such implant all the virtues in the human psyche.[31] Wisdom is thus clearly the Archetypal Torah, the תורה קדומה of the Kabbalists, of which the Mosaic Law is but an imperfect image. A similar notion is reflected in

---

Posidonius. Volume 1: The Fragments (Cambridge: Cambridge University Press, 1972).

[30] R. B. Todd, *Alexander of Aphrodisias on Stoic Physics* (Leiden: Brill, 1976), 34-37.

[31] Winston, *Wisdom of Solomon*, 42-43.

the statement of Rav Avin (4th c.) that the Torah is an incomplete form (*novelet*, premature fruit) of the Supernal Wisdom (*Gen. Rab.* 17.5 and 44.12).

5. *The Fourth Book of Maccabees*

In 4 Macc (probably 1st cent. CE) we have an overtly philosophical discourse on the theme of the mastery of religious reason over the emotions, illustrated, in what constitutes the major portion of the text, by a panegyric of the martyrs (Eleazar, the seven brethren, and their mother), which the author, a skilled rhetorician, binds to the discourse (the first 3 chapters) by repeated references to his main thesis.[32] The essential component in the book's argument is that the Torah, the Divine Nomos, is consistent with the world order. In the confrontation between Antiochus and Eleazar, the king claims that the Jewish ban on eating pork shows that Judaism does not accord with nature (5:8-9). In his response, Eleazar, identified both as a philosopher and an expert in the Law (5:4), argues, in spite of the king's mockery of the Jewish philosophy and his assertion that it is contrary to reason, that in fact it inculcates in its followers the virtues of temperance, courage, justice, and piety (5:22-25). His reasoning is couched in the language of Greek natural law theory: "For believing that the Law has been established from God, we know that the Creator of the world, in laying down the Law, feels for us (ἡμῖν συμπαθεῖ) in accordance with [our] nature (κατὰ φύσιν) and commands us to eat whatever is well suited to our soul" (5:25-26, my translation). The thrust of Eleazar's statement is that νόμος and φύσις deriving as they do from one Creator, cannot be mutually antagonistic. The Law is perfectly rational, and the term λογισμός, reasoning, as Redditt has noted, occurs characteristically 73 times, for the most part in the context of the author's recurring theme that human reason is sovereign over the emotions.[33]

Gutman[34] (1949) and Hadas[35] think that Eleazar's position is modelled

---

[32]   J. C. H. Lebram ("Die literarische Form des Vierten Makkabaerbuchs," *VC* 28 [1974]: 81-96) identifies the genre of the narrative on the martyrs with that of the ἐπιτάφιος λόγος or funeral oration.

[33]   P. L. Redditt, "The Conception of Nomos in Fourth Maccabees," *CBQ* 45 (1983): 249-70. Moreover, six times reason is modified by the adjective εὐσεβής. religious, and, as Redditt has correctly remarked, "the three terms νόμος, λογισμός, and εὐσέβεια form a circle of interrelated concepts."

[34]   Y. Gutman, "The Mother and Her Sons in the Aggadah and in II and IV Maccabees," in *Commentationes Iudaico-Hellenisticae in Memoiam Iohannis Lewy* (eds. M. Schwabe and J. Guman; Jerusalem: Magnes Press, 1949), 25-37 (Hebrew).

[35]   M. Hadas, *The Third and Fourth Books of Maccabees* (New York: Harper and Brothers,

on that of Socrates in Plato's *Gorgias,* where, in answer to Callicles'
objection that the tyrant can subject his victim to torture, Socrates insists
that "any injustice against me and mine is both worse and more shameful
for the man who does the injustice than for me who suffers it" (508e).[36]
Moreover, at the final judgment, says Socrates, relating an ancient tale as
the word of truth, the soul, stripped of its body, will be subjected to the
ultimate scrutiny of justice. Similarly, the author of 4 Maccabees justifies
the fate of the martyrs by emphasizing the immortality of the soul and its
future vindication. Victory in their contest, he says, was "incorruption in
long-lasting life," and "they now stand beside the divine throne and live the
life of the age of blessing, for Moses says (Deut 33:3), 'All the holy ones are
under your hands'" (17:12-19, cf. 18:23, and Wis 3:1).

Although there are clear echoes of Stoic teaching in the book, this may
merely indicate that the author's philosophical orientation is that of the
highly stoicized Middle Platonism of the age. The well-known Stoic definition of wisdom as "knowledge of things divine and human and of their
causes" (*SVF* 2.35) is reproduced in 1:15-17, where wisdom is identified
with the education given by the Law; the famous Stoic paradox that the
sage is not merely free but also a king (Cicero, *Acad.* 2.136) is echoed in
2:23; 7:23, and 14:2; and the martyrs are said to behave with true Stoic
apathy (9:17; 11:25; 15:11, 14). Wolfson argued that "by the time of Philo,
the question whether virtue means the extirpation of the emotions or only
their control seems to have been a subject of discussion among Hellenistic
Jews. Guided by Jewish tradition, the author of 4 Maccabees comes out in
opposition to the Stoics."[37] Renehan has correctly pointed out, however,
that the platonizing Middle Stoic Posidonius had also maintained that the
passions cannot be eradicated.[38] But the Middle Platonists generally
followed the Middle Stoa in this matter, so once again the author's
philosophical orientation points in the direction of Middle Platonism.[39]

1953), 115-18.

[36] Translation from Plato, *Gorgias: translated with notes by Terence Irwin* (Oxford:
Clarendon; New York: Oxford University Press, 1979).

[37] H. A. Wolfson, *Philo: Foundations of Religious Philosophy in Judaism, Christianity and
Islam* (2 vols.; Cambridge: Harvard University Press, 1948), 2:270-71.

[38] Edelstein and Kidd, *Posidonius,* 143, F161 and F187; A. A. Long and D. N. Sedley, eds.,
Hellenistic Philosohpers (2 vols.; Cambridge; New York: Cambridge University Press, 1987),
1:413-17. See R. Renehan, "The Greek Philosophical Background of Fourth Maccabees,"
Rheinisches Museum für Philologie 115 (1972): 223-38. Panaetius, too, seems to have taken
the same position (Cicero, *Off.* 1.102).

[39] Interestingly, in this case, Philo does not follow the Middle Platonic view but considers
ἀπάθεια the higher ideal (*Leg.* 3.129, 134), although he does on one occasion attribute
μετριοπάθεια to the sage Abraham (*Abr.* 257; cf., however, *QG* 4.73, where he says that

6. *Pseudo-Aristeas*

It was the Greek Bible that ultimately provided the occasion for a large-scale penetration of Greek philosophy into Hellenistic Jewish thought. Although the *Letter of Aristeas* (2nd cent. BCE) purports to be the eye-witness account by a courtier of Ptolemy II (283-247 BCE) of the events connected with the Greek translation of the Pentateuch, scholars are agreed that the book is a literary fiction, and that the author is in reality an Alexandrian Jew seeking to demonstrate the superiority of the Jewish faith and the possibility for mutual respect and peaceful coexistence between Jews and Greeks. In a letter to the High Priest Eleazar, Ptolemy announces his resolve to have the Hebrew Bible translated into Greek so that it could find its rightful place in the great library at Alexandria (34-40). Aristeas refers to the High Priest as the "true gentleman" (καλὸς καὶ ἀγαθός) and makes him use the same expression in his description of the 72 elders chosen to execute the translation (46). Not only did the latter have a thorough knowledge of the literature of the Jews, but they possessed equal mastery of Greek literature as well, "zealously cultivating the quality of the mean (τὸ μέσον) and eschewing any uncouth and uncultivated attitude of mind" (121-22).[40]

Interrupting the narrative of the translators' departure from Jerusalem, is an important digression consisting of the High Priest's rationale of the Law (128-72). In view of the fact that creation is one, asks the Greek delegation, why is it that some things are regarded by Scripture as unclean? To this the High Priest replies that the Lawgiver has enclosed his people with unbreakable palisades to prevent them from mingling with other nations and to keep them pure in body and spirit. Like Aristobulus, Pseudo-Aristeas asserts that "nothing has been set down in Scripture heedlessly or in the spirit of myth but only with the intent that we practice justice towards all people and be mindful of God's sovereignty" (168). The dietary rules are meant to promote holy contemplation and perfection of

---

Abraham experienced on the death of his wife Sarah not a πάθος but a προπάθεια (for the Greek fragment, see Marcus, LCL, 220). According to Petit, this fragment should be restored to Eusebius of Emesa (4th cent.): "Eusebius was certainly inspired by *QG* 4.73, but he has completely modified the redaction of his source" (See Francoise Petit, *Quaestiones in Genesim et Exodum: fragmenta graeca*, PAPM, v. 33, p. 168. Cf. James R. Royse, *The Spurious Texts of Philo of Alexandria* (Leiden: Brill, 1991) 25, n. 51). See now also Margaret Graver, "Philo of Alexandria and the origins of the Stoic Προπάθειαι", *Phronesis* 44.4 (1999): 300-25. See D. Winston, "Philo's Conception of the Divine Nature," in *Neoplatonism and Jewish Thought* (ed. L. E. Goodman; New York: State University of New York Press, 1992), 41 n. 51, and S. R. C. Lilla, *Clement of Alexandria* (London: Oxford University Press, 1971), 99-103.
[40] Charlesworth, *OTP*, 2:21.

character, for the permitted animals are gentle and clean, whereas those forbidden are wild and carnivorous. By way of allegory, the "parting of the hoof" and the "cloven foot" that characterize the permitted animals symbolize discrimination in our actions with a view to what is right. "Chewing the cud", on the other hand, signifies memory, admonishing us to remember "what great and marvelous things the Lord thy God did in thee" (Deut 10:21), that is, the marvelous construction of the human body and the acuity and infinite scope of the intellect. Furthermore, the character of "the weasel and the mouse and the rest of the forbidden animals is one that is prone to evil. Weasels, for example, conceive through the ears and give birth through the mouth, and this is taken to symbolize the maleficent actions of informers, who hear rumors and give body to them by word of mouth. This bit of physiological folklore was widespread in the ancient world, and an analogous symbolic interpretation of it can be found in Plutarch, where it is said to portray the creation of speech.[41] This kind of allegorizing by Pseudo-Aristeas may owe something to the influence of the Pythagoreans, who also possessed unusual dietary rules, which they later sought to justify philosophically.[42] Although there is considerable similarity here with Philo's allegorization of the dietary regulations, there is as yet nothing remotely resembling the Philonic "allegory of the soul." On the other hand, in insisting that these strange food laws have been legislated "with a view to truth and as a token of right reason" (161), he anticipates Philo's firm conviction that the Mosaic Law is no arbitrary set of decrees handed down from on high, but rather the truest reflection of the Logos.

The section on the seven banquets (187-294), in which the king's 72 questions are answered, one each, by the Jewish envoys, forms the largest single unit of the book, and its special significance is indicated by the author's emphasis on the king's bedazzled admiration for every answer and

---

[41] Plutarch, *Is. Os.* 381a; cf. Aristotle, *Gen. an.* 756b30; Antoninus Liberalis, *Metam.* 29.

[42] Diogenes Laertius 8.18, 24, 34; Porphyry, *Vit. Pyth.* 42; Aristotle F195 and F1972 (in *The Complete Works of Aristotle* [ed. J. Barnes; 2 vols.; Princeton; Princeton University Press, 1984], 2:2442). See I. Heinemann, *Philons griechische und jüdische Bildung* (Breslau: M. & H. Marcus, 1932), 498-500, and R. M. Grant, "Dietary Laws Among Pythagoreans, Jews, and Christians," *HTR* 72-73 (1979-80): 229-310. Interestingly, as in Philo, the ethical interpretations stand side by side with the literal. According to Heinemann, the Pythagoreans had the same prohibition of the weasel and gave the same justification for it that Pseudo-Aristeas provides. Cf. Philo, *Prob.* 2: "Now we are told that the saintly company of the Pythagoreans teaches among other excellent doctrines this also, 'walk not on the highways' [Diogenes Laertius 8.17]. This does not mean that we should climb steep hills — the school was not prescribing foot-weariness — but it indicates by this figure that in our words and deeds we should not follow popular and beaten tracks" (Colson, LCL). For the Pythagorean symbolism of salt, see Philo, *Spec.* 1.175, and Diogenes Laertius 8.35.

the incessant applause at the end of each banquet. Indeed it is part of the author's strategy to provide his reader with a list of distinguished gentile "witnesses" attesting the excellence and "philosophical purity" of the divine lawbooks of the Jews. In addition to the Egyptian priests who have dubbed the Jews "men of God" (reproducing the Egyptian expression *rmt ntr*) as distinguished from "men of food, drink, and raiment" (140), the list of witnesses includes Demetrius of Phalerum, Hecataeus of Abdera, and the philosopher Mendemus of Eretria (10, 31, 200-01). The king himself is perhaps the strongest witness, filling the Jerusalem Temple with sumptu-ous gifts (51-82), calling the translators "God-fearing" (179), acknowledg-ing that the highest God (i.e. the God of Israel) has preserved his kingdom in peace and honor (37), bowing down seven times before the Torah scrolls, his eyes suffused with tears of joy (177-78), and confessing at the conclusion of the banquet that he had been given "a lesson in kingship" (294). As Boccaccini has perceptively remarked, Pseudo-Aristeas is not even concerned to make Greek *paideia* dependent on the greater antiquity of Jewish *paideia*, a path well trodden by many oriental and Hellenistic Jewish authors, including the redoubtable Philo. The road to salvation is fully open to the gentiles, for it is rooted in the "love of learning" (φιλομά-θεια), "the supreme human quality, through which a pure disposition of mind is acquired, by seizing upon what is noblest" (2).[43]

Tcherikover has observed that the remarkable thing about the 72 answers of the Jewish sages is the absence in them of any trace of Jewish particularism.[44] The Torah, Moses, Sinai, the Jewish nation, Palestine — none of these appear. The one strikingly Jewish feature that characterizes every answer is the reference of all things to God, and even when that reference degenerates into a mere "tag", the impact of this emphasis on God as the ultimate source and standard of right remains undiminished, and it is just this "making God the starting-point of their reasoning" that wins the king's approval and is seconded by the philosopher Menedemus of Eretria, a member of the Megarian school, known for its skill in dialectics and its assertion that the good is a unity, "though called by many names," and that God, too, was but another name for the goodness that was knowledge (Diogenes Laertius 2.106).

The God-centeredness aside, much of the conceptuality of the 72 answers is essentially Greek.[45] Typically Greek, for example, are the

---

[43] See the excellent discussion in G. Boccaccini, *Middle Judaism: Jewish Thought 300 BCE to 200 CE* (Minneapolis: Fortress, 1991), 161-85, esp. 177-79.

[44] V. Tcherikover, "The Ideology of the Letter of Aristeas," *HTR* 51 (1958): 59-85.

[45] Some few answers, however, as Zuntz ("Aristeas Studies I: The Seven Banquets," *JSS* 4 [1959]: 23) has pointed out, "are entirely rooted in Jewish tradition. Ptolemy's fifth

statements that persuasion (τὸ πεῖσαι) is the object of discourse (266), that a clear conscience gives freedom from fear (243), that one should not be carried away by impulses but moderate one's emotions (the Peripatetic ideal of μετριοπάθεια) (256; cf. 223), and that one should not covet the unattainable (ἀνέφικτον).[46] It is especially noteworthy that in making mercy a key divine attribute, the term used repeatedly by Pseudo-Aristeas is not ἐλεήμων (which occurs only in Let. Aris. 208; cf. LXX Ex 34:6), but ἐπιεικής (192, 207, 211), which means equitable or fair, thus avoiding (at least from the vantage point of the modified position of the Middle and Late Stoa) the embarrassment occasioned by the former term for one who is aware of the Stoic philosophical objection to its irrational character. This is especially striking, since even the author of the Wisdom of Solomon and Philo frequently speak of God's ἔλεος. Equally striking is Pseudo-Aristeas' unusually strong emphasis on divine grace, which includes the notion that all effective moral action is wholly dependent on God (231, 236-38). The same conception is found in Wis 8:21-9:6 (cf. Prov 2:6), in Plato, Leg. 715e, and in the pseudo-Platonic Epin. 989d. Philo, in particular, never tires of insisting that without God's bounteous help, a human being could accomplish nothing, and that one who ascribes anything to his own powers is a godless villain.[47]

The door opened by Pseudo-Aristeas very likely contributed greatly to the formation of an entire school of Jewish philosophical exegetes of Scripture, and though the major part of its output has virtually disappeared, its single most outstanding and sparkling representative has largely survived the wholesale shipwreck. It is to this lone survivor and one of his precursors that we now turn.

7. Aristobulus: Precursor of Philo

The elaborate biblical commentaries of Philo were undoubtedly part of a flourishing Jewish Alexandrian scholastic tradition of biblical interpretation, as can readily be inferred from his frequent allusions to earlier and contemporary fellow exegetes.[48] Unfortunately, only one such predecessor

---

question (Let. Aris. 193), 'how to be invincible in war', elicits the answer, 'if he did not place his trust in unlimited power but throughout invoked God to give success to his enterprises.' Never was an answer like this given by a Greek adviser to a Greek king. It is in the spirit of Ps 20:8."

[46] Cf. Philo, Leg. 1.75; Conf. 7; Spec. 1.44

[47] Post. 136; Det. 60; Cher. 127-28; cf. m. Abot 3:7

[48] D. M. Hay, "Philo's Reference to Other Allegorists," SPh 6 (1979-80): 41-75.

is known to us by name. Aristobulus (2nd cent. BCE), descended from the High-Priestly line, inaugurates an interpretative philosophical approach to Scripture that dimly prefigures that of Philo.[49] Like the latter, his aim is to establish that the Torah's teaching is in accord with philosophical truth. To this end, he takes great pains to interpret anthropomorphic descriptions of God allegorically. He thus maintains that the biblical expression "hand of God" signifies the divine power, the 'standing of God" (Gen 28:13; Exod 17:6) refers to the immutability of God's creation, and the "voice of God" to the establishment of things, for as Moses continually says in his description of creation, "And God spoke and it came to pass." As for God's resting on the seventh day, this does not signify the end of his work but only that "after he had finished ordering all things, he so orders them for all time" (cf. Philo, *Leg.* 1.6), and the "work of the six days" only refers to the establishment of the course of time and the hierarchical structure of the universe.[50]

Although Aristobulus wishes the reader to understand the Torah philosophically (φυσικῶς) and "not slip into the mythological mode," and chides those who cling to the letter for their lack of insight and for providing a reading of the Torah in the light of which Moses fails to appear to be proclaiming great things,[51] there is no evidence that the biblical text as a whole ever became for him an allegory in the Philonic manner. Aristobulus further asserts that if anything unreasonable remains in the biblical text, the cause is not to be imputed to Moses but to himself. This seems to indicate his awareness of using a relatively new exegetical method and that he could not rely on a well-established tradition.[52]

8. *Philo of Alexandria*

Hellenistic Jewish philosophy reaches its climax in the subtle synthesis produced by Philo (ca. 20 BCE to ca. 50 CE) through his elaborate philosophical commentary on Scripture. Scion of a wealthy Jewish family and possibly of priestly descent like his forerunner Aristobulus, he played an important public role by heading a Jewish embassy to Gaius Caligula in 39-40 CE. His Atticized Greek displays a wide variety of rhetorical figures and styles, including a special fondness for the diatribe, the popular moral

---

[49] See 2 Macc 1:10; J. A. Goldstein, *II Maccabees* (AB 41A; Garden City, N.Y.: Doubleday, 1983), 168; and Gutman, *The Beginnings of Jewish Hellenistic Literature*, 1:187 (Hebrew).

[50] Fragments 2, 4, and 5, in Charlesworth, *OTP*, 2:837-42.

[51] Cf. *b. Qidd.* 49a: "R. Judah said, If one translates a verse literally, he is a liar."

[52] N. Walter, *Der Thoraausleger Aristobulos* (Berlin: Akademie Verlag, 1964), 124-29.

invective so characteristic of the Greco-Roman age. Although fully acquainted with the Greek philosophical texts at firsthand, Philo is not to be
regarded as an original philosopher, nor did he claim that distinction
himself. He saw his task more modestly as that of the great reconciler who
would bridge two disparate traditions that were both close to his heart.
Although there is still no consensus, it is likely that the apparent
eclecticism of his thought is in fact representative of Middle Platonism, a
philosophical tradition marked by Stoicizing and Pythagorizing tendencies,
including a strong dose of number symbolism.

The vast Philonic corpus may be divided into three groups: exegetical,
historical/apologetic, and philosophical. The exegetical writings, which
constitute the main body of Philo's work, can be subdivided into three
Pentateuchal commentaries: (1) the so-called Allegory of the Law, a series
of treatises that provide verse by verse commentary on biblical texts taken
from Gen 2:1-41:24, but constantly incorporate related texts that are in
turn investigated at length; (2) the so-called Exposition of the Law, constituted by a series of treatises organized around biblical themes or figures,
generally following the chronology of the Pentateuch; (3) Questions and
Answers on Genesis and Exodus (surviving only in Armenian and some
Greek fragments).

The fundamental goal of his great biblical commentary was to uncover
the hidden meaning of the Mosaic text, using allegorical interpretation,
the "method dear to men with their eyes opened" (*Plant.* 36). Greek alle-
gorism had its start towards the end of the sixth century BCE, in the
writings of Theagenes of Rhegium, who, in an apparent effort to defend
Homer against his detractors, interpreted his description of the inter-
necine battle of the gods as the antagonism of three pairs of opposites:
dry/wet, hot/cold, light/heavy. Philo was especially indebted to Stoic
allegorizing of the last two centuries BCE, such as that of Crates of Mallos,
who found in Homer's description of the shield of Agamemnon (*Iliad*
11.32-37) an image of the cosmos. A characteristic feature of the Stoic
exegetical technique, of which Philo was particularly fond, was the etymologizing of names, a direct outgrowth of the school's linguistic theory,
according to which names exist by nature, "the first articulate sounds being
imitations of things."[53] Philo was thus heir to an exuberant allegorizing tradition, which served him well in his heroic task of defending his ancestral

---

[53] *SVF* 2.146. A good example of Crates' playful manipulations of words in the manner of
Stoic etymologizing (similar to the rabbinic אל תקרי) is his interpretation of *Odyssey* 12.62-
63, where the pigeons (πέλειαι), which are said to carry ambrosia to Zeus are converted
into the Pleiades (Πλειάδες), since it is beneath Zeus' dignity to imagine that the birds
bring him ambrosia (Athenaeus, *Deipn.* 11.490b-e).

heritage. It should be noted, however, that Stoic and Middle Platonic allegoresis did not include the recognition of different levels of interpretation, and Philo is the earliest extant example of a writer who tries to maintain the validity of both the literal and the allegorical levels.

8. *Logos and Psychic Ascent*

Since Philo's mystical theology bars a direct approach to God's essence, we must seek it out through the oblique traces disclosed by its noetic aspect, the Divine Mind or Logos. Thus in Philo's hierarchical construction of reality the essence of God, though utterly concealed in its primary being, is nevertheless made manifest on two secondary levels, the intelligible universe constituting the Logos, which is God's image, and the sensible universe, an image of that image.[54] Philo further delineates the dynamics of the Logos' activity by defining its two constitutive polar principles, Goodness or the Creative Power, and Sovereignty or the Ruling Power, which are clearly reminiscent of the principles of Unlimit and Limit in Plato's *Philebus* (23c-31a), and reappear in Plotinus' two logical moments in the emergence of Intellect, where we find unlimited Intelligible Matter proceeding from the One and then turning back to its source for definition (*Enn.* 2.4.5; 5.4.2).[55]

Although the human soul, as a fragment of the Logos, might be thought to have a natural claim on immortality, the latter can be forfeited if the soul is not properly assimilated to its divine source. From Philo's Platonist perspective, the body is a corpse entombing the soul, which at its death returns to its own proper life (*Leg.* 1.107-08).[56] Alternatively, its sojourn in the body may be taken to be a period of exile (*QG* 3.10), a theme undoubtedly familiar to Philo from Middle Platonic exegesis of Homer's Odyssey, according to which Odysseus' arduous homeward journey symbolizes the soul's labors in its attempt to return to its original home (Plutarch, *Mor.* 745-46). The gradual removal of the psyche from the sensible realm and its ascent to a life of perfection in God is represented for Philo by two triads of biblical figures, the first (Enosh, Enoch, Noah) symbolizing the initial stages of the striving for perfection, the second (Abraham, Isaac, Jacob) its culmination (*Abr.* 759; *Praem.* 10-66). The Abraham of Philo is a mystical philosopher who, after having mastered the general studies (symbolized by

---

54 *Somn.* 1.239; *Conf.* 147-48; *Opif.* 25.
55 Philo, *Cher.* 27-28; *Sacr.* 59; *Her.* 166; *Abr.* 124-25.
56 Cf. M. Aurelius 4.41; Plato, *Resp.* 585b; *Tim.* 96b; *Soph.* 228-29; *Gorg.* 493a.

Hagar), in which stage all he could produce was Ishmael or sophistry, has abandoned the realm of sense (symbolized by his parting with Lot) for the intelligible world and, despite his initial flirtation with Chaldean (i.e. Stoic) pantheism, has attained to the highest vision of Deity, resulting in his transformation into a perfect embodiment of natural law.[57]

9. God and Creation

Philo defines two paths leading to a knowledge of God's existence. The first involves an apprehension of God through his works by those who are not yet initiated into the highest mysteries and are thus constrained to advance upward by a sort of heavenly ladder and conjecture his existence through plausible inference. The genuine worshipers and true friends of God, however, are "those who apprehend him through himself without the cooperation of reasoned inference, as light is seen by light" (*Praem.* 41). This formula is precisely that used later by Plotinus, when he speaks of "touching that light and seeing it by itself, not by another light, but by the light which is also its means of seeing" (*Enn.* 5.3.17.34-37 [Armstrong, LCL]).[58] Although there is no consensus concerning the precise meaning of Philo's second and superior path to God, some arguing that it results from a special grace of God, whose illumination flashes into the human psyche from without, it is, in my opinion, very likely based on the notion of a direct and continuous access of the human mind to God from within and may perhaps be viewed as an early form of the ontological argument, as it had already been formulated by the Stoics.[59]

Whether or not Philo's overpowering conviction of God's existence owes something to the Stoic ontological argument or perhaps to a Middle

---

[57] *Abr.* 68-71, 119-32; *Migr.* 1-12, 176-95; *Somn.* 1.41-60; *Gig.* 62-64. See S. Sandmel, *Philo's Place in Judaism* (Cincinnati: Hebrew Union College Press, 1956), 96-211.

[58] In *Leg.* 1.38, Philo writes: "For how could the soul have conceived of God had he not infused it and taken hold of it as far as was possible?" Cf. R. A. Nicholson (*The Mystics of Islam* [London: Routledge and Keegan Paul, 1963], 50): "This is what [the Caliph] 'Ali meant when he was asked, 'Do you see God?' and replied: 'How should we worship One whom we do not see?' The light of intuitive certainty (*yaqin*) by which the heart sees God is a beam of God's own light cast therein by Himself; else no vision of Him were possible. Tis the sun's self that lets the sun be seen." See also Spinoza's *Short Treatise* 1.1.10 : "But God, the first Cause of all things, and also the cause of himself, makes himself known through himself" (E. Curley, *The Collected Works of Spinoza* [Princeton: Princeton University Press, 1985], 65).

[59] D. Winston, *Logos and Mystical Theology in Philo of Alexandria* (Cincinnati: Hebrew Union College Press, 1985), 43-47.

Platonist version of it, his doctrine of creation clearly echoes the Stoic way of formulating that issue. Having attained philosophy's summit, Moses, according to Philo, recognized that there are two fundamental causes of being, the one active, the other passive (*SVF* 2.300, 312), the former an absolutely pure universal mind, beyond virtue and knowledge, the latter lifeless and motionless (*Opif.* 7-9). God thus created the universe by means of his "all-incising" Logos (λόγος τομεύς), out of a qualityless primordial matter, containing in itself nothing lovely and so utterly passive as to be virtually nonexistent. All things were created simultaneously and the sequential creation account in Genesis is meant only to indicate the logical order in God's design. As to whether the act of creation is understood by Philo as having a temporal beginning or as an eternal process, this continues to be a highly controversial issue, though a very substantial case can, I think, be made for the latter view.[60]

10. *Mysticism*

Dodds has correctly noted that the ecstatic form of prophecy as defined by Philo is not a description of mystical union, but a state of temporary possession.[61] Philo, however, speaks also of another form of prophecy, which may be designated 'hermeneutical' or 'noetic' and is mediated not through ecstatic possession but through the divine voice. Whereas in the state of possession the prophet's mind is entirely preempted, it is clear from Philo's analysis of the giving of the Decalogue, the paradigm of divine-voice prophecy, that in the latter the inspired mind is extraordinarily quickened. Since ecstatic possession is employed by Philo for the explanation of predictive prophecy alone, whereas the core of the Mosaic prophecy, the particular laws, are delivered by him in his role of hermeneutical or noetic prophet, it is in this form of prophecy that we must locate Philo's conception of mystical union. In his allegorical interpretation of the divine voice as the projection of a special "rational soul full of clearness and distinctness" making unmediated contact with the inspired mind that "makes the first advance," one can readily discern a reference to the activation of the human intellect (*Decal.* 37, 35). In Philo's noetic prophecy, then, we may detect the union of the human mind with the

---

60 Idem, "Review of D. T. Runia, *Philo of Alexandria and the Timaeus of Plato,*" *Ancient Philosophy* 12 (1992): 222-27. idem, "Creation Ex Nihilo."

61 E. R. Dodds, *Pagan and Christian in An Age of Anxeity* (Cambridge: Cambridge University Press, 1965), 70-72.

divine mind, or, in Dodd's terms, a psychic ascent rather than a supernatural descent.[62]

A series of Philonic passages contain most of the characteristic earmarks
of mystical experience: knowledge of God as one's supreme bliss and
separation from him as the greatest of evils; the soul's intense yearning for
the divine; its recognition of its nothingness and of its need to go out of
itself; attachment to God; the realization that it is God alone who acts; a
preference for wordless contemplative prayer; a timeless union with the All
and its resulting serenity; the suddenness with which the mystical vision
occurs; the experience of sober intoxication; and, finally, the ebb and flow
of the mystical experience. These passages go well beyond a merely
spirited religiosity, revealing instead what constitutes at the very least an
intellectual or theoretical form of mysticism but may well represent a
genuine inner experience that envelops Philo's psyche and fills it with
God's nearness.[63] Whether we can go further and attribute to him mystical
happenings involving union with the Divine Mind must remain uncertain
in view of the absence of anything more than vague descriptions of
personal psychic states that may represent only incipient forms of mystical
experience.[64]

---

[62] D. Winston, "Two types of of Mosaic Prophecy According to Philo of Alexandria," *JSP*
4 (1989): 49-67.
[63] Idem, *Philo of Alexandria: The Contemplative Life, the Giants, and Selections* (New York:
Paulist, 1981), 164-74.
[64] See *Migr.* 34-35; *Cher.* 27; *Leg.* 2.32, 85; *Somn.* 2.252.

PART TWO

BEN SIRA

CHAPTER TWO

Theodicy in Ben Sira and Stoic Philosophy

It has often been claimed that Ben Sira is engaged in a running polemic with Hellenism. Although Rudolf Smend's view that Sirach "hated Hellenism and the Greeks with all his heart" has been echoed to some extent by M. Hengel and more fully by V. Tcherikover, few modern scholars would now subscribe to that position. As J. Goldstein has pointed out, "the words 'Greek' and 'Greece' nowhere appear in Ben Sira's work ... Ben Sira does not tell his fellow Jews that they must not imitate foreigners, nor does he tell Jews to shun pagans." Goldstein believes that "Hellenism was simply not an issue for Ben Sira, since there were few if any Greeks in the country to imitate."[1] J. T. Sanders has correctly observed that Ben Sira "is entirely open to Hellenic thought as long as it can be Judaized."[2] Nevertheless, one can readily detect in his conception of human knowledge a considerably more modest assessment of the human capacity to master natural science than that espoused by the author of the Wisdom of Solomon. Although Ben Sira's blast in Sir 3:21-24 is probably directed against cosmogonic and extra-terrestrial speculations, which he considered potentially dangerous, he does not seem to share the very bold and enthusiastic confidence that the author of Wisdom has in his ability to attain "an unerring knowledge of existent being" (Wis 7:17). In contrast to Ben Sira who alludes to humanity's inability to count "the days of unending time" (Sir 1:2), the author of Wisdom knows "the beginning, and end, and middle of times" (Wis 7:17), a phrase with a distinctively cosmogonic ring and one deriving from the Orphic theogony.[3] But this denotes only a difference of degree and in no way indicates any reluctance on Ben Sira's part to adapt Hellenistic learning whenever it suited his purposes.

There can be little doubt that Ben Sira's opus is marked by a consistent effort to effect a new synthesis of ideas. In an age when Hellenic wisdom

---

[1] Jonathan Goldstein, "Jewish Acceptance & Rejection of Hellenism," in *Jewish and Christian Self-Definition* (ed. E. P. Sanders et al., 3 vols.; Philadelphia: Fortress, 1981), 1:73, 75; Rudolf Smend, *Die Weisheit des Jesus Sirach* (Berlin: Reimer, 1906), xxiv.

[2] J. T. Sanders, *Ben Sira & Demotic Wisdom* (Chico: Scholars Press, 1983), 58. Cf. J. L. Crenshaw, *Old Testament Wisdom: An Introduction* (Atlanta: John Knox, 1981), 159.

[3] Otto Kern, *Orphicorum Fragmenta* (Berlin: Weidmann, 1922), 91, 201.

dominated the civilized world, he did his best to broaden the bounds of the Mosaic Law so that it would encompass every manifestation of wisdom. As Collins has correctly pointed out, Ben Sira's so-called nationalization of wisdom constituted in reality the universalization of the Torah.[4] More than subordinating wisdom to the Law, he assimilated the Law to universal wisdom. The key note in his writing is that of didactic wisdom rather than the Law. The Torah is refracted for Ben Sira through the lense of wisdom, and the case for its legitimacy is made in wisdom's terms. "All wisdom is the fear of the Lord, and in all wisdom is fulfillment of the Law" (Sir 19:20).[5]

It is especially, however, in his confrontation with the problem of evil that Ben Sira moves beyond the earlier wisdom tradition and is actively engaged in adapting Stoic arguments for the formulation of his main solution to this puzzling paradox, namely, that nature is to be seen as a harmony of opposites. Although Platonism did not arrive in Alexandria before the first century BCE, some knowledge of Stoic philosophy does appear to have penetrated the Alexandrian intellectual scene already in the third century BCE, for we are told that when Cleanthes, scholiarch of the Stoic School from 263 to 232, refused the invitation of Ptolemy Philadelphus, he sent his pupil Sphaerus there instead (Diogenes Laertius 7.185). Sphaerus was later the counsellor of Cleomenes III of Sparta, who ended his days in Alexandria, and it is possible that he returned with him there, although the evidence is uncertain.[6] The visit of an isolated Stoic philosopher does not constitute a major presence and it is therefore unlikely that in the absence of a flourishing Stoic center such as those found in Rhodes and in Tarsus, Ben Sira would have possessed a detailed and technical knowledge of the Stoic philosophy. But the broad outlines of their thought and the chief elements of their major doctrines were probably well known to him. Although he does not speak explicitly of the harmony of the universal order, his words clearly imply it. The unity of creation was a given for biblical monotheism, so that Ben Sira faced the same dilemma that stalked the Stoics, whose single-minded monism was their philosophical trademark. Both he and they were constrained to explain the warring dualities that seem to mar the unity of being. In Sir 33:7-14, he seeks to reconcile the unity of creation with a divine plan that consistently discriminates between pairs of opposites: good and evil, life

---

[4] See Collins, "The Biblical Precedent for Natural Theology"; and Winston, *Wisdom of Solomon*, 36.

[5] See von Rad, *Wisdom in Israel*, 246-57.

[6] See Fraser, *Ptolemaic Alexandria*, 1.481; 2.695, n. 17; Pautrel, "Ben Sira et le Stoicisme."

and death, the sinner and the godly. In his effort to explicate the dietary laws, Pseudo-Aristeas had also noted the paradox that, in spite of the fact that creation was one, some things are regarded by the Torah as unclean for food and some even to the touch, and in the course of his explanation of this surprising fact he pointed out that although all things are to the natural reason similarly constituted, being all administered by a single power, in every case there is a profound logic for our abstinence from the use of some things and our participation in the use of others (*Let. Aris.* 129, 143). Ben Sira similarly indicates that although every day has its light from the sun, certain days were by the Lord's decision distinguished and made holy, and though all people were created out of earth, some, in God's great wisdom, were hallowed and brought near to Him, while others were cursed and removed from their place. "Look at all the works of the Most High," he concludes, "they go in pairs, one the opposite of the other" (Sir 33:15).[7] All this evidently implies that the universe consists of a harmony of opposites in accordance with a mysterious divine design.

The Stoics taught a similar doctrine. First, like Ben Sira, they declared that divine providence is "chiefly directed and concentrated upon three objects, namely to secure for the world, first, the structure best fitted for survival; next, absolute completeness (*ut nulla re egeat*); but chiefly, consummate beauty and embellishment of every kind" (Cicero, *Nat. d.* 2.58).[8] Then too, like Ben Sira, they taught that this is the best possible world that could be produced (Cicero, *Nat. d.* 2.87), and that notwithstanding apparent imperfections here and there, Nature so organized each part that harmony is present in the whole.[9] As for the evil of natural disasters, "it has a rationale peculiar to itself, for in a sense it too occurs in accordance with universal reason, and so to speak, is not without usefulness in relation to the whole. For without it there could be no good" (Chrysippus, in Plutarch, *Comm. not.* 1065B). M. Aurelius finds comfort in the belief that

---

[7] Cf. Qoh. 7:14; *T. Naph.* 2:7; *T. Ash.* 1:4-5; *Midr. Temurah* chap. 1; Philo, *Opif.* 33.

[8] Cf. Sir 42:17, "So that the universe may stand firm in his glory"; 42:23, "Everything liveth and abideth forever"; 42:24, "He has made nothing superfluous"; 42:22, "How beautiful is all that he has made"; 43:1, 9, 11. Cf. also Philo, *Spec.* 3.189; *SVF* 2.1009; Xenophon, *Cyr.* 8.7.22; Cicero, *Nat. d.* 2.93.

[9] Epictetus, *Diatr.* 1.12.16: "Instruction consists precisely in learning to desire each thing exactly as it happens. And how do they happen? As he that ordains them has ordained. And he has ordained that there be summer and winter, and abundance and death, and virtue and vice, and all such opposites, for the harmony of the whole ..."; Seneca, *Nat.* 7.27.4: "Do you not see how opposite the elements are among themselves? They are heavy and light, cold and hot, wet and dry; all the harmony of this universe is formed out of discordant elements." Cf. Hengel, *Judaism and Hellenism*, 1:147-49.

everything contributes to some grand universal scheme: "Nothing is harmful to the part which is advantageous to the whole. For the whole contains nothing which is not advantageous to itself ... As long as I remember that I am a part of such a whole I shall be well content with all that happens" (10.6). Ben Sira's attitude is quite similar: "No one should ask 'What is that?', or 'Why is that?' Everything has been created for its own purpose" (Sir 39:21). Indeed, the very elements that are "good for the godfearing turn to evil for sinners" (39:21; cf. Wis 16:24). "Fire and hail, famine and deadly disease, all these were created for retribution; beasts of prey, scorpions and vipers, and the avenging sword that destroys the wicked" (Sir 39:29-30). The Stoics had also pointed out that providence either watches over earthly affairs or cleanses them by floods and con-flagrations (Origen, *Cels.* 4.64 = *SVF* 2.1174).[10]

The more recalcitrant problem, however, was presented not so much by natural as by moral evil, and here again both Ben Sira and the Stoics employ the same approach. Logic requires the existence of both good and evil. In the fourth book of his treatise *On Providence*, Chrysippus argued as follows: "There is absolutely nothing more foolish than those men who think that good could exist, if there were at the same time no evil. For since good is the opposite of evil, it necessarily follows that both must exist in opposition to each other, supported as it were by mutual adverse forces; since as a matter of fact no opposite is conceivable without something to oppose it. For how could there be an idea of justice if there were no acts of injustice?" (Aulus Gellius, *Noct. att.* 7.1.2-4).[11]

Finally, Ben Sira's grateful response to the wonders of creation and his urgent call for man's acknowledging praise of their divine Author (Sir 42:15-43:33), goes hand in hand with his optimistic assessment of this best of all possible worlds: "All the works of the Lord are good, and he supplies every need as it occurs. No one should say, 'this is less good than that,' for all things prove good at their proper time. Come then, sing with heart and voice, and praise the name of the Lord" (39:33-35). Precisely the same

---

[10] Cf. Philo, *Prov.* 2.31-32: God employs famine, pestilence or earthquake out of his concern for virtue; and 2.104: Venomous animals are prepared by God for punishment of the errant.

[11] In 17:31 Ben Sira writes: "Is anything brighter than the sun? Yet the sun suffers eclipse. So flesh and blood have evil thoughts." Philo similarly writes: "It must needs be that mortal man shall be oppressed by the nation of the passions and receive the calamities which are proper to created being, but it is God's will to lighten the evils which are inherent in our race" (*Her.* 272-74). Cf. Seneca, *Ira* 2.28.4: "For it is not by the power of the gods, but by the terms of our mortality that we are forced to suffer whatever ill befalls."

blend of ideas characterizes the Stoic position. For the latter it is a matter of justice to render thanks for God's innumerable benefactions, and it is therefore the human task to hymn the praises of the Deity: "Why, if we had sense, ought we to be doing anything else, publicly and privately, than hymning and praising the Deity, and rehearsing his benefits? .. This is my task; I do it, and will not desert this post, as long as it may be given me to fill it; and I exhort you to join me in this same song" (Epictetus, *Diatr.* 1.16.15-21). The special suitability of hymns for singing the praises of God had already been emphasized by Cleanthes: "Bare prose does not have expressions suitable to the divine majesty, nor the meters, melodies, and rhythms to approach as closely as possible to the truth of the contemplation of divine things" (*SVF* 1.486, cf. Plato, *Resp.* 607a).[12] In sum, in dealing with the very thorny problem of theodicy, Ben Sira seems to have consciously followed in the footsteps of the Stoics, who had already exerted all their ingenuity in order to resolve the many challenges that must have been constantly hurled at them in the face of their self-satisfied and supremely optimistic faith in a perfect all-embracing Nature.[13]

Another aspect of the theodicy issue in regard to which Ben Sira seems to have followed the Stoic lead is in his formulation of the paradox of freedom and determinism. The older wisdom literature did not feel this contradiction too keenly, and was content to assert that all was determined by the gods in advance, and yet at the same time to insist that success and failure, and punishment and reward were conditioned by human behavior. In Egyptian writings, not only do the gods inspire people to act in all kinds of situations, but they are also said to cause them to commit destructive actions. In the inscriptions of Petosiris, who lived at the dawn of the Ptolemaic era, we read: "God places it [the evil thought] into the heart of him whomever he hates in order to give his goods to another whom he loves."[14] The same idea is already found, however, in the *Instruction of Ptahhotep* (from the Period of the Old Kingdom): "His guilt was fated in the

---

[12]   The use of hymns to the deity in Ben Sira is paralleled by the employment of a hymn to the creator-god in the *Instruction of Papyrus Insinger*, chap. 24, which is entitled "the teaching of knowing the greatness of the god so as to put it in your heart." According to Miriam Lichtheim, both *Papyrus Insinger* and Ben Sira were influenced by Hellenistic wisdom writings.

[13]   For a good general treatment of theodicy in Ben Sira, see James Crenshaw, "The Problem of Theodicy in Sirach: On Human Bondage," in *Theodicy in the Old Testament* (ed. J. L. Crenshaw; Philadelphia: Fortress, 1983), 199-240.

[14]   G. Lefebvre, *Le Tombeau de Petosiris* (Cairo: Impr. de l'Institut francais d'archeologie orientale, 1923-4), 2.91 (inscription 127, line 6); cited by S. Morenz, *Egyptian Religion*, (trans. A. W. Keep; London: Methuen, 1973), 66. Cf. Eccles. 2:26.

womb; He whom they guide cannot go wrong, whom they make boatless cannot cross" (12 = 210ff).[15] In the epilogue to that work it is said: "He who hears is beloved of god, He whom god hates does not hear. The heart makes of its owner a hearer or non-hearer ..." (540-50). An individual's career is similarly predetermined. In the Middle Kingdom *Teaching of Khety* it is said: "Lo, I have set you on god's path, A scribe's Renenet [a goddess of bounty and good luck] is on his shoulder on the day he is born.... The Meshkenet [goddess who presided over births] assigned to the scribe, she promotes him in the council."[16] Thus the deities Meskhenet and Renenet determined at a child's birth how successful he was to be in his pro-fessional career.[17] On a larger scale, the social status of a person is also determined by the god: "Man is clay and straw, The God is his builder. He tears down, he builds up daily. He makes a thousand poor by his will, He makes a thousand men into chiefs, when he is in his hour of life."[18] In the *Admonitions of Ipuwer*, dating from the period after the collapse of the Old Kingdom, a number of deplorable events are explained as having been determined at a very early stage by the gods: "This was predestined for you in the time of Horus, in the age of the Ennead."[19] According to *Ptahhotep*, "people's schemes do not prevail. God's commandment is what prevails; Live then in the midst of peace, what they (= gods) give comes by itself" (115-18).[20] The Demotic *Instruction of Anchsheshonqy* is particularly empha-tic concerning the absolute divine control over all human events: "There is imprisonment for giving life. There is release for killing. There is he who saves and does not find. All are from the hand of the fate and the god" (26.5-8).[21]

One passage in *Ptahhotep* seems to imply that one can immunize oneself from the vice of greed, but once having become infected with this disease, one can no longer free oneself from it: "If you want a perfect conduct, To be free from every evil, Guard against the vice of greed: A grievous sickness without cure, There is no treatment for it" (298). This has been taken to indicate the author's attempt to qualify his doctrine of absolute deter-minism.[22] In fact, however, what this passage asserts is the exact equivalent

---

[15] See Lichtheim, *Ancient Egyptian Literature*, 1:67.

[16] *The Satire of the Trades*, or *Teaching of Khety, Son of Duauf*, in Lichtheim, *Ancient Egyptian Literature*, 1:191.

[17] Morenz, *Egyptian Religion*, 67.

[18] *Instruction of Amenemope* 10.13-18, in Lichtheim, *Ancient Egyptian Literature*, 2:160.

[19] See Morenz, *Egyptian Religion*, 68.

[20] Lichtheim, *Ancient Egyptian Literature*, 1:65.

[21] Lichtheim, *Late Egyptian Wisdom Literature*, 90-91.

[22] Lichtheim, *Ancient Egyptian Literature*, 1:68. The interpretation is that of M. Fox, *The Book of Qohelet and its Relation to the Wisdom School* (Ph.D. diss., Hebrew University of

of Aristotle's similar discussion in *Ethica Nicomachea* 3.1114a, where it is argued that before a person's disposition is formed, he is apparently in a position to act in different ways, but once it is formed, this is no longer true.[23] What all this amounts to is that even what might be considered the relative freedom people ordinarily possess is no longer available to them once they have allowed themselves to acquire incorrigibly diseased dispositions. The theoretical question, however, of whether their initial freedom of action is to be considered absolute or relative is not explicitly resolved by Aristotle, but is turned aside instead by an *ad hominem* argument (1114a31-b25). In any case, the passage cited above from *Ptahhotep* does not necessarily soften the deterministic sentiments quoted earlier from that work.

It has been pointed out that the Demotic wisdom Instruction known as *Papyrus Insinger* was the first such Egyptian writing to deal consciously and explicitly with the freedom/determinism dilemma. Except for the paradoxical chapter endings, which describe human beings as totally dependent on God and divine emissaries, Fate and Fortune (*Shay* and *Shne*),[24] all of *Papyrus Insinger*'s teachings affirm humanity's moral freedom. H. Brunner argued that the belief in the regular connection between deed and result had been abandoned in *Papyrus Insinger*, but as Lichtheim has correctly remarked, if this were the case "it would be impossible to understand the Demotic writer's intention when he composed his long Instruction in which that connection is continuously reiterated." What we find in Papyrus Insinger is very much like the paradoxical formulation of the Stoics that everything is in accord with Heimarmene, yet our actions are in our power (ἐφ' ἡμῖν). In the light of the various Hellenistic elements in *Papyrus Insinger* it is very likely that in this case too we are dealing with such an influence. Lichtheim has enumerated the following examples of Hellenistic borrowings: *Papyrus Insinger*'s loose aphoristic form combined with an attempt to impose some order; the choice of themes (similarity with Pseudo-Plutarch's *De liberis educandis*); "character" as a key term and the drawing up of a typology of characters; the concept of disposition and its explanation by examples drawn from three classes of things, substances, animals, and people (similar to Stoic theory); the Greek τόπος "count no man happy till his death"; two kinds of shame; not to slight small things

Jerusalem, 1972), 51 (Hebrew).

23 See the excellent discussion of this Aristotelian passage in David J. Furley, *Two Studies in the Greek Atomists* (Princeton: Princeton University Press, 1967), 184-95.

24 *Papyrus Insinger* 5.9 reads: "There is curse and blessing in the character that was given him."

(ὀλιγωρία); the fallibility of the wise man; the teaching of the right mean; and finally, the self-presentation of the author. In view of such a considerable number of striking similarities between *Papyrus Insinger* and Ben Sira, it is reasonable to assume that the similar formulation of the freedom/determinism paradox found in both these authors was due to their common use of Stoic sources.[25]

Although a palpably deterministic strain does run through the book of Proverbs, it nevertheless lacks an explicit and conscious expression of the freedom/determinism paradox. Thus the author of Proverbs teaches that the sage will acquire wisdom, while the fool will hold it in contempt, thereby implying that their life course is fixed in advance.[26] There is even a verse that asserts that God has created all, including the fool, for a special purpose (16:4).[27] Nowhere, however, does the book of Proverbs declare unequivocally, as does Ben Sira, that God has determined a person's character even before birth (Sir 1:14-15), or that a human being was fashioned by God as clay in the power of the potter, so that in accordance with an eternal cosmic plan, the godly or blessed stand over against the sinner or the cursed (Sir 33:10-15). Moreover, Ben Sira includes, along with his starkly predestinarian passages, emphatic statements concerning humanity's freedom to choose his life-path accompanied by explicit warnings against blaming God for causing him to sin.[28] The book of Proverbs, on the other hand, like most of the earlier Near Eastern wisdom instructions, does not explicitly articulate the contradiction between the all-determining divine will and the apparent freedom of choice enjoyed by human beings.[29]

It may fairly be said that the Hellenistic elements utilized by Sirach are generally in the service of a conventional wisdom view of things, and there is no sign that he was willing to strike out in radically new directions. He undoubtedly found that the manner in which the Stoics dealt with the problem of theodicy was most congenial to the Jewish approach to things, and was therefore quite happy to adopt a number of their formulations in this regard. The author of Wisdom, on the other hand, was clearly a much

---

[25] See Lichtheim, *Late Egyptian Wisdom,* 107-96.

[26] Prov 14:6; 17:16; 9:7; 13:19; 20:12.

[27] See Fox, *Book of Qohelet,* 53-54.

[28] See Winston, *Wisdom of Solomon,* 48-49.

[29] I am therefore unable to accept J. T. Sanders' judgment that the book of Proverbs already contained the freedom/determinism paradox that characterizes Ben Sira. Moreover, his citation of Prov 22:2 as an expression of the deterministic view is inapt, since that verse refers not to the divine determination of a person's ethical character, but of his economic status. See Sanders, *Ben Sira & Demotic Wisdom,* 55, n. 127.

greater enthusiast of Greek philosophy and science, bold enough to conceive of Wisdom as an eternal emanation (ἀπόρροια) of God's glory, and even ready to adopt elements of Stoic physical theory in order to explicate biblical miracles. Much of this new spirit, however, must be ascribed to the new social and intellectual context in which that author found himself.

CHAPTER THREE

Freedom and Determinism in Greek Philosophy and Jewish Hellenistic Wisdom

Introduction

Say not: "From God is my transgression", For that which he hateth made He not. Say not: "(It is) He that made me to stumble," for there is no need of evil men. Evil and Abomination doth the Lord hate, and He doth not let it come nigh to them that fear Him (Sir 15:11-13).[1]

In a monotheistic creed there is almost an ineluctable tendency to fault omnipotent deity for human sin. The rabbis, for example, put the following critique into the mouth of Cain:

Master of the world, if I have killed him, it is thou who hast created in me the Evil Yezer. Thou watchest me and the whole world. Why didst thou permit me to kill him? It is thou who hast killed him ... for if thou hadst received my sacrifice I would not have become jealous of him (*Midr. Ha-gadol*, Gen 4:9).

That the rabbis took this critique seriously is made clear by the statement of Rabbi Simeon b. Yohai,

It is a thing hard to say, and it is impossible for the mouth to utter it. It is to be compared to two athletes who were wrestling in the presence of the king. If the king wills, he can have them separated; but the king wills not; in the end one overwhelmed the other and killed him. And the dying man shouted: "Let my case be examined before the king" (*Gen Rab.* 22:9).[2]

The rabbis similarly plead in favor of the brothers of Joseph, "When thou didst choose, thou didst make them love; when thou didst choose, thou

---

[1] Translations of Sirach in this essay are from *APOT* (ed. R. H. Charles; 2 vols.; Oxford: Clarendon, 1913), unless otherwise noted.

[2] The midrashic analogue of an athletic contest seems to be drawn from Greek sophistic discussions. Plutarch, for example, tells us that a certain athlete had hit Epitimus the Pharsalian with a javelin, accidentally, and killed him, and Pericles squandered an entire day discussing with Protagoras whether it was the javelin or rather the one who hurled it or the judges of the contests, that ought to be held responsible for the disaster (*Per.* 36).

didst make them hate" (*Gen. Rab.* 84:18). Elijah, too, spoke insolently towards heaven (literally, "hurled words against the height") saying to God, "Thou hast turned their heart back again," and God later confessed that Elijah was right (*b. Ber.* 31b; cf. *Sanh.* 105a).[3] A similar critique is voiced with almost consistent monotony by the author of 4 Ezra, "This is my first and last word; better had it been that the earth had not produced Adam, or else, having once produced him, (for thee) to have restrained him from sinning" (4 Ezra 7:116).[4] The author of the Apocalypse of Abraham is equally exercised over the divine license for evil to invade the human psyche, "O Eternal, Mighty One! Wherefore hast thou willed to effect that evil should be desired in the hearts of men, since Thou indeed art angered over that which was willed by Thee ..." (*Apoc. Ab.* 23).[5] Even in the polytheistic ambience of the Homeric human being we find an analogous attempt to put the burden of sin on Zeus. "Not I was the cause of this act," cries Agamemnon,

> but Zeus and my portion and the Erinys who walks in darkness: they it was who in the assembly put wild ἄτη in my understanding, on that day when I arbitrarily took Achilles' prize from him. So what could I do? Deity will always have its way (*Il.* 19.86).

That this is no idiosyncratic whim of Agamemnon is attested by the understanding response of Achilles:

> Father Zeus, great indeed are the ἄται thou givest to men. Else the son of Atreus would never have persisted in rousing the θυμός in my chest, nor obstinately taken the girl against my will (*Il.* 19.270ff.)[6]

In a sense, the Bible itself encouraged this feeling that God is ultimately responsible for humanity's wicked deeds. A distinct complex of historic

---

[3] See S. Schechter, *Some Aspects of Rabbinic Theology* (New York: Macmillan, 1936), 264-92.

[4] Translation from *APOT* 2:591; cf. 3:8, 20-22; 7:47-48; 8:42-44.

[5] *The Apocalypse of Abraham* (ed. G. H. Box; London: SPCK, 1919), 71

[6] Cf. Herodotus 1.45 (Godley, LCL): "But it is not you that I hold the cause of this evil [says Croesus to Adrastus], save in so far as you were the unwilling doer of it: rather it is the word of a god, the same who told me long ago what was to be"; Homer, *Od.* 1.32-34 (Murray, LCL): "Look you now [says Zeus], how ready mortals are to blame the gods. It is from us, they say, that evils come, but they even of themselves, through their own blind folly, have sorrows beyond that which is ordained." See E. R. Dodds, *The Greeks and the Irrational* (Berkeley: University of California, 1959), 3; Willy Theiler, "Tacitus und die antike Schicksalslehre, " *Phyllobolia für Peter von der Mühll* (Editiones helveticae. Series graeca 4. Basel: Helbing & Lichtenhahn, 1946), 56-7; M. Pohlenz, *Freedom in Greek Life and Thought* (Dordrecht: D. Reidel, 1966), 124-60; E. Wust, "Von den Anfängen des Problems der Willensfreiheit," *Rheinisches Museum* 101 (1958): 95. Gregory Vlastos, *Plato's Universe* (Oxford: Clarendon, 1975), chapter 1.

events is explicated in Scripture through the primitive but potent concept
of psychic invasion. God directly intervenes in Pharaoh's inner delibera-
tions, "hardening his heart" in order to demonstrate ultimately his divine
might (Exod 10:1; cf. Sir 16:15). He similarly hardens the heart of Sihon,
king of the Amorites (Deut 2:30), and applies the same divine strategy to
the Canaanites (Josh 11:20: "It was the Lord's purpose that they should
offer an obstinate resistance to the Israelites in battle, and that thus they
should be annihilated without mercy and utterly destroyed, as the Lord
had commanded Moses"). Inversely, God does not permit Abimelech, King
of Gerar, to sin with Abraham's wife Sarah (Gen 20:6). In an encounter
with Saul, David is ready to suggest that perhaps it is the Lord who has
incited Saul against him (1 Sam 26:19), and when the Lord's anger is
kindled against Israel, we are told that he incites David to count them (2
Sam 24:1; cf. 1 Chr 21:1). God prevented Eli's sons from taking their
father's admonitions seriously, because he wished to slay them (1 Sam
2:25), and in order to fulfill his word to Ahijah the Shilonite spoken to
Jeroboam (1 Kgs 11:31), he induced Rehoboam to refuse the people's
request that he lighten their yoke (1 Kgs 12:15). Isaiah takes up the same
theme. "Make the heart of this people fat, and their ears heavy, and shut
their eyes; lest they see with their eyes, and hear with their ears, and understand with their hearts, and turn and be healed" (Isa 7:10 [RSV]; cf. 29:10).
Finally, both Jeremiah and Ezekiel foresee God's direct future intervention
in order to transform the human psyche and redeem it from its congenital
misery.[7] In the light of this background of ideas, (in addition, of course, to
the deterministic elements running through ancient Near Eastern wisdom

---

[7] Jer 31:30-33; 32:39-40; Ezek 36:16-30; 20:32-44; cf. Deut 30:6; *Jub.* 1:23; 5:12. See W.
Lütgert, *Das Problem der Willensfreiheit in der vor christlichen Synagoge* (Beiträge zur Forde-
rung christlicher Theologie 10.2; Gütersloh: Bertelsmann, 1906); Y. Kaufmann, *History of
Israelite Religion* (4 vols.; Tel-Aviv: Mosad Bialik, 1966 or 1967) 3:2, 438, 560-61 (Hebrew).
Cf. also 2 Chr 25:20; Pseudo-Philo, *L.A.B.* 12:3: "And when he [Aaron] said this, they
hearkened not unto him, that the word might be fulfilled which was spoken in the day
when the people sinned in building the tower, when God said: 'And now if I forbid them
not, they will adventure all that they take in mind to do, and worse'" (M. R. James, trans.,
The Biblical Antiquities of Philo [New York: Ktav, 1971], 111) (See also 21:2, 22:7). Many of
the above quoted biblical verses later came under the attack of the Gnostic Marcion. See
Adolf von Harnack, *Marcion* (Darmstadt: Wissenschaftliche Buchgesellschaft, 1960), 272,
278; A. Marmorstein, *Studies in Jewish Theology* (London: Oxford University Press, 1950), 1-
47. For the Greek notion of psychic intervention, see Dodds, *The Greek and the Irrational,*
10ff.; and for the Greek notion of ἄτη as a deliberate deception which draws the victim on
to fresh error whereby he hastens his own ruin (the grim doctrine that *Quem deus vult
perdere, prius dementat*), see Dodds, *The Greeks and the Irrational,* 38-9. Cf. also the Muslim
notion of "sealing" (Qur'an 2:5-6; 7:92-99). See W. M. Watt, *Free Will and Predestination in
Early Islam* (London: Luzac, 1948), 15-16.

literature and more especially the book of Ecclesiastes), it is not difficult to see how Ben Sira (ca. 180 B.C.E) could come to emphasize the decisive importance of God's prior gift of wisdom in determining a person's moral character. We shall now attempt to show that the quotation from Ben Sira with which we began does not necessarily constitute an inner contradiction in his doctrine on this point, and that his teaching (which reached its fullest development in the Dead Sea Scrolls) had a considerable impact on the author of the Wisdom of Solomon.

Ben Sira

Ben Sira clearly states that God has predetermined a person's character from birth.

> To fear the Lord is the beginning of Wisdom, and with the faithful was she created in the womb. With faithful men is she, and she hath been established from eternity, and with their seed shall she continue (Sir 1:14-15).

This is but part of the larger cosmological picture that our author depicts.

> When God created His works from the beginning, after making them He assigned them (their) portions. He set in order his works forever, and their authority unto their generations. They hunger not, neither are they weak, and they cease not from their works. Not one thrusteth aside his neighbour, they never disobey His word (Sir 16:26-28).[8]

The notion of portions recurs throughout the book. "Praise is not seemly in the mouth of the wicked, For it hath not been apportioned him by God (Sir 15:8).[9] A more detailed account of God's fashioning of human beings spells out the polar plan of creation that provides for two antithetical categories of people.

> Likewise also all men are made from the clay, and Adam was created of earth. In His great wisdom God distinguished them, and differentiated their ways. Some He blessed and exalted, and others He hallowed and brought nigh to Himself. Some He cursed and abased, and overthrew them from their place. As the clay is in the power of the potter, to fashion it according to his good pleasure; so is man in

---

[8] Cf. *t. Yoma* 2:7, "From this Ben Azzai deduced: you will be given that is yours, by your name you will be called, and in your place you will be set; there is no lapse of memory before God; no one can touch what is prepared for his fellow" (see parallels in *y. Yoma* 3:9; *b. Yoma* 38a).

[9] Cf. Sir 40:1; 38:1; 17:7; 41:3; 11:22; *1 Enoch* 67:1; *Pss. Sol.* 5:6.

the power of his creator, to make him according to His ordinance.[10]
Over against evil (stands) the good, and against death life; Likewise
over against the godly the sinner. Even thus look upon all the works of
God, each different, one the opposite of the other (Sir 33:10-15).[11]

Moreover, the hopeless condition of the sinner is explicitly related to his
genetic endowment. "(As for) the wound of the scorner [i.e., his lack of
wisdom], there is no healing for it, for an evil growth is his plant" (Sir
3:28).[12]

How can we now reconcile this stark predestinarianism with the equally
emphatic teaching of Ben Sira concerning human freedom to choose life's
path? "God created man from the beginning," he writes,

> And placed him in the hand of his יצר. If thou (so) desirest, thou
> canst keep the commandment, and (it is) wisdom to do His good
> pleasure. Poured out before thee (are) fire and water. Stretch forth
> thine hand unto that which thou desirest. Life and death (are) before
> man. That which he desireth shall be given to him. Sufficient is the
> wisdom of the Lord. (He is) mighty in power, and seeth all things. . .
> He commanded no man to sin, nor gave strength to men of lies (Sir
> 15:14-20).

To answer this question we must examine the development of the free
will problem in Greek philosophy. Even a cursory reading makes it at once
evident that before Epicurus the well-known polemics concerning freedom
and determinism are absent from Greek thought. Plato and Aristotle seem
to be content with a notion of "relative" free will,[13] but their virtual unconcern with the classical dilemmas that came to characterize the later
debates over this issue has caused modern commentators no little trouble
in elucidating their positions. Unfortunately, the objective cool with which
the classical period was able to approach this question gave way in the early
Hellenistic age to an earnest and impassioned anxiety. A feeling of helpless

---

[10] Cf. Isa 45:9; Jer 18:6; *T Naph.* 2:2-7; 1QH[a] I, 21; III:23; IV:29; Rom 9:20; *Amen-em-opet* 25
(*ANET*, J. B. Pritchard, ed. [Princeton University Press, 1955], 424).

[11] Cf. Sir 18:3; *1 Enoch* 41:8; *T. Naph.* 2.7; *T. Ash.* 1.4-5.

[12] Cf. Sir 11:14-17; 4 Ezra 3:22; 4:30; Wis 12:11: σπέρμα γὰρ ἦν κατηραμένον ἀπ᾽ ἀρχῆς ;
Pseudo-Philo, *L.A.B.* 25:5.

[13] See, for example, Wolfson, *Philo*, 1:430; D. J. Furley, *Two Studies in the Greek Atomists*
(Princeton: Princeton University Press, 1967), 210-26; Richard Loening, *Geschichte der
strafrechtlichen Zurechnungslehre*, Vol. 1: *Die Zurechnungslehre des Aristoteles* (Jena: G. Fischer,
1903), ch. 18; D. J. Allan, "The Practical Syllogism," in *Autour d'Aristote; recueil d'études...
offert à Monseigneur A. Mansion* (Bibliothèque philosophique de Louvain 16; Louvain:
Publications universitaires, 1955), 325-40, esp. 332-36. For Socrates, see W. K. C. Guthrie,
A History of Greek Philosophy (6 vols.; Cambridge: University Press, 1962-81), 3:459-62.

fatality, even of unreality begins to take hold of people,[14] and Epicurus, whose major concern was the liberation of humanity from the grip of myth and superstition, could no longer ignore the new challenge to humanity's freedom. In Epicurus, for the first time in Greek philosophy (according to one interpretation),[15] we encounter the concept of absolute free will. The absence of primary sources, however, makes it difficult to determine the exact nature of Epicurus' doctrine of the atomic swerve. If we follow the Giussani-Bailey interpretation,[16] according to whom Epicurus posited an atomic swerve for every instance of free action, it would be necessary to classify Epicurus' doctrine as one of absolute free will. The latter teaches that voluntary motion is uncaused, and that no fixed inner structure of the will determines action. We find a similar doctrine in the writings of Alexander of Aphrodisias (early third century CE), according to whom free will depends upon causeless motion (ἀναίτιος κίνησις) and this in turn depends upon an admixture of non-being. Non-being destroys uniform and consistent action and accounts for the fact that persons of similar

---

[14] See, for example, W. Gundel, *Beiträge zur Entwicklungsgeschicte der Begriffe Ananke und Heimarmene* (Giessen: Brühl, 1914); F. Cumont, *Astrology and Religion among the Greeks and Romans* (New York: Dover, 1960); Dom David Amand, *Fatalisme et liberté dans l'antiquité grecque* (Louvain: Bibliothèque de l'Université, 1945); A. D. Nock, *Sallustius, Concerning the Gods and the Universe* (Hildesheim: Olms, 1966), lxx ff.

[15] The expression *libera potestas* occurs first in Lucretius 2.256. Cf. Pamela Huby, "The first Discovery of the Free Will Problem," *Philosophy* 42 (1967): 353-62. (Cf., however, M. Pohlenz, *Die Stoa* [2 vols.; Göttingen: Vandenhoeck & Ruprecht, 1955], 2:59-60, who thinks that Epicurus dealt with the free will problem under the impetus of Zeno.) Huby's explanation, however, for the Epicurean preoccupation with this problem (she considers it a reaction to the thoroughgoing determinism of Democritus) seems to be inadequate. (Moreover, her assertion that "it was possible for men like Plato and Aristotle to hold many educational and psychological beliefs in common with us without being aware of any free will problem because they had no notion of thoroughgoing psychological determinism," is naive.) In addition to the fillip imparted by the encroaching forces of astrological fatalism, we should like to point to an inner motivation for Epicurus' free will doctrine. It would seem to us that the soteriological thrust of Epicurus' teachings required a clear hope for human salvation grounded in the theoretical principles of his atomic system. Since, on the one hand, the infinite causal atomic chain could be easily misconstrued by the common person as precluding even the slightest possibility of achieving happiness by special human efforts, and the realistic limitations of human character, on the other hand, would dampen the prospects of any substantial success on the part of Epicurus with most people, it suddenly became essential to find a way to guarantee the effectiveness of the atomic world view in securing human happiness. The atomic swerve allowed the new teaching to break through the causal nexus that shaped a person's character and moral destiny from an infinitely remote past and permitted the Epicurean philosophy to espouse a hopeful and confident meliorism.

[16] See Cyril Bailey, *The Greek Atomists and Epicurus* (Oxford: Clarendon, 1928), 432-37; C. Giussani, *Studi Lucreziani* (Turin, 1896).

endowments and breeding frequently differ from one another.[17] If, on the other hand, we follow Furley's interpretation[18] (by far the likeliest), according to which Epicurus taught that the motions of the psyche are not determined *ab initio*, because discontinuity is brought about by the atomic swerve thus allowing new patterns of motion to emerge that cannot be explained by the initial constitution of the psyche, we should have to classify his doctrine as a relative free will theory of the "modified causal" and "melioristic" type. The latter teaches that a person's volitional motion, though unconstrained by an external force and thus relatively free, is a product nonetheless of the individual's own psyche, which is not a completely autonomous agent. In the causal variety of this doctrine, the autonomy of the psyche is severely limited by the universal causal chain (Stoics), whereas in its "non-causal" variety it is limited by the irrational motions of the body (Plato, Middle Platonism, Neoplatonism), and in its predestinarian variety, it is God who ultimately determines its nature. In the "modified causal" version of the Epicureans, although the atomic soul cluster is a part of the causal nexus, the latter can be broken through and hence training and conditioning in the light of the Epicurean teachings could more or less rectify improper proportions in the soul and thus secure the ultimate sovereignty of reason in the life of a person (Lucretius 3.307-22).[19] The "non-causal" and "non-melioristic" variety of relative free

---

[17] *De Anima* in *Alexandri Aphrodisiensis praeter commentaria scripta minora. De Anima liber cum mantissa* (Ivo Bruns, ed.; Supplementum Aristotelicum II; Berlin: G. Reimer, 1887-92), 170-71; 22-27. Cf. Roger A. Pack, "A Passage in Alexander of Aphrodisias Relating to the Theory of Tragedy," *AJP* 58 (1937): 418-36. Cf. the solution of Thumama b. Ashras (d. 828), who argued that generated effects have no author at all. See Majid Fakhry, *History of Islamic Philosophy* (New York: Columbia University Press, 1970), 68. For a modern example, cf. the Russian Orthodox thinker Nicholas Berdyaev who developed the notion of "meontic" freedom; see F. Nucho, *Berdyaev's Philosophy* (New York: Anchor, 1966), 37-40.

[18] Furely, *Two Studies*, 161-237.

[19] It ought to be noted, that if Furley's interpretation of Epicurus is correct (and to this writer it seems by far the most reasonable interpretation so far proposed), then we must conclude that, aside from a few isolated passages in Alexander's commentary on Aristotle's *De Anima* that embody a concept of ἀναίτιος κίνησις rooted in the μὴ ὄν and based on a farfetched interpretation of Aristotle's notion of the συμβεβηκός as ἐγγύς τι τοῦ μὴ ὄντος (*Metaph.* 6:1026b, 15ff.), there was nowhere in ancient Greek philosophy (as far as we know) a doctrine of absolute free will. Moreover, Alexander's notion of causeless motion found no echo in subsequent Greek thought, and was actually inconsistent with his own discussion of the free will problem in his Περὶ εἱμαρμένης. In Sharples' opinion, the doctrine expressed in Alexander's *mantissa* 169-72 is unlikely to be one to which Alexander would have subscribed and is probably the work of a pupil. For a full translation and analysis of this passage, see R. W. Sharples, "Responsibility, Chance and Not-Being," *Bulletin of the Institute of Classical Studies*, University of London, 22 (1975): 37-64. For the text, see idem, *Alexander of Aprhrodisias On Fate* (London: Duckworth, 1983): 212-14.

will is represented by Carneades (214-129 BCE),[20] Pseudo-Plutarch, Alcinous, Pseudo-Apuleius (second century CE),[21] and the Peripatetic Alexander of Aphrodisias in his Περὶ Εἱμαρμένης (De Fato). These thinkers denied that there was a universal causal chain that encompassed even acts of will (it did, however, encompass the results of acts of will), and insisted that voluntary motion was its own cause. According to Alcinous, for example, acts of will belong to the category of the "possible" (δυνατόν) which is "indeterminate" (ἀόριστον), and the soul is its own master (ἀδέσποτον).[22] Probably, however, these thinkers would not have disagreed with Plato that the soul is subject to contamination by the body and that if the latter is radically diseased, the soul might not always succeed in becoming sufficiently decontaminated so as to be restored to complete health.[23]

---

[20] See Cicero, Fat. 11-14; Victor C. L. Brochard, Les sceptiques grecs (Paris: J. Vrin, 1969) 148-53.

[21] See W. Theiler, "Tacitus," 67ff.; C. Andresen, "Justin und der mittlere Platonismus," ZNW 44 (1952-53): 183ff.

[22] Cf. Plato, Resp. 10.617e; Epicurus, Ep. Menoeceus 133

[23] Alcinous [Albinus], Epit. 26:3; Apuleius, Dogm. Plat. 1:12; Pseudo-Plutarch, De Fato (ed., Ernesto Valgiglio; Rome: A. Signorelli, 1964). The polemical thrust of Carneades, Alexander, and the Middle Platonists was directed mainly against the Stoics and their doctrine of the universal causal chain. The attackers apparently felt that the subtle distinction of the Stoics would undoubtedly be lost on the average man, who would thus succumb to the so-called ἀργὸς λόγος (or "lazy argument") and resign himself to fate (cf. Alexander Aphrodisias, Fat. 16). Alexander thus argues that the Stoic causal chain theory is too rigidly conceived and must be modified to allow for the contingent and possible (chaps. 22-24). Not even the gods, he argues, would be able to predict the future completely, but would "foreknow possible things (τὰ ἐνδεχόμενα) only as possible." The popular character of Alexander's argumentation becomes emphatically clear when he proceeds at one point to defend his free will theory by claiming after the manner of Pascal's famous "wager" that "men would not err in their actions by reason of the conviction of free will (even if it did not exist). But, on the other hand, supposing that some power of free will does exist ... if we are persuaded that we have no control over anything, we shall let many things go that should be done by us" (ch. 21). It is this popular and polemical spirit that dominates Alexander's treatise and robs it of the ability to do even scant justice to the precise argumentation of the Stoics that provided for the first time in Greek philosophy an adequate analysis of the free will problem with all its confusing dilemmas. (See A. Gercke, Chrysippea [Jahrbuch für klassische Philologie, Suppl. 14; Leipzig: Teubner, 1885], 694; G. Verbeke, "Aristotélisme et Stoicisme dans le De Fato D'Alexandre d'Aphrodisias," Archiv für Geschichte der Philosophie 50 [1968]: 73-100; A. A. Long, "Stoic Determinism and Alexander of Aphrodisias' De Fato," Archiv für Geschichte der Philosophie 52 [1970]: 247-68. Long correctly concludes that Alexander's treatise is "... a defence of some freedom in human action, and a generalised attack on determinism, based upon Aristotle with some borrowing from Stoic language and thought. In much the same way Pseudo-Plutarch's De Fato and Calcidius' In Timaeum [142-190] combine a form of Platonism with a rather large quantity of Stoic doctrine ... Many of the views he attacks will have been held by Stoics, but Alexander does not attempt a systematic presentation and critique of Stoic determinism.") It is unlikely, however, that in

Turning to rabbinic literature, although the general rabbinic teaching appears to be an implied absolute free will doctrine,[24] there is a distinct rabbinic tendency that must be classified as one of relative free will of the predestinarian type. The latter appears to be an adaptation of the causal version of the Stoics, which insisted that voluntary motion is caused both by εἱμαρμένη or the universal causal chain[25] as well as a person's inner character, which in its turn is of course also a part of that chain.[26] The Stoics maintained that our choices are within our power (ἐφ' ἡμῖν) by distinguishing between the proximate cause (προκαταρκτικὴ αἰτία) and the principal cause (αὐτοτελὴς αἰτία), and asserting that εἱμαρμένη provides

---

pressing their attack against the Stoics, our critics meant to assert a doctrine of absolute free will. Such an assertion would have to provide an explicitly emphatic statement to the effect that the soul can overcome the contaminating influences of the body in an absolute manner, thus rendering itself immune from all possible pathological seizures. At any rate, there seems to be insufficient warrant for deducing such a conclusion from the formulations that have survived. Even the statement in Calcidius' *In Timaeum* 181, is insufficiently explicit to justify the conclusion that "the healthfulness of reason and deliberation" can restore the soul's absolute sovereignty over the body. See J. den Boeft, *Calcidius On Fate* (Leiden: Brill, 1970), 107-08. The same may be said for Alcinous [Albinus], *Epit.* 31.2: καὶ τὸ ἀκούσιον ἐν ἀγνοίᾳ τινὶ ἢ πάθει κεῖται, ἅπαντα δὲ τὰ τοιαῦτα ἔξεστιν ἀποτρίψασθαι καὶ λόγῳ καὶ ἤθεσιν ἀστείοις καὶ μελέτῃ. It can be argued that Alcinous [Albinus] is merely emphasizing that education and training can have a decisive influence on one's moral actions. He is in no way, however, confronting the ultimate question of whether or not there may be some residual recalcitrance in a soul encased in a body diseased by heredity and environment that cannot be completely overcome. (Cf. Aristotle, *Eth. nic.* 3.5.18-23.) Aristotle here sidetracks the issue, by emphasizing the practical results of making vice ultimately depend on a man's natural endowments ("If this is true," he writes, "how will virtue be any more voluntary than vice?").

[24] I say "appears," for in asserting, for example, that "all is in the hands of Heaven, except the fear of Heaven" (*b. Ber.* 33b and parallels), the Rabbis may have meant simply that whereas God's providence in every other aspect of a person's life involves direct intervention and guidance, this does not apply to the deliberative process governing a person's moral life. In any case, the rabbinic statement quoted above could at best only "imply" that God is not the ultimate cause of an individual's choices. The Sadducees, on the other hand, if we can rely on the all too brief account of Josephus, seem to have held an absolute free will theory based on the explicit denial of divine providence (cf. Sir 16:17-23). See David Flusser, "The Pharisees and Stoics according to Josephus," *Iyyun* 14-15 (1963-64): 318-29 (Hebrew); L. Wächter, "Die unterschiedliche Haltung der Pharisäen, Sadduzäen und Essener zur Heimarmene nach dem Bericht des Josephus," *ZRGG* 21 (1969): 97-114.

[25] Εἱμαρμένη is described as συμπλοκὴν αἰτιῶν (H. Diels, *Doxographi graeci* [Berlin: G. Reimer, 1879] 322). Cf. εἱρμὸν αἰτιῶν τουτέστι τάξιν καὶ ἐπισύνδεσιν ἀπαράβατον (Diels, *Doxographi*, 324); Philo, *Her.* 301, *Aet.* 112; *SVF* 2.915-21; Plotinus, *Enn.* 3. 2. 1; M. Aurelius, 10.5.1; Seneca, *Ben.* 4.8. 2 [Basore, LCL]: "series implexa causarum"; Cicero, *Div.* 1. 225 [Falconer, LCL]: "ordinem seriemque causarum."

[26] H. Diels, *Doxographi graeci*, 322: ἐν ᾗ συμπλοκῇ καὶ τὸ παρ' ἡμᾶς, ὥστε τὰ μὲν εἱμάρθαι, τὰ δὲ συνειμάρθαι. Cicero, *Fat.* 30 ("confatalis"); cf. *SVF* 2. 979, 991, 1000.

only the proximate causes of a person's actions, while the individual himself provides the principal causes thereby participating in the process that initiates action.[27] Wolfson has shown that this was also St. Augustine's position, who could thus say paradoxically that a person sins freely, even though the sinning is predetermined by his irresistible concupiscence.[28] In the light of the Stoic position, it is easy to understand the famous paradox of Rabbi Akiba: "Everything is foreseen, yet man has the capacity to choose freely" (Aboth 3:15). This was simply a Jewish version of the well-known Stoic paradox, adapted to a predestinarian framework, in the same manner as the later version of St. Augustine.[29] Rabbi Akiba could thus boldly declare on the one hand that God created both the righteous and the wicked (b. Hag. 15a; b. B. Bat. 16a),[30] and on the other hand, he could

---

[27] Cf. Chrysippus, in Aulus Gellius, Noct. att. 7.2. An excellent analysis of the Stoic position is given by A. A. Long, "Freedom and Determinism in the Stoic Theory of Human Action," in Problems in Stoicism (ed. A. A. Long; London: Athlone Press, 1971), 173-99. See also Otto Rieth, Grundbegriffe der stoischen Ethik (Problemat 9: Berlin: Weidmann, 1993), 134-68; J. M. Rist, Stoic Philosophy (London: Cambridge University Press, 1969), 112-32; M. Reesor, "Fate and Possibility in Early Stoic Philosophy," Phoenix 19 (1965): 288-97; M. Pohlenz, Grundfragen der stoischen Philosophie (Göttingen: Vandenhoeck & Ruprecht, 1940), 105-08; M. Pohlenz, Die Stoa, 1.101-06. See now Susanne Bobzien, Determinism and Freedom in Stoic Philosophy (Oxford: Clarendon, 1998).

[28] H. A. Wolfson, Religious Philosophy (Cambridge: Harvard University Press, 1951), 158-76.

[29] The adaptation to a predestinarian framework was facilitated by the fact that the Stoics themselves equated fate with God. See Augustine, Civ. Dei 5. 8 (CCSL 136): "[fatum] louem appellant, quem summum deum putant, a quo conexionem dicunt pendere fatorum": Seneca, Ben. 4.7.2 [Basore, LCL]: "Hunc eundem [deum] et Fatum si dixeris, non mentieris." (It may be noted that according to Pohlenz, Die Stoa 1.100, Zeno got his idea of divine providence from his Semitic background, though such an assumption is unnecessary.) Cf. Pss. Sol. 9:4; 5:4; see E. Schürer, History of the Jewish People in the Age of Jesus Christ (rev. and ed. G. Vermes; trans. T. A. Burkill; 3 vols.; Edinburgh: T&T Clark, 1979), 2:393, n. 40; M. Hengel, Judentum und Hellenismus (Tübingen: Mohr, 1969), 256. For the Stoic terminology in Josephus' description of the Pharisaic doctrine of will (e.g. εἱμαρμένη, ὁρμή, ἐκλογή, ἐφ' ἡμῖν) see G. F. Moore, "Fate and Free Will in the Jewish Philosophies According to Josephus," HTR 22 (1929): 371-89; Flusser, "Pharisees and Stoics". Flusser emphasizes the differences between the Pharisaic and Stoic doctrines. For Stoic influence in rabbinic thought, see Armand Kaminka, Studies in Scripture, Talmud, and Rabbinical Literature, (2 vols.; Tel Aviv: Debir, 1938, 1951), vol. 2 (Hebrew); J. Bergmann, "Die stoische Philosophie und die Jüdische Frömmigkeit," in Judaica. Festschrift zu Hermann Cohens 70. Geburtstage (ed. H. A. Fischel; Berlin: Bruno Cassirer, 1912; repr., New York: Ktav, 1977), 145-66; S. Lieberman, "How much Greek in Jewish Palestine?" in Biblical and Other Studies (ed. A. Altman; Cambridge: Harvard University Press, 1963), 123-41; J. Goldin, "The School of R. Yohanan b. Zakkai", H. A. Wolfson Jubilee Volume (Jerusalem: A. Kohut Memorial Foundation and L. N. Littauer Foundation, 1965), Hebrew section, 69-92.

[30] Cf. b. Sota 22a; 1QH^a IV, 38; 2 Enoch 49:2; 2 Bar. 42:7.

insist that a person has free will. The predestinarian emphasis is made especially explicit in the following passage from the *Mekilta*:

> We find that the names of the righteous and their deeds are revealed before God even before they are born, as it is said, "Before I formed thee in the belly I knew thee" (Jer 1:5). We thus learn that the names of the righteous and their deeds are revealed before God. How about those of the wicked? Scripture says: 'The wicked are estranged from the womb' (Ps 58:4 [3]; *Pisha* 16).[31]

We are now in a position to resolve the apparent contradiction that we found in Ben Sira. Although loyal to traditional Judaism, Ben Sira often absorbs Hellenistic ingredients that are thoroughly assimilated to his own thinking. It has been correctly pointed out, for example, that the polarity principle that he uses to good advantage is a characteristically Greek pattern (cf. Heraclitus), that his statement that God is all (Sir 43:27) bears

---

[31] Cf. *y. Ber.* 4.2: "It is revealed and known before thee that we have not the strength to resist him (The Evil Yezer); but may it be thy will, O Lord ... that thou wilt remove him from us, and subject him, so that we may do thy will as our will." (See S. Schechter, *Some Aspects*, 264-92). Cf. *Gen. Rab.* 3.8: "From the beginning of the world's creation God foresaw the deeds of the righteous and the deeds of the wicked ... 'And God separated the light from the darkness,' between the deeds of the righteous and the deeds of the wicked. 'God called the light Day,' these are the deeds of the righteous, 'and the darkness He called Night,' these are the deeds of the wicked." Here (as in Ben Sira and the Dead Sea Scrolls) we have once again the splitting of humanity into two camps. Cf. the great Sufi mysic Ibn al-Farid (12th-13th c.), who cites the tradition that when Allah created Adam, he drew forth his posterity from his loins in two handfulls, one white as silver and one black as coal, and said, "These are in Paradise and I care not, and these are in Hell and I care not" (*Ta'iya* 746). Cf. also *Tanhuma* 4: "... So, too, said Adam before the Holy One blessed be He, Lord of the universe, two thousand years before you created your world, the Torah was beside you, like a master workman [Prov 8:30], and in it is written, 'This is the procedure: when a person dies in a tent,' Had you not decreed death for man, would you have thus written in it? But you have come to hang the libel [עלילה] on me. This is meant by 'He is terrible in His doing [עלילה] toward the children of men'" (Ps. 66:5). (See Efraim E. Urbach, *The Sages, Their Concepts and Beliefs* [Jerusalem: Magnes, 1969], 227-53 [Hebrew].) With this one may compare Al-Bukhari, *Qadar* b. 11: "The Prophet of God said that Adam and Moses maintained a debate before God, and Adam got the better of Moses who said, 'Thou art that Adam whom God created and breathed into thee his own spirit, and made the angels bow down before thee, and placed thee in Paradise; after which, thou threwest man upon the earth, from the fault which thou didst commit.' Adam replied: 'Thou art that Moses, whom God selected for his prophecy and to converse with, and he gave thee twelve tablets, in which are explained everything, and he made thee his confidant and the bearer of his secrets; Then how long was the Bible written before I was created? Moses said 'forty years.' Then said Adam: Didst thou see in the Bible that Adam disobeyed God? 'Yes." 'Dost thou reproach me on a matter which God wrote in the Bible before creating me?'" (See E. Sell, *The Faith of Islam* [London: SPCK, 1880], 173; Morris S. Seale, *Muslim Theology* [London: Luzac, 1964], 23). For alternative interpretations of R. Akiba's statement, see Urbach, *Sages*, 229ff.; Schechter, *Some Aspects*, 285.

a distant echo of Stoic terminology, and that his doctrine of the purpose-fulness of all created things was common Stoic teaching.[32] It is, therefore not unlikely that in dealing with the free will problems, which by that time had begun to become troublesome, he made use of the well-known Stoic formula. Hence, he could maintain the wisdom tradition that emphasized predestinarianism, and still admonish his readers not to attribute their sins to God.[33]

The Wisdom of Solomon

We turn now to an examination of the impact of Ben Sira's pre-destinarianism on the Wisdom of Solomon. It is only to be expected that the latter would find ample occasion to follow in the footsteps of the former. We shall give a few illustrations not involving the predestinarian concept. The author of Wisdom declares, for example, that the children of adulterers shall not reach maturity (Wis 3:16). Similarly, Ben Sira declares: "Her children shall not spread out their roots, And her branches shall bear no fruit" (Sir 23:25).[34] Furthermore, virtually identical images are used in both books to describe their authors' ardent pursuit of wisdom.[35] Again the author of Wisdom declares that God loves all things and abhors nothing that he made, "For never couldst thou have formed anything if thou didst hate it" (Wis 11:24 [APOT 1.554]). Similarly, Ben Sira declares, "For that which He hateth made He not" (Sir 15:11). Returning to our theme of predestinarianism, we find that according to the author of Wisdom the impious summoned death themselves and made a covenant with him (Wis 1:16; cf. Isa 28:15) because they are worthy to be his portion (μερίς) (Wis 2:24; Apoc Ab. 22:14; 2 Bar. 42:7). The idea of being worthy either of wisdom or of death recurs more than once. Wisdom goes about seeking them that are worthy of her (Wis 6:16). Grace and mercy are to

---

[32] See Hengel, *Judentum und Hellenismus,* 263ff.; R. Pautrel, "Ben Sira et le Stoicisme," 535-49; Johann Marböck, *Weisheit im Wandel* (Bonner Biblische Beiträge 37; Bonn: Hanstein, 1971), 162-73.

[33] Cf. Gerhard Maier, *Mensch und freier Wille* (WUNT 12; Tübingen: Mohr, 1971), 24-164. The paradox of human freedom locked into a deterministic scheme that characterizes Jewish apocalyptic, may be similarly resolved by the realization of the relative character of that freedom. Although this relative freedom generally suffices to absolve God from responsibility for human evil, in books like *2 Bar.* and *4 Ezra,* under the impact of the catastrophe of the year 70, the ultimately inscrutable divine determination of human moral choices is boldly probed and challenged. See also Schürer-Vermes 2.393-94.

[34] Cf. 1 Enoch 10:9; *b. Yebam.* 78b.

[35] Wis 6:12-24; 7:7-14; cf. Sir 15:2; 51:26; 51:13.

God's chosen (ἐκλεκτοῖς, Wis 3:9; cf. *1 Enoch* 5:7). In contrast to the wicked, the righteous were found by God to be worthy of himself (Wis 3:5).[36] Moreover, the children of the impious are wicked and their generation (γένεσις) is accursed (Wis 3:12). Of the Canaanites, he asserts that their generation was evil and their wickedness inborn, and their way of thinking could not change forever. For it was a seed accursed from the beginning (Wis 12:10-11).[37] Furthermore, were it not for divine grace (Wis 8:21), which bestows on humanity a divine wisdom, characterized as an inner member of the celestial court sitting by the very throne of God (Wis 9:4; *1 Enoch* 4:3; Sir 1:1), even one who is born with the best natural endowments (εὐφυής), possessing a good soul united with an undefiled body (Wis 8:19-20), is to be accounted as nought and is rejected from among God's children (Wis 9:4,6). For even the best body is corruptible and thus weighs down the soul by filling the mind with distracting cares, thereby depriving it of the ability adequately to search out the knowledge of affairs terrestrial, let alone matters celestial (Wis 9:15-17).[38] Hence, only when God sends his wisdom down from its heavenly abode can a person's paths upon the earth be made straight and salvation be achieved (Wis 9:17-18).[39]

Although the predestinarian character of Wisdom is not as explicit as that of Ben Sira, the tone of his diction makes it difficult to avoid the impression that the two books are not far apart on this matter. The final clue, however, is to be found in Wisdom's statement that it was through the devil's envy that death entered into the world, and that they who belong to his party experience it (Wis 3:24).[40] Here, as in Ben Sira, we are once again confronted with the splitting of humankind into two camps, those who are sought out by Wisdom, and those who belong to the portion of Satan. With the latter concept we come much closer to the Dead Sea Scrolls.

---

[36]   Cf. Wis 11:25: "And how would anything have endured, except thou hadst willed it? or that which was not called by you (μὴ κληθέν) be preserved?" Cf. Eccl 6:10; *4 Ezra* 10:57; *Mek.*, *Pisha* 16; Rom 8:28; CD 2:11.

[37]   Cf. *Jub.* 22:20-21; Bar 3:26-28; CD 2:7; *b. Yoma* 87a

[38]Cf. *4 Ezra* 4:10-11, 21; *T. Job* 36.8; *b. Sanh.* 39a; Pseudo-Callisthenes, Βίος Ἀλεξάνδρου 1:14; Plato, *Phaed.* 81c

[39]   Cf. 1QH^a X, 5-7; IV:22, 31. With Wis 7:16 cf. 1QH^a I, 29.

[40]   Cf. Wis 1:13-14: "For God made not death, nor does he delight in the destruction of the living. For he created all things that they might have being, and the created things of this world preserve their being [καὶ σωτήριοι αἱ γενέσεις τοῦ κόσμου]; cf. the Stoic theory of οἰκείωσις, Diogenes Laertius 7. 85; Philo, *Mos.* 1.96], and there is not in them the poison of destruction." Cf. *1 Enoch* 69:11; *4 Ezra* 8:60.

PART THREE

THE WISDOM OF SOLOMON

CHAPTER FOUR

The Book of Wisdom's Theory of Cosmogony

To illustrate God's omnipotence, the author of The Wisdom of Solomon speaks of his "all-powerful hand that created the world out of formless matter."[1] In his commentary to this verse, Reider remarks, "ἄμορφος ὕλη is a Greek philosophical term which is entirely foreign to Jewish thought and conception. The Jews believed in creation out of nothing; the Greeks believed in creation out of formless matter which was eternal. On the one hand religious monism (God alone is eternal); on the other philosophic dualism (God and matter are eternal). It is difficult to assume that the author of Wisdom, who was far more Jewish than Philo, would adhere to the Greek view of creation. Undoubtedly the allusion is casual and not dogmatic."[2] Altmann, on the other hand, observes more accurately "that in rabbinic Judaism opinion oscillated for some time between accepting and rejecting the notion of primordial matter or elements." He adds, however, that "the discussion between R. Gamaliel II and a philosopher recorded in *Gen. Rab.* 1.9 shows that the doctrine of *creatio ex nihilo* was considered the sound orthodox view towards the end of the first century CE."[3] We shall attempt to show that not only was an unambiguous doctrine of *creatio ex*

---

[1] Wis 11:17, ἡ παντοδύναμός σου χεὶρ καὶ κτίσασα τὸν κόσμον ἐξ ἀμόρφου ὕλης. (All translations from the Wisdom of Solomon are my own and are based on the text edited by J. Ziegler in *Sapientia Salomonis*, [Septuaginta Vetus Testamentum Graecum 12.1; Göttingen; Vandenhoeck and Ruprecht, 1962]). For the phrase cf. Aristotle, *Phys.* 191a.10, ἡ ὕλη καὶ τὸ ἄμορφον; Plato, *Tim.* 50d; and Posidonius, in H. Diels, *Doxographi graeci*, (4th ed.; Berlin, W. de Gruyter, 1965), 458: τὴν τῶν ὅλων οὐσίαν καὶ ὕλην ἄποιον καὶ ἄμορφον εἶναι.

[2] J. Reider, *The Book of Wisdom* (New York: Harper, 1957), 145. His last sentence is actually a quotation from A. T. S. Goodrick's edition (*The Book of Wisdom* [London; Rivington's, 1913], 248); the rest is a prarphrase of J. A. F. Gregg's edition (*The Wisdom of Solomon in the Revised Version* [rev. ed.; Cambridge: Cambridge University Press, 1909], 110). R. Marcus, on the other hand, thinks that the author of Wisdom is only giving an "elegant rephrasing of Genesis 1:2" (quoted by R. M. Grant, *Miracle and Natural Law in Graeco-Roman and Early Christian Thought* [Amsterdam: North Holland, 1952], 138). Gregg had already made the same suggestion.

[3] A. Altmann, *Studies in Religious Philosophy and Mysticism* (Ithaca, N.Y.: Cornell University Press, 1969), 129.

nihilo missing in Jewish-Hellenistic literature, but that even in rabbinic literature such a doctrine appeared at best only in a polemical context, and that the more common view was probably the doctrine of creation out of primordial matter.

Wolfson has already shown that the creation references in *Letter of Aristeas* 136 and 2 Maccabees which have often been taken to indicate *creatio ex nihilo* are in reality inconclusive.[4] In 2 Macc 7:28 the martyr mother admonishes her son as follows, "I beg of you, my child, to look up to heaven and earth and see all that is therein, and know that God did not make them out of existing things."[5] Now ὄντα may simply refer to the visible world of particulars. Diogenes of Apollonia, for example, writes πάντα τὰ ὄντα ἀπὸ τοῦ αὐτοῦ ἑτεροιοῦσθαι ("all existing things are created by the alteration of the same thing").[6] The text in 2 Maccabees would then only be saying that God did not fashion heaven and earth from formed things but from some unformed primordial matter. Similarly, when Pseudo-Aristeas makes Eleazar say, "That anyone should be made a god because of some invention he has contrived is altogether foolish; for such persons only took things already created and put them together (τῶν γὰρ ἐν τῇ κτίσει λαβόντες τινὰ συνέθηκαν) and showed that they possessed further usefulness, but they did not themselves create the objects" (τὴν κατασκευὴν αὐτῶν οὐ ποιήσαντες αὐτοί), he may mean only that, unlike

---

[4] Wolfson, *Philo*, 1:302-3; H. F. Weiss, *Untersuchungen zur Kosmologie des hellenistischen und palästinischen Judentums* (Berlin: Akademie-Verlag, 1966), 34, 72ff.; cf. G. Scholem, "Schöpfung aus nichts und Selberverschränkung Gottes," *ErJb* 25 (1956): 97; Altmann, *Studies*, 129.

[5] ὅτι οὐκ ἐξ ὄντων ἐποίησεν αὐτὰ ὁ θεός. According to J. Moffatt, (*On the Epistle to the Hebrews* [ICC; New York: Scribner, 1924], 161, n. 2) the οὐκ here goes with the verb (unlike Heb 11:3, where the μή goes with φαινομένων). But even if the οὐκ went with ὄντα (see F. Blass and A. Debrunner, *Grammatik des neutestamentlichen Griechisch* [12 ed.; Göttingen: Vandenhoeck & Ruprecht, 1965], §433 n. 3), it could still be interpreted to mean relative nonbeing. According to Aristotle (*Phys.* 1.9.192a), the Platonists, who refer to matter as "the great and the small," identified it with τὸ μὴ ὄν. Indeed, Aristotle himself is willing to speak of things coming to be in a way ἐκ μὴ ὄντος, in an incidental sense (κατὰ συμβεβηκός). Philo, too, apparently referred to creation out of preexistent matter as creation ἐκ τοῦ μὴ ὄντος (e.g., *Mos.* 2.267; *Spec.* 2.225). It depends, of course, on which interpretation of Philo's cosmogony one follows. Cf. H. Wolfson, "The Kalam Problem of Non-Existence and Saadia's Second Theory of Creation," *JQR* n.s.36 (1946): 371-91; and also below notes 21 and 40. Cf. Gersonides, *Milhamot Adonai* 6.17, "the only remaining alternative is that the world is in one respect 'ex nihilo' and in another 'ex aliquo' (מיש ש) [a distinction that had escaped the ancients]: it is from something inasmuch as it is made from matter; it is ex nihilo inasmuch as it is made from matter lacking all form."

[6] Cf. Anaximander B1; Protagoras of Abdera B1. Diels and Kranz (*Die Fragmente der Vorsokratiker*) divide the textual evidence on each presocratic philosopher into categories: A, testimonia; B, the actual fragments. I use this reference in these notes.

human inventors who make new combinations of formed things, God made the very form and structure of matter.

Turning to rabbinic literature, we find the question of creation a subject of discussion between Rabban Gamaliel II and a "philosopher": "A philosopher said to R. Gamaliel: Your God was a great craftsman, but he found himself good materials[7] which assisted him: Tohu wa-Bohu, and darkness, and wind, and water, and the primeval deep. Said R. Gamaliel to him: May the wind be blown out of that man [a euphemism for 'drop dead']; Each material is referred to as having been created. Tohu wa-Bohu: 'I make peace and create evil' (Isa 45:7); darkness: 'I form the light and create darkness' (Isa 45:7); water: 'Praise Him, ye heavens of heavens, and ye waters' — why? — 'For He commanded, and they were created' (Ps 148:4-5); wind: 'For, lo, He that formeth the mountains, and created the wind' (Amos 4:13); the primeval deep: 'When there were no depths, I was brought forth' (Prov 8:24)."[8] It is essential to note that the "philosopher" insists that God, though a great craftsman, was "assisted" (שסייעוהו) by five materials, all of which had a cosmogonic function in pagan mythology.[9]

---

[7] סמנים may mean colors or pigments, and, in general, any artist's materials. Cf. the picturesque simile of the painter's palette with which Empedocles illustrated the production of infinite variety out of the same few elements (earth, water, air, fire) (B23). The simile gains precision, as Guthrie points out, from the fact that Greek painters worked in terms of four basic colors (white, black, yellow, red) (W. K. C. Guthrie, *History of Greek Philosophy* [6 vols; Cambridge: Cambridge University Press, 1962-81], 2:148-49; cf. Philo, *Mos.* 2.88; *QE* 2.85; *Congr.* 116; Josephus, *Ant.* 3.183; *J.W.* 5.212-14).

[8] *Gen. Rab.* 1.9. The translation is based on the edition of J. Theodor and C. H. Albeck (*Midrash Rabbah. Genesis* [3 vols.: Jerusalem; Vahrman, 1965]). For the word שסייעוהו cf. *Exod. Rab.* 43.6, "Lord of the universe, they have provided you with assistance (סיוע), and you are angry with them? The calf which they have made will be of assistance to you (יהיה מסייעך)."

[9] See for example, S. G. Kirk and J. E. Raven, eds., *The Presocratic Philosophers* (1st ed.; Cambridge: Cambridge University Press, 1957), 8-72; S. G. F. Brandon, *Creation Legends of the Ancient Near East* (London: Hodder & Stoughton, 1963). There are strong echoes both in Scripture and in rabbinic midrash of the once-dynamic role ascribed to the primeval waters in early mythology (see S. Loewenstamm, *The Tradition of the Exodus in Its Development* [Jerusalem: Magnes, Hebrew University, 1965], 101-29 [Hebrew]). See esp. *Exod. Rab.* 15.22, where creation is described as unable to proceed unitl God tramples "Ocean" and slays him (cf. *Exod. Rab.* 24.1; *b. B. Bat.* 74b; *Midr. Pss.* 114; *Mek.* on Exod 14.21). There are also vague echoes of the semiautonomous character of darkness, "Why did the Holy One blessed be He create the world in Nisan, and not in Iyyar? Because when He created His world, He said to the prince of darkness: 'Begone from before me, for I wish to create the world with light'" (*Pesiq. Rab.* 95a; cf. Philo, *Opif.* 33). For a second-century parallel to the semiautonomous cosmological role of the elements, compare the cosmogony of Bardaisan (154-222 CE) who maintained that the world was formed from five elements: light, wind, fire, water, and darkness. By chance they came into movement and mingled with one another, so that confusion arose and the darkness also had an

The violent reaction of Rabban Gamaliel II is inexplicable on the assumption that the "philosopher" merely alludes to creation from formless matter. As a matter of fact, both Bar Kappara and Rabbi Judah b. Pazzi interpreted the Genesis account as describing creation out of primordial matter.[10] Bar Kappara's use of the formula "were it not written, it would be impossible to say so" indicates, however, his great concern for the danger lurking in such a scriptural formulation. What bothered the rabbis were the Gnostic heresies that insisted on multiple creative powers. Many passages attest to the continuing rabbinic debate with these Gnostics. We read, for example, in *b. Sanh.* 38a (*t. Sanh.* 8.7), "Man was created alone, so that the Sadducees [i.e., heretics] might not say: There are multiple sovereignties in Heaven." "Adam was created [last of all beings] on Sabbath eve, lest the Sadducees say: The Holy One, blessed be He, had a partner in cosmogony." On 39a we further read, "The Emperor [var. read.: an infidel] said to R. Gamaliel: He who created the mountains did not create the wind, for it is written, 'For lo, there is a former (יוצר) of mountains and a creator (ברא) of wind' (Amos 4:13)." A pointed admonition

---

opportunity to mingle with them. The pure elements call upon their Lord, who sends the Logos to create some order in chaos. See H. J. Drijvers, *Bardaisan of Edessa* (Assen: Van Gorcum & Comp., 1966), 98-104, 219-20; cf. also the Sethian cosmological triad of light, darkness, and uncontaminated spirit (H. A. Wolfson, *Philosophy of the Church Fathers* (2d rev. ed.; Cambridge: Harvard University Press, 1964), 526-27; J. Doresse, *The Secret Book of the Egyptian Gnostics* (New York: Viking, 1960), 146-54).

[10] *Gen. Rab.* 1.5, "R. Huna said in the name of Bar Kappara: 'Were it not written it would be impossible to say so; God created the heaven and the earth — from what? — from 'and the earth was without form.'" *y. Hag.* 2.1, "R. Judah b. Pazzi taught: At first the world was a watery chaos [lit. water within water]; how do we know this? since it is written, 'and the spirit of God was hovering over the waters'; He then turned it into snow, as it is written 'He casteth forth his ice like crumbs' (Ps 147:17)." Cf. *Exod. Rab.* 15.7, 22; 50.1; *Qoh. Rab.* 13.15. A more elaborate formulation (with Platonic echoes) is found in Rabbi Yohanan's statement in *Gen. Rab.* 10.3 (cf. Rav's statements in *b. Hag.* 12a; *Gen. Rab.* 4.9), that God created the world by taking two coils of fire and snow and joining them together (Altmann, *Studies*, 129). According to Rav Hama there were six coils, stretching forth in six directions. Cf. the irrational motions (i.e., the rectilinear "wandering motions" in all six directions) which, according to Plato, characterized the "traces" or "copies" of the four elements in the Receptacle (*Tim.* 34a; 43b). Yet another formulation, interpreted by Altmann as an emanation theory of creation, is the statement of R. Simeon b. Jehosadaq in *Gen. Rab.* 3.4 that "the Holy One, blessed be He, wrapped himself in a white garment, and its splendor shone forth from one end of the world to the other" (cf. H. J. Schoeps, *Urgemeinde-Juden-christentum-Gnosis* [Tübingen: Mohr, 1956], 47). Moreover, the recurring "aggadic" expression, "I will return the world to tohu wa-bohu" (*b. Sabb.* 88a), would also seem to imply that God would return the world to the primordial chaos from which he had once made it emerge. Cf. the Egyptian Book of the Dead, where Atum is represented as threatening "I shall destroy all that I have made, and this land will return unto Nun, into the floodwaters, as in its first state" (*ANET*, 9).

against heretical cosmological speculation seems to be reflected in the statement of Rabbi Simon b. Menasya, a contemporary of the Patriarch Rabbi Judah I: "Drink of the water of thy Creator and not turbid water, so that you may not be dragged into heretical teachings" (*Sipre Deut.* 48, on Prov 5:15).[11] Moreover, we know that the Gnostics actually tried to find biblical identifications for many of their various "aeons." According to the Valentinians, the first eight aeons, the Ogdoad, can be found in Genesis, where Beginning, God, Heaven, and Earth are mentioned first (the first Tetrad), then Abyss, Darkness, Water, and Spirit (the second Tetrad) (Irenaeus, *Haer.* 1.18.1). There seems to be a reference to this in a homiletical teaching of Nahum of Gimzo (*b. Hag.* 12a; cf. *Gen. Rab.* 1.14), "If it had said, 'heaven and earth,' I would have said that Heaven and Earth were names of the Holy One, blessed be He. But now that it says: (את) the heaven and (את) the earth,' heaven means the actual heaven, and earth means the actual earth." There is even a spirit called "Thauthabaoth" in Ophite sources, an obvious variant of Tohu wa-Bohu (Origen, *Cels.* 6.31).[12]

In the light of all this, there can be little doubt that the emphatic reference to filth and refuse in the parable of Rabbi Eleazar points very specifically to Manichaean gnosis. We read in *y. Hag.* 2.1, "It is analogous to a king who had built a palace in a place of sewage, refuse, or stench. Whoever comes and says that this palace is in a place of sewage, refuse, or stench, does he not blemish [it]: Even so, whoever says that the world was originally a watery chaos blemishes [it]."[13] The analogy drawn by Rabbi Eleazar is meaningless without its Manichaean background, for the concept of מים במים ("a watery chaos") contains in itself no implication whatever of sewage or stench. Manichaean dualism, however, had ascribed the material creation to the powers of darkness and filth, and it is this ambiance of dualistic heresy that informs the parable of Rabbi Eleazar. "The difference between these two principles [i.e., light and darkness],"

---

[11] Cf. *Gen. Rab.* 1.3, 8.8; *y. Ber.* 9.1; *b. Sanh.* 38b ad fin.; Justin, *Dial.* 62. According to the Pseudo-Clementine Homilies 16.11, Simon Magus pointed out to Peter that the Bible itself admits two or more deities since it says, "Let us make man in our image"; "Now that man has become like one of us" (see A. Büchler, *Studies in Jewish History* [Oxford: Oxford University Press, 1956], 245-74).

[12] See M. Joel, *Blicke in die Religionsgeschichte* (Breslau: Verlag Schottlaender, 1880), 1:168; R. Grant, *Gnosticism and Early Christianity* (2d ed.; New York: Columbia University Press, 1966), 47, 52.

[13] Cf. *b. Hag.* 16a; *Gen. Rab.* 1.5. For R. Eleazar's distaste for esoterics, see *b. Hag.* 13a, and *y. Hag.* 2.1 (Eleazar was a student of Rav). See also H. Graetz, *Gnosticismus und Judenthum* (Krotoschin; B. L. Monasch 1846), 29-35.

says Severus of Antioch, "is like that between a king and a pig. Light dwells in a royal abode in places suitable to its nature, while the dark like a pig wallows in mud and is nourished by filth and delights in it."[14] In the course of extracting the absorbed Light from the Archons, the Living Spirit "flayed them and made the sky from their skins, and out of their excrement he compacted the earth, and out of their bones he made the mountains."[15] An interesting parallel may be found in the Mandaean cosmogony, where Ptahil-Utra, who had emerged from the black waters (*dmn mia siauia sliq*) and along with him all hateful and destructive works, is enjoined by Bhaq-Ziwa to create a world. He goes "below the Skinas, to the place where there are no longer any (Light-) Worlds. He stepped into the murky mire, into the turbid water (*qam bkita dsiana uqambun bmia tahmia*)."[16] In another passage, Ptahil complains in the world of darkness to which he had been banished, "What have I sinned against my father Abatur, that he has sent me into the deep, which is full of stench (*l'umqa dkulh 'sruta*)?"[17]

It is this type of Gnostic teaching that also explains the strong opposition of Rav to those who boast that they deal in cosmology. "Rav said, 'Let the lying lips be dumb' (Ps. 31:18): may they be bound, muted, and struck dumb; 'which speak insolently against the righteous'; who articulate concerning the Righteous One of the world things he concealed from his creatures; 'in pride and contempt': this refers to one who boasts that he speculates on matters of cosmology; he thinks he is exalting, whereas he is only insulting" (*y. Hag.* 2:1, cf. *Gen. Rab.* 1.5). Now Rav is himself the author of a number of cosmological statements,[18] and in this

---

[14] F. C. Burkitt, *The Religion of the Manichees* (Cambridge: Cambridge University Press, 1925), 17. Cf. Plotinus, *Enn.* 1.6.6.

[15] Burkitt, *Religion of the Manichees*, 27; H. Puech, *Le Manichéisme* (Paris: Civilisations du Sud, 1949), 79; G. Widengren, *Mani and Manichaeism* (London: Holt, Rinehart & Winston, 1961), 55 (cf. J. de Menasce, ed. and tr., *Skand-gumanik vicar* [ed. and tr., J. de Menasce; Fribourge en Suisse: Librairie de l'Universite, 1945], 253, 231-32). For a good elucidation of the Mandaean doctrine that Ahreman does not exist in *getih*, or the corporeal world, see S. Shaked, "Some Notes on Ahreman, the Evil Spirit, and His Creation," *Studies in Mysticism and Religion presented to G. Scholem* (Jerusalem: Magnes, Hebrew University, 1967), 227-34.

[16] See K. Rudolph, *Theogonie, Kosmogonie und Anthropogonie in den mandaischen Schriften* (Göttingen: Vandenhoeck & Ruprecht, 1965), 125, 139.

[17] Rudolph, *Theogonie*, 126. For *'sruta* see also *y. Hag.* 2.1 (במקום הסריות). "Mani grew up in a Southern Babylonian gnostic, more explicitly Mandaean, baptist community," writes Widengren (*Mani and Manichaeism*, 26). For a summary of the present state of Mandaean studies, see K. Rudolph, "Problems of a History of the Development of the Mandaean Religion," *HR* 8 (1969): 210-35.

[18] *b. Hag.* 12a; W. Bacher, *Die Aggada der Babylonischen Amoräer* (Budapest: Kon. Ung.

he was only following the ruling of Rabbi Ishmael that (in opposition to that of Rabbi Akiba) permitted such speculation.[19] The extreme irritability that he exhibits in the passage just quoted can therefore only be understood as a reaction to the Gnostic challenge. In sum, there is no evidence that the normative rabbinic view was that creation was *ex nihilo*. Rabban Gamaliel II's formulation came only under the impact of a polemic with someone who was undoubtedly a Gnostic. In the context of such a confrontation, it would only be natural for Rabban Gamaliel II to counter with the notion that even the apparently primordial elements to which the Gnostic ascribed a dynamic cosmogonic function were created by God. Nothing may be inferred from this discussion as to the common rabbinic view of creation.[20]

The first explicit formulation of *creatio ex nihilo* appeared in second-century Christian literature, where the argument for a "double creation" theory is made on the grounds that creation out of an eternal primordial

---

Univers., 1878), 16-21; G. Scholem, *Jewish Gnosticism* (New York: Jewish Theological Society of America, 1960), 27-28.

[19] *y. Hag.* 2.1; cf. Joel, *Religionsgeschichte*, 1:156-57; B. Bacher, *Agodot ha-Tannaim* (4 vols; Berlin; Jerusalem; Devir, 1922), 1:75; H. Albeck, *Seder Moed* (Jerusalem 1954) supplemental notes, 510. All agreed, however, that it was forbidden to speculate concerning the worlds that preceeded the creation of our own world (cf. S. Lieberman, *Tosefta Kifshuta* [New York: Louis Rabinowitz Research Institute in Rabbinics at the Jewish Theological Seminary of America, 1955-1962], 5:1296). A convenient summary of rabbinic views on creation may now be found in E. Urbach, *Hazal: Pirke Emunoth we-Deoth* (Jerusalem: Magnes, Hebrew University, 1969), 161-89 (Hebrew).

[20] Most recently, Urbach (*Hazal*, 164) repeats the usual interpretation that the "philosopher" who argues with Rabban Gamaliel II holds the doctrine of creation out of primordial matter. In so sensitive an area as this, however, the "philosopher" would hardly have chosen a verb that could easily be construed to mean "actively assisted" (i.e., in the act of creation) had he merely intended to derive from the text of Genesis a doctrine of creation out of primordial matter. Moreover, strictly speaking, Rabban Gamaliel II's formulation does not necessarily imply creation *ex nihilo*; כלם כתוב בהם בריאה might conceivably mean that they were all passive elements that were endowed with power and activity only through the divine word. But even if he did mean to imply a creation *ex nihilo*, it would reflect not the common rabbinic view but rather an *ad hominem* response in the heat of a debate with someone who seriously challenged Jewish monotheism (cf. Weiss, *Untersuchungen*, 177). Once formulated, however, it was bound to be repeated (cf. *b. Hag.* 12a ["R. Judah said in the name of Rav: Ten things were created on the first day: heaven and earth; Tohu wa-Bohu; light and darkness; wind and water; the measure of day and the measure of night"]); *Exod. Rab.* 15.22. Moreover, there is a passage in *Mekilta, Shirata* 8, which provides strong prima facie evidence that the rabbis did not subscribe to creation *ex nihilo*. Ten examples are given there for the uniqueness of God's acts in contrast to those of humanity. The best example of all: that God can create *ex nihilo*, is not given. Furthermore, example six states that to make a roof a human being requires wood, stones, dirt, and water, whereas God has made of water a roof for his world. cf. *Gen. Rab.* 4.1. (I owe this reference to Professor Judah Goldin).

element would compromise the sovereignty of God.[21] Although this mode of argumentation became a commonplace in medieval philosophy (it was already accepted by Saadia), it was explicitly rejected by both Maimonides and Gersonides.[22]

---

[21] Tatian, *Orat.* 5; Theophilus of Antioch, *Autol.* 2.4, 10 ad fin. (cf. Origen, *Princ.* 2.1.4). Again, it was probably the Gnostic challenge that had set up other powers by the side of God that gave rise to this cautionary defense of God's sovereign power (cf. Weiss, *Untersuchungen,* 149-50). The statement in Herm. *Mand.* 1:1 ("who created everything from non-existence into existence") is still not an explicit *ex nihilo* formulation, and Tertullian (*Herm.* passim), who explicitly teaches creation *ex nihilo*, employing (against Hermogenes) the same arguments used by Tatian and Theophilus, does not hold to a double-creation theory. (By "double creation" is meant that God first created a primordial matter out of which he then proceeded to create the world.) Saint Augustine (*Conf.* 12.8, *Gen. Man.* 1.10) accepted the double-creation theory, but insisted that God created matter and form simultaneously (see E. Gilson, *The Christian Philosophy of St. Augustine* [New York: Random House, 1960; London: V. Gollacanz 1961], 197-205). Cf. Calcidius (first half of fourth century CE), *in Tim.* 276-78. Another second-century formulation of *creatio ex nihilo* is that of the Alexandrian Gnostic teacher Basilides, who flourished during the reign of Hadrian (117-38), but his extreme version involves a "non-existent God" making "a non-existent cosmos out of the non-existent" (Hippolytus, *Haer.* 7.20.2-21) (see Wolfson, *Church Fathers,* 551; idem, "Negative Attributes in the Church Fathers and the Gnostic Basilides," *HTR* 50 [1957]: 145-56; G. Quispel, "Gnostic Man: The Doctrine of Basilides," in *The Mystic Vision* [trans. R. Manheim ; Bollingen Series 30; Papers from the Eranos Yearbook, vol. 6; Princeton, N.J.; Princeton University Press, 1968], 210-46). For the ambiguity of the phrase *ex nihilo*, see the penetrating analysis of Wolfson, "The Meaning of Ex Nihilo in the Church Fathers, Arabic and Hebrew Philosophy and St. Thomas," *Medieval Studies in Honour of J. D. M. Ford* (ed. U. T. Holmes and A. J. Denomy; Cambridge: Harvard University Press, 1948), 355-67; idem, "The Meaning of Ex Nihilo in Isaac Israeli," *JQR* 50 (1959): 1-12. (Wolfson explains why Saadia, and following him Maimonides and Aquinas, formulated the doctrine of *ex nihilo* as creation שׁי מן לא ["not from a thing"]. He feared that לא מן שׁ אלא ["from no-thing"] could be taken to mean, as it was by one school of the Kalam, from "relative" nothing, i.e., matter. Indeed, Saadia virtually indicates this himself in his *Commentary on Sefer Yetzirah.* Cf. Fredegisus [d. 834], who, in his *Epistola de nihilo et tenebris,* maintained that nothingness and darkness are something, and not simply the absence of something. Creation *ex nihilo*, therefore, means creation from an undifferentiated matter from which God molded everything; E. Gilson, *History of Christian Philosophy in the Middle Ages* [New York: Random House, 1955], 111-12.) Crescas, too, uses the formula מדבר לא or "not from something" (*Or Adonai* 3.1.5). See also, Grant, *Miracle and Natural Law,* 135-52.

[22] See H. A. Wolfson, "The Platonic Aristotelian, and Stoic Theories of Creation in Halevi and Maimonides," *Essays in Honour of J. Hertz* (London: E. Goldston, 1942); Maimonides, *Guide* 2.13; Gersonides, *Milhamot* 6.18. With the arguments of Maimonides and Gersonides, compare those of Hermogenes in Tertullian, *The Treatise against Hermogenes* (ed. J. H. Waszink; London: Longmans, Green & Co., 1956), 5, 31 ff. The rabbis were apparently untroubled by the implied compromise of God's sovereignty posed by an eternal matter until the Gnostics began quoting Scripture to support their doctrine of multiple creative powers (see also, H. A. Wolfson, "Plato's Preexistent Matter in Patristic Philosophy," in *The Classical Tradition* [ed. L. Wallach; Ithaca, N.Y.: Cornell University Press, 1966], 409-20; Weiss, *Untersuchungen,* 139-80).

Returning to the author of the Wisdom of Solomon, it is now clear that there is no reason to doubt the plain meaning of his statement that creation was out of formless matter. Moreover, there is some internal evidence that makes this interpretation all but certain. First, as Grimm had pointed out long ago,[23] it was the author's object to adduce as great a proof as possible of the power of God. Since creation *ex nihilo* would be an even greater marvel than that of conferring form on an already existent matter, he could hardly have failed to have specified the former had he thought it possible. Second, in his account of the various miracles performed by God on behalf of the children of Israel, the author employs a Greek philosophical principle in order to make the notion of miracles more plausible. The pre-Socratics had already taught the mutual interchange of elements. Pythagoras, for example, taught that "the elements interchange and turn into one another completely" (μεταβάλλειν δὲ καὶ τρέπεσθαι δι' ὅλων) (Diogenes Laertius 8.25). The principle behind this doctrine was stated with especial clarity by Diogenes of Apollonia, "For if the things now existing in this world, earth and water and air and fire and all other things that are observed to exist in this world, if any one of these were different from another — really different in its own nature, and not the same real thing that changes and is altered in many ways — then they would be unable to mingle with one another at all, or to be any help or harm to another; neither would any plant grow from the earth nor any animal or any other thing be born, if they were not so constituted as to be really the same thing. But all these things arise by alteration out of the same thing, become different at different times, and return back to the same thing."[24] By the Hellenistic age it was a commonplace in Greek philosophy that the stuff of which the world is made is ἄποιος ὕλη, and that therefore the elements were mutually interchangeable.[25] The Stoics, in their attempt to explicate divination and the various miracle stories it involved, made especial use of this principle to show that the gods could accomplish anything without violating the laws of nature. "For you [sc.

---

[23] C. Grimm, *Das Buch der Weisheit* (Kurzgefasstes Exegetisches Handbuch zu den Apokryphen des A.T.; Leipzig: Hirzel, 1857), 213.

[24] Diels and Kranz, *Die Fragmente der Vorsokratiker*, 64, B2. Cf. Plato, *Tim.* 49b-c; *Phaed.* 72b, where the change of one thing into another is described as "going round as it were in a circle"; Aristotle, *Gen.corr.* 377, 1-7. See C. Kahn, *Anaximander and the Origins of Greek Cosmology* (New York, 1960), 119-65.

[25] Sextus Empiricus, *Math.* 2.312; Diogenes Laertius 7.150; 8.25; Epictetus, *Diatr.* 3.24.10; frg. 8; Diels, *Doxographi graeci*, 308; cf. Calcidius, *in Tim.* 283-301; *SVF* 2:405-11. Grant, *Miracle and Natural Law*, 184, refers more specifically to a passage from Cleanthes (*SVF*, 1.497) which describes the intermingling of the elements at the time of the ἐκπύρωσις.

Stoics] yourselves are fond of saying that there is nothing that a god cannot accomplish, and that without any toil; as man's limbs are effortlessly moved merely by his mind and will, so, as you say, the gods' power can mould and move and alter all things. Nor do you say this as some superstitious fable or old wives' tale, but you give a scientific and systematic account of it: you allege that matter, which constitutes and contains all things, is in its entirety flexible and subject to change, so that there is nothing that cannot be moulded and transmuted out of it however suddenly, but the moulder and manipulator of this universal substance is divine providence, and therefore providence, whithersoever it moves, is able to perform whatever it will."[26]

The author of Wisdom similarly explains the miracle of the passage of the Red Sea, "For the whole creation was formed over again in its particular nature, submitting to your divine command, so that your children might be preserved unharmed" (19:6). "For the elements were 'transposed' (i.e., their potency or tension [τόνος] was increased or diminished) as the notes in a psaltery vary the beat while holding to the melody, as one may accurately surmise from the sight of what happened. For land animals were changed into water animals, and natant creatures migrated onto the land. Fire retained its own force in the water, and water forgot its quenching nature. Conversely, flames did not waste the flesh of perishable creatures that walked among them, nor was the easily-melted ice-like kind of heavenly food dissolved" (19:18-20).[27] Returning to our argument, had the author of Wisdom held the doctrine of *creatio ex nihilo*, he could hardly have been troubled by lesser miracles and sought a philosophical principle to explain them, for *creatio ex nihilo* is the miracle of miracles. It quickly

---

[26] Cicero, *Nat. d.* 3.39.92; assigned by Von Arnim to Chrysippus (*SVF* 2.1107). Grant, *Miracle and Natural Law*, 128, assigns this passage to Posidonius. In any case, this passage should not be taken to mean that according to the Stoics, God can act arbitrarily. The Stoics were probably only insisting that the so-called miracles associated with divination are not really miracles, but have a natural explanation. As a matter of fact, the interest of the Stoics in divination in the first place may have been motivated by their search for empirical evidence to back up their theory of universal causality (see S. Sambursky, *Physics of the Stoics* [London: Routledge and Kegan Paul, 1959], 65-71). Cicero's formulation is undoubtedly misleading, but as Guthrie has noted elsewhere, "The picture given [in *Nat. d.*] of many philosophical theories is a deliberate travesty" (Guthrie, *History of Greek Philosophy*, 2.480). Cf. L. Edelstein (*The Meaning of Stoicism* [Cambridge: Harvard University Press, 1966], 33): "At any rate, the Stoic God is not absolute. Unlike the Jewish God he does not bring forth the world by fiat."

[27] Wis 19:6: ὅλη γὰρ ἡ κτίσις ἐν ἰδίῳ γένει πάλιν ἄνωθεν διετυποῦτο. Wis 19:18: Δι' ἑαυτῶν γὰρ τὰ στοιχεῖα μεθαρμοζόμενα, ὥσπερ ἐν ψαλτηρίῳ φθόγγοι τοῦ ῥυθμοῦ τὸ ὄνομα διαλλάσσουσιν, πάντοτε μένοντα ἤχῳ. For a detailed discussion see Appendix to this essay.

became the paradigm for God's miraculous powers, and its denial was taken to betoken the undermining of revealed religion.[28]

The attempt to explicate miracles on the basis of God's ability to transform the nonexistent is already found in Philo (*Opif.* 26.81; *Mos.* 2.267). Moreover, it would appear at first sight that like the author of Wisdom, Philo, too, explains some of the biblical miracles through the physical principle of the interchangeability of the elements. A closer look, however, shows that, although he describes some of the biblical miracles in terms of an interchange in the functioning of the elements (*Mos.* 2.267, "Changing round the elements [μεταβαλὼν τὰ στοιχεῖα] to meet the pressing need of the occasion, so that instead of earth the air bore food for their nourishment"), and reproduces the actual language of Wis 19:6 (*Mos.* 1.201, "But God has subject to Him not one portion of the universe, but the whole world and its parts, to minister as slaves to their master [ὡς δεσπότῃ δοῦλα ὑπηρετήσοντα]," he ascribes this reassignment of functions solely to the absolute power of the divine will, making no reference to a material principle. He argues that if God could fashion the world out of nonbeing, surely he could reapportion the various operations of the elements [*Mos.* 2.267]). The author of Wisdom, on the other hand, makes God first fashion the elements anew by transposing them (there seems to be a vague allusion here to a change in the relative proportions of their pneumata) in order to achieve the desired reassignment of roles.[29]

Philo's argument for miracles from God's power to create from the nonexistent became a potent weapon in the arsenal of those who sought to explain the very difficult miracle of resurrection. If God could bring the world into being out of nothing, the argument went, surely he could accomplish the easier task of restoring the dissolved elements of the corpse.[30] The pagan philosopher Celsus (ca. 178-80 CE), on the other

---

[28] Cf. Maimonides, *Guide*, 2:22; 2:25; Albo, *Ikharim* 1.12.1; Abravanel, *Mif 'alot Elohim* 6a.

[29] Grant's assertion, then (*Miracle and Natural Law*, 185) that Philo reproduces Wisdom's explanation of miracles, is unwarranted.

[30] See *b. Sanh.* 91a; Tertullian, *Res.* 11; Augustine, *Civ.* 21; Grant, *Miracle and Natural Law*, 235-45; "Maimonides, *Ma'amar Tehiyyat ha-Metim*," ed. J. Finkel, *PAAJR* 9 (1938-39): 30. For Iranian parallels, see my article, "The Iranian Component in the Bible," *HR* 5 (1966): 211; H. Chadwick, "Origen, Celsus and Resurrection," *HTR* 41 (1948): 83-102. For Islamic parallels, see R. Walzer, *Greek into Arabic* (Cambridge: Harvard University Press, 1962), 181-87. As G. Gnoli correctly points out (contra Casartelli, Gray, Moulton, Jackson, and Bailey), the Iranian parallels need not imply that Ahura Mazda creates *ex nihilo*. The argument for resurrection would stand even if God only brings things into being from a state of relative nonexistence, i.e., from an unshaped preexistent matter (Gnoli, "Osserva-zioni," 163-93. I owe this reference to Professor Shaked). The same may be said of the Jewish and Islamic parallels (cf. Qur'an 19:66-67; 22:5; 86:5-8). The earliest argument for resurrection based explicitly on God's capacity to create *ex nihilo* seems to be that of

hand, reacted violently to this kind of argumentation. "For what sort of body," he wrote, "having once been completely destroyed, can return to its previous nature...? Having no reply they escape to a most outrageous refuge by saying that 'anything is possible with God.' But God can neither do what is shameful or what is contrary to nature ... For he himself is the reason of everything that exists; therefore he is not able to do anything contrary to reason or his own character."[31] Galen similarly criticizes Moses' account of creation which omits the material principle and ascribes everything to God's arbitrary will. "For Moses it seems enough to say that God simply willed the arrangement of matter and it was presently arranged in due order; for he believes everything to be possible with God, even should he wish to make a bull or a horse out of ashes".[32] We, however, do

---

Tertullian cited above.

[31] Origen, *Cels.* 5.14, 23. Origen, too, excludes from the general principle that all things are possible to God things that are nonexistent, or inconceivable, or disgraceful, but maintains that resurrection, especially as he understands it, is none of these. See R. Walzer, *Galen on Jews and Christians* (London: Oxford University Press, 1949), 31. The idea of omnipotence was already expressed by Homer, θεοὶ δέ τε πάντα δύνανται (*Od.* 10.306). Cf. Matt 19:26; Mark 10:28; Philo, *Opif.* 46 (πάντα θεῷ δύνατα); Gen 18:14, rendered in the LXX, "Shall anything be impossible with the Lord?" Aristotle, however, cites the poet Agathon in support of his view that not even God can change the past (*Eth. nic.* 6.2.6); and Pliny the Elder gives us a list of things that God cannot do, "Not even for God are all things possible — for he cannot, even if he wishes, commit suicide ... nor bestow eternity on mortals or recall the deceased, nor cause a man that has lived not to have lived or one that held high office not to have held it — and that he has not power over what is past save to forget it, and ... that he cannot cause twice ten not to be twenty, or do many things on similar lines" (*Nat.* 2.27). Cf. Plato, *Resp.* 2.381c, "It is impossible then even for a god to wish to alter himself"; Seneca, *Ben.* 6.2.2-3 (see Grant, *Miracle and Natural Law*, 127-34). On the other hand, in answer to Saint Jerome who had stated (*Epist.* 22, *Ad Eustochium*) that although God is omnipotent he could not restore virginity to a girl who had lost it, Peter Damian (1007-72) replied that the laws of nature and of logic are founded by God, who can undo them whenever he so wishes. God can thus undo what is done, for he dwells in an eternal present. Hence, "God in his invariable and most constant eternity can so bring it about that what will have been done in our transitory world may not be done; so that we can say: God can so act that Rome, which was founded in ancient times, will not have been founded" (*De Divina Omnipotentia*, chap. 15). See J. Endres, *Petrus Damiani und die weltliche Wissenschaft* (Münster: Aschendorf, 1910), 16-30. Similarly, Karl Barth repeats again and again that nonsense may be given sense by an act of sheer omnipotence on the part of God. For a discussion of Descartes' radical voluntarism, according to which even mathamatical theorems are contingent upon God's will, see A. Funkenstein, "Descartes, Eternal Truths and the Divine Omnipotence," in *Descartes: Philosophy, Mathematics and Physics* (ed. Stephen Gaukroger; Sussex: Harvester, 1980), 181-95.

[32] Cf. Lucretius 1.163-4: A denial of the principle that nothing is created out of nothing would imply that anything could be created out of anything without seed, e.g., men from the sea, or cattle from the desert; Epicurus, *Ep. Herod.* 38. (See also Lieberman, *Greek in Jewish Palestine* [New York: Jewish Theological Seminary of America, 1942], 113-14: "They [i.e., the Israelites] took the sand from the 'footprints of the ox of the Merkabah' and

not hold this; we say that certain things are impossible by nature and that God does not even attempt such things at all but that he chooses the best out of the possibilities of becoming" (*UP* 11).[33] In ignoring the properties of matter, Moses, in Galen's view, is virtually denying the principle of causality, and is thus attributing the impossible to God.[34] The argument that even God cannot do the impossible recurs in Alexander of Aphrodisias,[35]

---

recreated him." Cf. L. Ginzberg, *Al Halaka wa-Agada* [Tel Aviv: Devir, 1960], 243.) It is interesting to note that Galen apparently does not find a creation *ex nihilo* in Genesis, but rather a divine will arbitrarily arranging some sort of primordial matter. Cf. Julian, *Galil.* 49D-E.

[33] Cf. Aristotle, *Cael.* 288a, 2. See Walzer, *Galen,* 11-12; 23-37. Saadia, too, refused to attribute the logically absurd to God and argued that this did not diminish his power, for "the absurd is nothing" (Saadia Gaon, *Book of Beliefs,* 134). Cf. Maimonides, *Guide* 1:75; 2:13,19; 3:25 ("He wills only what is possible, and not everything that is possible, but only that which is required by His wisdom to be such"); Crescas, *Or Adonai* 5.2.3; Albo, *Ikharim.* Cf. Saint Anselm, "And as, when God does a thing, since it has been done it cannot be undone, but must remain an actual fact; still, we are not correct in saying that it is impossible for God to prevent a past action from being what it is. For there is no necessity or impossibility in the case whatever but the simple will of God, which chooses that truth should be eternally the same, for he himself is truth" (*Cur Deus Homo* 2:18a; cf. Augustine, *Civ.* 5.10). Similarly, Saint Thomas writes, "sub omnipotentia dei non cadit aliquid, quod contradictionem implicat" (*S.T.* 1.9.25a, 4). On the question "utrum Deus possit virginem reparare," Thomas says, "solum id a Dei potentia excluditur, quod repugnat rationi entis, et hoc est simul esse et non esse, et eiusdem rationis est: quod fuit non fuisse" (*Quodlib.* 5a, 3). For a modern discussion see Arthur Prior, *Past, Present and Future* (Oxford: Clarendon, 1967).

[34] The Stoics and Epicureans explicitly equated *creatio ex nihilo* with the denial of causality (Alexander of Aphrodisias, *Fat.* 192.14; Plutarch, *Mor.* 731D). The principle "gigni de nihilo nihilum, in nihilum nil posse reverti" (Persius 3:83), which was ultimately based on the logical argument of Parmenides (frg. B 8.7 ff.; cf. Plato, *Soph.* 237b-239c), was explicitly attributed to Democritus (Diogenes Laertius 9.44) and Anaxagoras (B5), and according to Aristotle (*Metaph.* 1062b; *Phys.* 1.4.187a, 27) was accepted by all the physicists. The only dissenting voice we hear of is that of the Sophist, Xeniades of Corinth (fifth century BCE) (Sextus Empiricus, *Math.* 7.53), who declared that "everything was false ... and that everything which comes to be comes to be from what is not and everything which is destroyed is destroyed into what is not." But see von Fritz, PW, ser. 2, vol. 9, pp. 1438-39, who finds Sextus's report unreliable. As to the Neoplatonist, Hierocles of Alexandria (fifth century CE), who has the Demiurge create out of nothing through sheer will, this may well have been due to Christian influence (Praechter, PW, 8.1479-87; H. Marrou, in *Conflict between Paganism and Christianity in the Fourth Century* [ed. A. Momigliano; Oxford: Clarendon, 1963], 138). See now Ilsetraut Hadot, *Le Problème du Néoplatonisme Alexandrin: Hiéroclès et Simplicius* (Paris: Études Augustiniennes, 1978), 86-92, who shows that there is no need to invoke Christian influence to explain Hierocles' position. See also Richard Sorabji, *Time, Creation and the Continuum* (Ithaca: Cornell University Press, 1983), 313-15.

[35] Alexander of Aphrodisias, *On Destiny* (trans. A. Fitzgerald; London: Scholartis 1931), chap. 30, 122-23. See also P. Thillet, "Un Traité inconnu d'Alexandre d'Aphrodise sur la Providence dans une version arabe inédite," in *L'homme et son destin, d'après les penseurs du*

"For things impossible by their very nature, preserve this same nature even in the presence of the gods. Surely it is impossible even for the gods either to make the diagonal [sc. of a square] commensurate with its side, or for twice two to make five, or for anything that has already happened not to have happened.[36] In fact the gods do not desire empire over the impossible." Moreover, "if one assumes that everything is possible for the gods, it would not be impossible for them to know the size of the infinite, which is absurd."

The identical argumentation of Alexander reappears in the mysticism of the school of Gerona. In Rabbi Ezra ben Shelomo's *Commentary on the Song of Songs* (falsely attributed to Nachmanides) we read, "This follows Plato's view who said that it was absurd to think that the creator should produce something out of nothing, and that there is a pre-existent matter ... His inability to create something out of nothing does not indicate any deficiency on his part, even as it does not indicate any deficiency on his part that He is unable to produce what is logically absurd, e.g., creating a square the diagonal of which is commensurate to its length or combining two contraries at the same instant. Just as this does not imply any deficiency in his power, in the same way no short-coming on his part is indicated by his inability to effect an emanation of something from nothing. For this belongs to the logically absurd ... King Solomon in his pure wisdom meant this when he said 'of the woods of Lebanon' — thence everything was emanated. The essence existed before, but the emanation was innovated."[37]

Moyen Age; actes du Premier Congrès international de philosophie médiévale. Louvaine-Brussels, Aug 28-Sept 4, 1958 (Lovain: Nauwelaerts, 1960), 319, where Alexander adds that eight cannot be less than one, three cannot equal four, nor can colors be perceived by the sense of hearing, even by divine fiat. Maimonides knew this treatise of Alexander and referred to it in his *Guide* (3.16) (see S. Pines's introduction to his translation of the *Guide of the Perplexed* [Chicago: University of Chicago Press, 1963], 65).

[36] Cf. *m. Ber.* 9:3, "If a man cries out to God over what is past, his prayer is vain"; *y. Ber.* 9:3; *Gen. Rab.* 72.6. An interesting analogy from rabbinic law (where a prior act of perfectly legitimate betrothal is actually undone) is the principle invoked in *b. Yebam.* 110a, *b. Ketub.* 3a, and *b. Git.* 33a: "Everyone who betrothes, does so in accordance with the sense of the Rabbis, and the Rabbis have annulled his betrothal." For examples in Roman law, see D. Daube, "Greek and Roman Reflections on Impossible Laws," *Natural Law Forum* 12 (1967): 1-84. The English deist, William Wollaston, quotes our Mishnah, but disagrees with it. God, he says, foreknows the petitions of man, and designs the course of happenings accordingly. (Wollaston was apparently unaware of the interpretation given our Mishnah in the Jerusalem Talmud.) But he also records the saying of the Sefer Hasidim, "that we should not pray for the impossible, or that which is contrary to nature, or the unseemly, or that God should change the world by way of miracle" (see Altmann, *Studies*, 224, 235; cf. *b. Sabb.* 53b).

[37] See *A Commentary on the Song of Songs by Moses ben Nachman* (Altona, 1764), 5b-6a

For the early Jewish mystics, creation out of nothing (i.e., out of absolute nothing) belonged to the realm of the logically absurd. They therefore reinterpreted it to mean creation from the essence of God.[38] Ironically, later Jewish mystics, such as Aaron of Starosselje (1766-1828) and Nahman of Bratzlav (1772-1811), unable to assimilate the paradox of the simultaneous existence and nonexistence of a finite universe, did indeed embrace the absurd, and maintained that God could do the logically impossible, "They write in their books: 'Is it possible for God to make a triangle into a square?' But our master [Rabbi Nahman] said: 'I believe that God can make a square triangle. For God's ways are concealed from us. He is omnipotent and nothing is impossible for Him.'"[39]

Thus we find that the explicit formulation of the doctrine of creation *ex nihilo* was not indigenously Jewish, but that under the influence of Christian-Muslim thought it penetrated into Jewish philosophical and religious literature.[40] Moreover, in its Christian-Muslim-Jewish formulation

---

(Hebrew). For a French translation, see G. Vajda, *Le commentaire d'Ezra de Gerona sur le Cantique des Cantiques* (Paris: Aubier-Montaige, 1969). See also G. Scholem, *Ursprung und Anfänge der Kabbala* (Berlin: DeGruyter, 1962), 329; and his "Te'uda hadasha le-toldot re' shit ha-Kabbala," *Sefer Bialik* (Tel Aviv: Hotsaat Vaad-ha-yovel uve-hishtatfut hotsaat Omanut, 1934), 155-62; A. Aptowitzer, "Heker Agada," *Bitzaron* 11 (1944): 198-99; Altmann, *Studies*, 137.

[38] The same kind of reinterpretation had been already worked out by Christian Neoplatonists, such as Pseudo-Dionysius and John Scotus (cf. Wolfson, "Meaning"; Scholem, "Schöpfung"; idem, *Major Trends in Jewish Mysticism* [New York: Schocken Books, 1946], 221). In the long version of the so-called Theology of Aristotle we already find the divine "Word" (*kalima*) designated as "nothing" (*laysa*) (since it is beyond motion and rest), and hence creation through the latter is a creation *ex nihilo*. A similar view is found among the Isma'iliya (e.g., Nasr al-Khosrau), the radical wing of the Shi'a; see S. Pines, "La longue recension de la théologie d'Aristote dans ses rapports avec la doctrine Ismaélienne," *Revue des études Islamiques* 22 (1954): 7-20; Scholem, *Ursprung*, 373-81.

[39] *Kunteros Yeme ha-Telaoth* (Jerusalem, 1933), 190. The logical antinomies have an ontic status, according to Rabbi Nahman; they are not errors of the mind. They are born in the very act of creation, the primordial act of divine contraction (צמצם). The ultimate paradox is thus constituted by two contradictory theological demands: that God be present in the world, and that he not be present in it. Only when the absolute antinomies assail faith, and faith withstands the attack, is "paradoxical faith" born. Faith does not resolve the antinomy, but only remains silent in its presence. Such a faith is absolutely free, for it is freedom from all rational determination. The messianic age will see the rational resolution of the antinomies, thereby also annulling our freedom of choice, and transforming men into angels (see J. G. Weiss, "Ha-Kushya be-Torath R. Nahman mi-Bratzlav," *Alei Ayin: The Salman Schoken Jubilee Volume* [Jerusalem, 1952], 245-91; L. Jacobs, *Faith* [New York: Basic Books, 1968], 201-9.

[40] Even if Wolfson (*Philo*, 1:302-10) is correct in his attempt to show that Philo taught a double creation theory, he certainly did not teach it unambiguously. For a critique of Wolfson, see Karl Bormann, *Die Ideen und Logoslehre Philons von Alexandrien* (diss., University of Köln, 1955), 35-44; Weiss, *Untersuchungen*, 59-72. Moreover, his influence on

it was a purely negative doctrine whose intent was only to deny the theories of creation out of matter or through emanation from God.[41] It was never meant to compete in the philosophical arena as an alternate theory that could explain how God, who was pure spirit, could create the material world. Its presumption is that this question is beyond the scope of either experience or reason, and hence unamenable to philosophical analysis. Hence, its acceptance served as the chief underpinning for the supernatural conception of deity.

Appendix

Wis 19:18 presents some difficulties for the translator. Omitting a translation of the ambiguous terms, we may render it as follows: "For the elements were μεθαρμοζόμενα, as in a psaltery, the notes change the name of the ῥυθμός, while sticking to the ἦχος." Now, the musical analogy employed by the author would be particularly sharpened if we were to translate the ambiguous terms in the following way: "For the elements were transposed — as in a psaltery, the notes vary the key (τόνος or τρόπος), while sticking to the melody." The author would thus be saying (following Stoic theory) that the τόνος of the elements was either heightened or lowered through a change in the relative proportions of fire and air constituting their pneumata, just as the τόνος of a musical mode is varied by the transposition of the notes within it. Both the elements and the

---

medieval Jewish thought was only an indirect one, and on rabbinic literature it was virtually nil. (Cf., however, S. A. Poznanski, "Philon dans l'ancienne littérature judéoarabe," *REJ* 50 [1905]: 10-31, who seeks to demonstrate that al-Moqammes [tenth century] made use of a translation of Philo [probably in Syriac], and even suggests that it is not inconceivable that Saadia, too, may have used it.) As for the formulation in Sefer Yezirah (עשסה את שאינו ישנו) it is still quite ambiguous, although it was readily exploited by Saadia as an expression of creation *ex nihilo* (see Scholem, *Ursprung*, 20-29).

[41] See, for example, J. B. Heinrich, *Dogmatische Theologie* (10 vols.; Mainz: Franz Kirchheim, 1872-1901), 5:20; E. Brunner, *Dogmatik* (3 vols.; Zurich; Stuttgart; Zwingli-Verlag, 1960), 2:20; Saint Thomas, *De Pot.* 3.1, ad 7; *S.T.* 1a, 45, 1, ad 3; cf. E. Gilson, *The Christian Philosophy of St. Thomas Aquinas* (New York: Random House, 1956), 121-22. Cf. Saint Augustine, "Like him who made the universe, the mode of making is hidden and incomprehensible to man" (*Civ.* 10.12); Weiss, *Untersuchungen*, 178. Saadia, too, speaks explicitly of the mystery of creation: "How can something be derived from nothing? [literally: not from something]. Our answer is that if mortal creatures had been in a position to conceive of how such a thing could come about, it would not have been necessary for our reason to attribute it exclusively to the eternal Creator" (Saadia, *Book of Beliefs*, 84). The analytical philosopher of today would undoubtedly object to such a use of the term "create," inasmuch as the aforementioned thinkers appear to have deprived it of all content, and were thus employing a vacuous, and therefore meaningless expression.

modes retain their identity despite the transposition, which only affects their tonos. For the author's tendency to view the transformation of nature in terms of a change in τόνος, see 16:24: ἡ γὰρ κτίσις σοὶ τῷ ποιήσαντι ὑπηρετοῦσα ἐπιτείνεται εἰς κόλασιν κατὰ τῶν ἀδίκων καὶ ἀνίεται εἰς εὐεργεσίαν ὑπὲρ τῶν ἐπὶ σοὶ πεποιθότων. The intent of this verse is that the elements of fire and water, through a heightening or lowering of their τόνος, underwent a sufficient inner transformation to account, on the one hand, for the miracle of the ice-like manna that "endured fire and melted not," and, on the other hand, for the punishment of the Egyptians by fire "flaming amid the hail and flashing in the showers" (16:22).[42]

The question of τόνοι is unfortunately one of the most troubled in the history of ancient Greek music. According to one widely accepted theory, however, the different τόνοι were different keys, that is, transpositions of one basic octave pattern to different pitch levels. Mountford and Winnington-Ingram, for example, write: "The Perfect Immutable System could as a whole be played at various pitches without any alteration of the internal sequence, just as our modern Major or Minor scale can be taken at various pitches. When associated with a given pitch, the Perfect Immutable System had a distinctive name and was called a τόνος or τρόπος. According to Aristoxenus there were thirteen such τόνοι, to which later theorists added two more."[43] Now there is evidence that a variety of modes were in use by Alexandrian Jews in their chanting of the psalms,[44] and Clement of Alexandria, who praised the majestic psalmody of the Alexandrian Jews, singled out one of these modes as the *Tropos Spondeiakos*, apparently a modification of the Dorian mode (Clement, *Paed.* 2, c. 4). The ethos of this τρόπος is described by all Greek authorities as dignified, quiet, and highly solemn.[45] In the light of this Jewish familiarity with modes, the author of Wisdom's use of a musical analogy referring to the latter is very understandable. As for his surprising use of the term ῥυθμός instead of τόνος or τρόπος (the latter, in its technical use, is first attested to

---

42 For ἐπίτασις and ἄνεσις, see Philo, *Mut.* 13.87; *QG* 2.64; *Her.* 156; *SVF* 3.92 and 525; Plato, *Resp.* 442a; *Phaed.* 86c, 94c. See Goodrick, n. 2 above, p. 334; J. Fichtner, *Weisheit Salomos* [Tübingen: Mohr, 1938], 69; G. Ziener, *Die theologische Begriffsprache im Buch der Weisheit* [Bonn: P. Hanstein, 1956], 155-58.

43 *OCD*, 707; R. P. Winnington-Ingram, *Mode in Ancient Greek Music* [Cambridge: Cambridge University Press, 1936], 48ff., esp. 71ff.

44 Saadia, for example, quoting an old rabbinic interpretation, writes: "The expression על השמינית demonstrates that the Levites used eight modes, so that each time one of their regular groups executed one mode" (see E. Werner and I. Sonne, "The Philosophy and Theory of Music in Judaeo-Arabic Literature," *HUCA* 16 [1941]: 295ff.).

45 See Pseudo-Plutarch, *Mus.* 1134f-1135b, 1137b-d; Winnington-Ingram, *Mode*, 22-24; E. Werner, "The Attitude of the Church Fathers to Hebrew Psalmody," *RR* 7 [1943]: 349-52.

by Dionysius Halicarnassensis, *Comp.* 19), this may perhaps be due to an attempt on his part to avoid technical musical terms and stick to common everyday usage. (Possibly, he was himself confused in an area where even experts rarely agreed with one another.) One may imagine the following development in popular usage. We know from Aristoxenus that within the Greater Perfect System there were seven different types or species (εἴδη τοῦ διὰ πασῶν) that could be distinguished by their different interval sequences. Each had its own distinctive name (Mixolydian, Lydian, Phrygian, Dorian, Hypolydian, Hypophrygian, Hypodorian). These may be regarded as heirs of the ἁρμονία (i.e., scales or modes) of which Plato (*Resp.* 398d-399c) and Aristotle (*Pol.* 1339) spoke. The modal names were attached to them — and even the term ἁρμονία. Now, the modes (which, strictly speaking, "involved the internal relationships of notes within a scale, especially of the predominance of one of them over all the others as a tonic") may be defined as "epitomes of stylized song, similar to the Chinese tyao, the Indian rag, and the Arabic maqam."[46] In a broad sense, they were probably patterns or general melodic types, with each of which certain specific rhythms and certain tetrachord genera were associated. Hence, common usage may have simply designated the ἁρμονίαι or εἴδη as ῥυθμοί.[47] See Philo, *Contempl.* 29, who writes of the Therapeutae of Egypt as follows: ὥστε οὐ θεωροῦσι μόνον, ἀλλὰ καὶ ποιοῦσιν ᾄσματα καὶ ὕμνους εἰς τὸν θεὸν διὰ παντοίων μέτρων καὶ μελῶν, ἃ ῥυθμοῖς σεμνοτέροις ἀναγκαίως χαράττουσι (cf. *Contempl.* 80); and Lydus, *Mens.* 2.3: πάντας τοὺς ῥυθμοὺς ἐκ τῆς τῶν πλανήτων κινήσεως εἶναι συμβαίνει. ὁ μὲν γὰρ Κρόνος τῷ Δωρίῳ, ὁ δὲ Ζεὺς τῷ φρυγίῳ, ὁ δ Ἄρης τῷ Λυδίῳ.[48] Moreover, the names with which the characters or the old modes were associated were used by Aristoxenus to describe the τόνοι. (Indeed, the terms ἁρμονία and τόνος were sometimes used interchangeably in the sense of modes.) Hence, it is conceivable that the latter, too, were popularly and indiscriminately referred to as ῥυθμοί.

In any case, the author of Wisdom may have been content with but a vague hint at the transposition scales and the very close analogy they would provide for someone who understood Stoic physics. (Nowhere does he

---

[46] Winnington-Ingram, *Mode*, 3, 21.

[47] It may be pointed out that Arabic music distinguished between melodic modes [*asabi*] and rhythmic modes [*iqa'at*]. This distinction was already made, for example, by Al-Kindi and the Ikhwan as-Safa. See H. G. Farmer, *A History of Arabian Music to the 13th Century* (London: Luzac & Co., 1929), 151; *L'épître sur la musique des Ikhwan Al-Safa*, ed. Amnon Shiloah (Extrait de la *Revue des études Islamiques*, 1967), 176ff. Dr. Shiloah informs me that the Arabic writers refer this distinction to Greek sources.

[48] I owe this reference to Professor Pines.

explicitly refer to the Stoic theory of πνεῦμα, although his language on occasion points to it.) For the average reader, it was sufficient to point to variations in rhythm which yet do not change the melody in order to illustrate the miraculous changes in the functioning of the elements on Israel's behalf. However we translate ῥυθμός, it is hard to resist the feeling that the analogy of the τόνοι was at least in the back of his mind, even if he did not explictly state it.

CHAPTER FIVE

Creation Ex Nihilo Revisited:
A Reply to Jonathan Goldstein*

In his article on "The Origins of Creation Ex Nihilo," Jonathan Goldstein takes issue with my assessment of the doctrine of creation *ex nihilo* in rabbinic literature. It is his view that Rabban Gamaliel II insisted unequivocally on that doctrine in his reply to a "philosopher's" challenge that creation was from pre-existent matter, and that the rabbi's statement was in no way a response to Gnostic views of cosmogony. To explain the origins of the *ex nihilo* formulation, he proposes the hypothesis that Jews and Christians came to insist on it "because of their ever stronger adherence to the belief in bodily resurrection, especially in its most extreme form: viz., that the dead will be resurrected with the same bodies they had in life" (p. 129). The evidence that he has adduced on behalf of this hypothesis, however, not only fails to support it, but indicates very clearly that Christian theologians did not feel the need to invoke the concept of creation *ex nihilo* in order to demonstrate the possibility of the resurrection of the flesh.

Goldstein claims that Tatian (c. 160 CE), "who is the first to state the doctrine of creation *ex nihilo* unambiguously,[1] used it immediately to justify the belief in bodily resurrection" (p. 132). Tatian, however, does no such thing. His argument runs as follows: "For just as, not existing before I was born, I knew not who I was, and only existed in the potentiality of fleshly matter, but being born, after a former state of nothingness, I have obtained through my birth a certainty of my existence, in the same way, having been born, and through death existing no longer, and seen no longer, I shall exist again just as before I was not, but was afterwards born.

---

* "The Origins of the Doctrine of Creation Ex Nihilo," *JJS* 35, 2 (1984): 127-35.

[1] Tatian does not actually employ that formula as such, but his explicit denial that matter is an eternal principle by the side of God would appear to imply that it was created by God *ex nihilo*. It cannot be said, however, that this doctrine is taught by him unambiguously, since his reference to the origin of matter from God as προβεβλημένη could be interpreted to mean that it is an emanation from God. See Alfred Adam, *Lehrbuch der Dogmengeschichte* (2d ed.; Gütersloh: Mohn, 1970), 155. On the other hand, Martin Elze (*Tatian und seine Theologie* [Göttingen: Vandenhoeck & Ruprecht, 1960], 84) and Gerhard May (*Schöpfung aus dem nichts* [Berlin; New York: De Gruyter, 1978], 152) deny this.

Even though fire destroy all traces of my flesh, the world receives the vapourized matter and though dispersed through rivers and seas, or torn in pieces by wild beasts, I am laid up in the storehouses of a wealthy Lord. And, although the poor and the godless know not what is stored up, yet God the Sovereign, when He pleases, will restore the substance that is visible to Him alone to its pristine condition" (*Oratio ad Graecos* 6). The context makes it quite clear that the state of nothingness that is referred to here is one of relative nothingness, i.e., the development of a human body from a drop of semen. Justin had already argued in a similar manner: 'But as in the beginning you would not have believed it possible that from a little sperm such persons could be produced, and yet you actually see that they are, so now realize that it is not impossible that human bodies, after they are dead and disseminated in the earth like seeds, should at the appointed time, at God's command, arise and assume immortality" (1 *Apol.* 19). Tatian's argument, then, is that just as God could form the human body originally from a drop of semen, so can he later restore it, after it has been vapourized by fire or torn to pieces by wild beasts, from the substance that remains and is deposited in the divine storehouses, where it is visible to God alone.[2] In any case, it is clear from Tatian's mode of argumentation

---

[2]   Cf. *b. Sanh.* 90b: "An emperor said to Rabban Gamaliel: 'Ye maintain that the dead will revive; but they turn to dust, and can dust come to life?' Thereupon his [the Emperor's] daughter said to him [the Rabbi]: 'Let me answer him: In our town there are two potters; one fashions [his products] from water, and the other from clay: who is the more praise-worthy?' 'He who fashions them from water,' he replied. 'If he can fashion man from water [viz. the sperm], surely he can do so from clay!' [i.e. the dust into which the dead are turned]" (trans. from *Sanhedrin* [trans. J. Schachter and H. Freedman; Hebrew-English edition of the Babylonian Talmud; Seder Nashim; London: Soncino, 1969]). Similarly, Zarathustra is represented as questioning his God concerning resurrection: "He who has passed away is torn apart by dog and bird and carried off by wolf and vulture; how will their parts come together again?" Ohrmazd's reply is that it is easier to reconstitute a wooden casket from the sundered parts of an old one than to make one out of nothing. Similarly, it is easier for God to gather and reconstitute the sundered parts of the human body from the five storekeepers who receive them (i.e. earth, water, plants, heavenly light, and wind), than to have created the human body when it was not (*The Selections of Zatspram* 34.1.7). For text and translation, see R. C. Zaehner, *Zurvan, A Zoroastrian Dilemma* (repr.; N.Y.: Biblo and Tannen, 1972), 348; also I. Scheftelowitz, *Die altpersische Religion und das Judentum* (Giessen: A. Topelmann, 1920), 204ff. Cf. Porphyry, in Macarius Magnes 4.24 (in *Kritik des Neuen Testaments von einem griechischen Philosophen Kdes 3. Jahrhunderts die im Apocriticus des Macarius Magnes enthaltenen Streitschrift* [ed. A. von Harnack; T.U. 37.4; Leipzig: J. Ch. Hinrichs, 1911], 92 [= fr. 94 in *Porphyrius, "Gegen die Christen," 15 Bucher. Zeugnisse, Fragmente und Referate* ed. A. von Harnack; Abhandlungen der königl. preuss. Adad. d. Wissenschaften, philos. hist. K1; Berlin: Verlag der Konigl. Akademie der Wissenschaften, 1916]); Qur'an 17.52; 22.5; 36.78-82; Saadia Gaon, *The Book of Beliefs and Opinions* (trans. by Samuel Rosenblatt; New Haven: Yale University Press, 1948), 277-78, 411. See Richard Walzer, *Greek Into Arabic* (Oxford: B. Cassirer, 1962), 181-87; Henry

in *Oratio* 5.3 that it was the perception that pre-existent matter could readily be seen as equal in power (ἰσοδύναμος) to God, and thus open the door to Gnostic dualism, that motivated his refusal to entertain the possibility of creation from such a primordial entity, rather than his need to establish the doctrine of resurrection.

Although Theophilus of Antioch (later second century) maintained the doctrine of creation *ex nihilo*, he nevertheless similarly argues for resurrection from God's ability to form a human "out of a small moist matter and a tiny drop, which itself previously did not exist" (*Autol.* 1.8). Tertullian (c. 160 to c. 225), on the other hand, does indeed argue for resurrection from God's ability to create from nothing, but is careful to point out that he does not really require that argument, for even if one maintains that God created the world from primordial matter (*de materia subiacenti*), "since the allegation would be that by the refashioning of the material he produced very different substances and very different species from the material itself, I should no less maintain that he brought them forth out of nothing, seeing he had brought forth things which had been in fact non-existent. For what does it matter whether a thing is brought forth out of nothing or out of something, so long as what was not comes into being, when even not to have been is to have been nothing? ... As it is, although it does matter, yet I win approval in either case. For if out of nothing God has built up all things, he will be able also out of nothing to produce the flesh reduced to nothing: or if out of material he has contrived things other than it, he will be able also out of something other than it to recall the flesh, into whatsoever it may have been drained away. And certainly he who has made is competent to remake, seeing it is a greater thing to make than to remake, to give a beginning than to give it back again. Thus may you believe that the restitution of the flesh is easier than its institution" (*Res.* 11).[3]

On the basis of the evidence examined above, which, as we have shown, actually points in a direction opposite to that posited by Goldstein, the latter concludes that 'wherever a believer in the extreme form of bodily resurrection says that the world was created from the non-existent, whether the word 'non-existent' is singular (τὸ μὴ ὄν) or plural (τὰ μὴ ὄντα), one should assume that the speaker means creation *ex nihilo* unless (as at 2

Chadwick, "Origen, Celsus, and Resurrection," *HTR* 41 (1948): 83-102. G. Gnoli has correctly pointed out that the Iranian parallels need not imply that Ahura Mazda creates *ex nihilo*, since the argument for resurrection would stand even if God only brings things into being from a state of relative non-existence. See G. Gnoli, "Osservazioni sulla dottrina mazdaica della creazione," Istituto Universitario di Napoli, *Annali* 13 (1963): 163-93.

[3] Translation by Ernst Evans, *Tertullian's Treatise on the Resurrection* (London: SPCK, 1960), 31-33.

Macc 7:22-29) the context proves that he did not. Thus Paul at Rom 4:17 probably asserts both creation *ex nihilo* and bodily resurrection" (p. 134). "Though Paul held that the resurrected body would be 'spiritual' not 'physical,' the physical body itself would be transformed into the spiritual" (p. 132). Although Paul's teaching in this matter is not unambiguous, it seems to me that Charles's interpretation is much more likely to be correct than that adopted by Goldstein. It is Paul's view that "man's present body is psychical (ψυχικόν σῶμα) as an organ of the psyche, whereas the risen or spiritual body (πνευματικόν σῶμα) is an organ of the spirit ... Hence between the bodies there is no exact continuity. The existence of the one depends on the death of the other. Nevertheless some essential likeness exists between them. This essential likeness proceeds from the fact that they are successive expressions of the same personality, though in different spheres. It is the same individual vital principle that organizes both."[4] From this perspective, Paul's view on the resurrection can hardly be seen as exemplifying that doctrine "in its extreme form," since it appears very unlikely that he held that "the physical body itself would be transformed into the spiritual."

In the light of the above, Goldstein's interpretation of *Gen. Rab.* 1.9 no longer seems reasonable. It is evident that those who sought to defend the doctrine of resurrection, even in its extreme form, did not require the support of the conception of God's ability to create *ex nihilo*. There is therefore no reason to suppose that the "philosopher's" statement would have provoked such an angry response from R. Gamaliel if all he meant to say was that creation took place from pre-existent matter. It is of no avail to assert that "the verb סיע ('to help') can be used of inanimate instruments," since, as we have already pointed out earlier,[5] in so sensitive an area as this the "philosopher" would hardly have chosen a verb that could easily be construed to mean "actively assisted" (in the act of creation) had he merely intended to derive from the text of Genesis a doctrine of creation out of primordial matter. But even if he was foolish enough to use such an ambiguous expression to no special purpose, there is every reason to believe that what provoked the rabbi's wrath was his taking the verb סיע to mean "actively assisted," for there is no evidence that the rabbis were especially attached to a doctrine of creation *ex nihilo*.[6] Indeed, there is

---

[4] R. H. Charles, *Eschatology* (repr.; N.Y.: Schocken Books, 1963), 452. Cf. the Gnostic *Treat. Res.* in which the author "in a manner remarkably like that of Paul, posits a radical discontinuity of form between the earthly and the resurrection of bodies, but continuity of identification" (*IDBSup*, 741).

[5] Winston, "Wisdom's Theory of Cosmogony," 191, n. 20.

[6] Ibid., 188, n. 10.

prima facie evidence that such a doctrine was far from being commonly accepted by them. Ten examples are given in *Mekilta, Shirata* 8, to describe the uniqueness of God's acts in contrast to those of human beings, but the best example of all, that God can make things out of nothing, is not given. Moreover, example six states that to make a roof a human requires wood, stones, dirt, and water, whereas God has made a roof for his world out of water. God's first act of creation thus presupposes the existence of water.

CHAPTER SIX

Wisdom in the Wisdom of Solomon

The quest for ultimate wisdom is deeply rooted in the human psyche, but views have widely differed as to both its legitimacy and its potential for actual attainment. The author of Job 28 entertains no hopes for the success of such an enterprise, and Qoheleth is sorely aggrieved at the fact that divinity has planted such a futile urge in the human heart (3:11). To plumb the mysteries of the cosmos presupposes an ability to comprehend deity, but as the author of the Babylonian poem *Ludlul Bel Nemeqi* (I will praise the Lord of Wisdom) had already put it, "Where have mortals learnt the way of a god?"[1] The author of the Wisdom of Solomon, however, disdainfully dismissing every trace of pessimism, exasperation, rage, or a placid contentment to remain within narrow bounds, summons his fellow mortals to espouse a bold and confident commitment to follow his lead and explore the uttermost limits of divine Wisdom.

Woman Wisdom: Literary Personification or Divine Hypostasis?

In his description of wisdom, the author invokes a female figure of cosmic beauty and grandeur, and employs a magnificent fivefold metaphor in which she is conceived as an eternal emanation of God's power and glory (7:25-26). She is no figment of his own imagination, having already made her appearance as a cosmic force in Proverbs 8 under the guise of a charming female playing always before Yahweh, after having been created by him at the beginning of his work, and having obvious roots in ancient Near Eastern myth. It appears she can be defined as a hypostasis if one follows the very broad definition of that term offered by W. O. E. Oesterly and G. H. Box: "a quasi-personification of certain attributes proper to God, occupying an intermediate position between personalities and abstract beings."[2] *Hu* and *Sia*, for example, are in Egyptian tradition the creative word and understanding of the high god Re-Atum, personified and separated

---

[1] W. G. Lambert, *Babylonian Wisdom Literature* (Oxford: Clarendon Press, 1960), 41.
[2] W. O. E. Oesterly and G. H. Box, *The Religion and Worship of the Synagogue* (London: Pitman, 1911), 169.

from their originator. Mythologically expressed, they are, as Helmer Ring-gren suggests, "the first begotten children of Re-Amun and his assistants in the creation of the world."[3] Similarly, Egyptian Maat is a personification of the concept *maat*, right order in nature and society (Hebrew יֹשֶׁר, "straight-ness" or "uprightness," is precisely equivalent), who became the daughter of Re and was vouchsafed a cult of her own. According to one text, "Re has created Maat, he rejoices over her, he delights in her, his heart is joyful when he sees her."[4] Examples from the Akkadian sphere are *Mesharu* and *Kettu*, "Righteousness" and "Right," who were conceived sometimes only as qualities of the sun-god or as gifts granted by him, and sometimes in a more concrete way as personal beings, even independent deities.[5]

Although R. B. Y. Scott has argued that, according to Prov 8:22, Yahweh "possessed" (קָנָנִי) wisdom as an attribute or faculty integral to his being from the very first, and "in or with his wisdom founded the earth,"[6] the Hebrew text is much too ambiguous to bear this interpretation with any degree of certainty. It is therefore fair to conclude that it is only in the book of Wisdom and in Philo, where Sophia is conceived of as an eternal divine emanation, that she appears for the first time in Hellenistic Jewish writings as a hypostasis in the sense defined above. Indeed, the most remarkable feature about the author of Wisdom's description of Sophia is that she is depicted as an effluence or emanation of God's glory, a notion that even the more philosophically ambitious Philo was loathe to express explicitly, preferring instead to use locutions that implied it. Although Philo does not apply the term ἀπόρροια, "effluence," to Logos/Sophia, he does employ the verbs ὀμβρέω and πλημμύρω in this connection. In *Somn.* 2.221, paraphrasing Exod 17.6, he has God say, "I stand ever the same immutable, before thou or aught that exists came into being, established on the topmost and most ancient source of power, whence showers forth the birth of all that is, whence streams the tide of wisdom."[7] Wis 7:25 is the earliest attestation of the term ἀπόρροια applied to Logos/Sophia as an emanation from God. It is very likely, however, that the notion of an overflow from God was already used by adherents of the Middle Stoa, perhaps by Posidonius, since Cicero writes: "And if humankind possesses

---

[3] H. Ringgren, *Word and Wisdom* (Lund: H. Ohlssons, 1947), 27.

[4] C. Bauer-Kayatz, *Studien zu Proverbien 1-9* (Neukirchen-Vluyn: Neukirchener Verlag, 1966), 98.

[5] See Ringgren, *Word and Wisdom*, 53-58.

[6] R. B. Y. Scott, *Proverbs and Ecclesiastes* (AB 18; Garden City, N.Y.: Doubleday & Co., 1965), 72.

[7] Cf. Philo, *Post.* 69; *Fug.* 198. At *Spec.* 1.40, the simile employed would seem to imply that the *logos* is an emanation from God.

intelligence, faith, virtue, and concord, whence can these things have flowed down (*defluere*) upon the earth if not from the powers above?" (*Nat. d.* 2.79; cf. *Sen.* 78; *Div.* 1.110; Seneca, *Ep.* 120.14). In any case, here the author finally makes good his promise in 6:22 to tell us how Wisdom came into being. Unlike Ben Sira (1:4; 24:9), who asserts that God has created Wisdom, he says not a word about her creation, but instead describes her in the present tense as a divine effulgence. The answer to πῶς ἐγένετο, how she came into being, thus turns out to be that she is in reality an eternal emanation of which one would have to say more precisely that she is ἀεὶ γιγνομένη καὶ γεγενημένη, ever being produced and in a state of having been produced (Proclus's formula in his *in Tim.* 290.3-25).[8]

In 7:22-24 the author proceeds to describe Wisdom by a series of twenty-one epithets (7 x 3, a triple perfection):

> For in her is a spirit intelligent (πνεῦμα νοερόν) and holy,
> unique of its kind yet manifold, subtle (λεπτόν), agile, lucid, unsullied,
> clear, inviolable, loving goodness, keen,
> unhindered (ἀκώλυτον), beneficent (εὐεργετικόν), humane (φιλάνθρωπον),
> steadfast, unfailing, untouched by care, all-powerful, all-surveying,
> and pervading all spirits, intelligent, pure, and most subtle.
> For wisdom is more mobile than any motion,
> she pervades and permeates all things by reason of her pureness.

There are numerous parallels for such serial lists in the ancient world. In the representation of the initiation into immortality delivered in the so-called Mithras Liturgy, part of the great Paris Magical Codex (presumably

---

[8] Some commentators (such as J. Schulthess, H. Ewald, and H. Bois) would supply ἐμοί before ἐγένετο in Wis 6:22 and translate "How I got her," since the author of Wisdom apparently nowhere tells us how Sophia actually came into being. Moreover, it is sometimes argued (most recently by Offerhaus) that if Wisdom is an eternal logos, we should require the very form γέγονε rather than ἐγένετο. Grimm and Goodrick understand ἐγένετο after the manner of Wisdom's creation according to Prov 8:24; Job 28:26; and Sir 1:24. I agree with Grimm that it is quite arbitrary to supply ἐμοί, since the author would hardly have omitted such an important modification if that were really his intent. On the other hand, it is not difficult to suppose that in introducing his boldly new conception of Wisdom as an eternal divine hypostasis, he would in his introductory remarks promising to expose Wisdom's origins use the usual expression πῶς ἐγένετο, not yet committing himself to this new conception, and then at the right moment launch into an over-powering literary effusion that does not speak explicitly either of Wisdom's creation or of her eternal emanation, but that leaves the reflective reader with the irresistible conclusion that the author wishes him to draw. See C. L. W. Grimm, *Das Buch der Weisheit* (Leipzig: S. Hirzel, 1860), 133-34; A. T. S. Goodrick, *The Book of Wisdom* (London: Rivingtons, 1913), 178-79; U. Offerhaus, *Komposition und Intention der Sapientia Salomonis* (Bonn: Self-published, 1981), 108-12; C. Larcher, *Le Livre de la Sagesse* (Paris: Gabalda, 1984), 2.434-35.

compiled in the early fourth century CE), Aion is similarly invoked with twenty-one epithets that consistently refer to him as god of light and fire.[9] Similarly, in its twenty-one words, the Ahuna Vairya, "the most sacred and probably the most ancient of the Zoroastrian formulas of devotion," contained in germ the whole revelation of the Good Religion and the twenty-one *nasks* of which it was composed.[10]

Wisdom's twenty-one epithets are borrowed largely from Greek philosophy, especially that of the Stoa. Posidonius defined God as "intelligent breath (πνεῦμα νοερόν) pervading the whole of substance" (F100),[11] and Stoics described the soul as a "subtle (λεπτομερές), self-moving body" (*SVF* 2.780). Moreover, according to Chrysippus, "since the universal nature extends to all things, everything that comes about in any way whatever in the whole universe ... will necessarily have come about conformably with that nature and its reason in due and unimpeded (ἀκώλυτος) sequence" (*SVF* 2.937). Chrysippus also referred to the gods as beneficient (εὐεργε-τικοί) and humane (φιλάνθρωποι, lit.: lovers of humanity) (*SVF* 2.1115). What characterizes the Stoic pneuma above all, however, is that it pervades (διήκει) and permeates (χωρεῖ) all things (*SVF* 2.416, 1021, 1033). According to Stoic cosmology, an active principle (the divine Logos) totally pervaded a passive principle (qualityless matter) as the passage of body through body. The pneuma's extension through matter is described as tensional motion (κίνησις τονική), characterized as a form of oscillation in which the pneuma "moves itself from itself and into itself" or backwards and forwards, a simultaneous motion in opposite directions.[12] This scientific theory appealed so strongly both to Philo and to the author of the Wisdom of Solomon that they were willing to take up this stark corporealism and adapt it to their own Platonist way of thinking, an adaptation undoubtedly made possible by their transposition of the materialist Stoic terminology into literary metaphor.

The author's emphasis on Wisdom's pervasiveness throughout the cosmos is balanced by his countervailing insistence that she nonetheless enjoys a symbiotic relationship with God, a condition of unbroken intimacy with the divine (8:3). It may therefore be said that there is an aspect of God's essence in everything (and in the human mind preeminently); yet

---

[9] See H. Lewy, *Chaldean Oracles and Theurgy* (rev. ed.; ed. M. Tardieu; Paris: Études Augustiniennes, 1978), 405.
[10] *Greater Bundahishn* 1.15. The twenty-one *nasks* were divided into three groups of seven each. See R. C. Zaehner, *The Dawn and Twilight of Zoroastrianism* (New York: G. P. Putnam's Sons, 1961), 261; idem, *Zurvan*, 314, 415.
[11] Edelstein and Kidd, *Posidonius*.
[12] See Todd, *Alexander of Aphrodisias*, 34-37.

for all that, this essence remains inseparable from God. The only comparable concept in ancient Jewish thought is Philo's similar notion of an all-penetrating divine Logos that reaches into each individual's mind, thereby converting it into an extension of the divine mind, albeit a very fragmentary one (*Det.* 90; *Gig.* 27; *Leg.* 1.37-38; cf. M. Aurelius, 8:57; *Corpus Hermeticum* 121).

Like Philo, the author of Wisdom evidently teaches that God created the world by means of Wisdom. Although his statement that "God made all things by his 'word' (λόγῳ), and through his 'wisdom' (σοφίᾳ) framed man" (9:1-2) is in itself ambiguous,[13] since it is by no means clear that "word" and "wisdom" here refer to Logos/Sophia, the matter is, I think, settled by his description of Wisdom as "chooser of God's works" (8:4), which clearly implies that Wisdom is identical with the divine mind through which the deity acts. In light of this, the assertion that "with you is Wisdom who knows your works and was present when you created the world" (9:9) undoubtedly signifies that Wisdom contains the paradigmatic patterns of all things (cf. 9:8) and serves as the instrument of their creation.

But if Wisdom is pervasively present in all things, and above all in the operations of human reason, what is the significance of humanity's hot pursuit of her and the need for special supplication to the Lord that he dispatch her from his heavenly throne (9:10)? The issue here is one of perspective. Since Wisdom is both immanent and transcendent, these modes of description are easily interchangeable, depending on the focus of the writer. To explain this double aspect, the platonizing Roman Stoic philosopher Seneca employs a vivid simile, which probably derives from the Middle Stoa, and, incidentally, recurs much later in the writings of Schneur Zalman of Liadi, founder of Habad Hasidism, who cites it from the Cabalistic tract *Pardes Rimmonim* (1548) of Moses Cordovero of Safed. Seneca states:

> Just as the rays of the sun do indeed touch the earth, but still abide at the source from which they are sent (cf. Wis 7:27), even so the great and hallowed soul, which has come down in order that we may have a nearer knowledge of divinity, does indeed associate with us, but still cleaves to its origin; on that source it depends, thither it turns its gaze and strives to go, and it concerns itself with our doings only as a being superior to ourselves (*Ep.* 41.5).[14]

---

13 Wis 8:5-6 is also somewhat ambiguous, and has been variously translated.

14 Cf. Philo, *QG* 2.40; *Det.* 90; M. Aurelius 8.57; Justin, *Dial.* 128.3-4; Tertullian, *Apol.* 21.10-13; Lactantius, *Inst.* 4.29.4-5.

The Neoplatonist Proclus (fifth century CE) later provides a concise expression of this bifocal perspective:

> The gods are present alike to all things; not all things, however, are present alike to the gods, but each order has a share in their presence proportioned to its station and capacity, some things receiving them as unities and others as manifolds, some perpetually and others for a time, some incorporeally and others through the body (*Inst.* 142).[15]

From the human viewpoint, the divine Wisdom enters the human being and departs; from the eternal perspective of God, however, it is ever present to us, though its consummation in any particular case is conditioned by the fitness of the recipient. Hence our author speaks in no uncertain terms of "desire for instruction" (6:17), "training in Wisdom's society" (8:18), and the need for predawn vigilance on her behalf (6:14-15).

Wisdom's Salvific Power

The greatest boon bestowed by Wisdom is the gift of immortality, a gift made possible by the fact that human beings enjoy kinship with her:

> After thinking this over in my mind, and pondering in my heart that there is immortality in kinship with Wisdom, and in her friendship sheer delight, and in the labors of her hands unfailing wealth, and in training in her society understanding, and great renown in the sharing of her words, I went about in search of how I might make her my own (Wis 8:17-18).

The theme of human kinship with God occurs in Plato and is a characteristic teaching of the Stoa. Plato writes: "We declare that God has given to each of us, as his daemon, the kind of soul that is housed in the top of our body and that raises us — seeing that we are not an earthly but a heavenly plant — up from earth towards our kindred in the heaven" (*Tim.* 90A). In the Pseudo-Platonic *Alcibiades I*, Socrates says that the part of the soul that is the seat of knowledge and thought resembles God, and those who look at this will gain thereby the best knowledge of themselves (133B-C).[16] Philo takes up the theme with equal vigor: "It is the human [being's] lot to occupy the place of the highest excellence among living creatures because his stock is near akin to God, sprung from the same source in

---

[15] Translation from Proclus, *The Elements of Theology* (2d ed.; trans. E. R. Dodds; Oxford: Clarendon, 1963).

[16] Cf. *Phaed.* 79D; *Resp.* 490B; 611E; *Leg.* 899D; Posidonius, F 187 (Edelstein and Kidd, *Posidonius*).

virtue of his participation in reason, which gives him immortality, mortal though he seems to be" (*Spec.* 4.14).[17]

In a fine ode to Wisdom's saving power in history (10:1-21), the author assimilates the old covenantal salvation-history with its miraculous and sudden divine irruptions to the immanent divine ordering of human events as mediated by the continuous activity of Wisdom. It is her generation-by-generation election of holy servants (7:27) that structures the life of Israel. Her saving and punishing power is illustrated by the enumeration of seven righteous heroes and their wicked counterparts: Adam and Cain; Noah and the Flood generation; Abraham and the confounded nations; Lot and the Sodomites; Jacob and Esau; Joseph and his critics; Israel led by Moses and the Egyptians led by pharaoh. The ode is marked by the use of anaphora, repetition of the same word at the beginning of successive verses. Wisdom is thus introduced throughout the chapter with the emphatic pronoun "she" (αὕτη), which marks off six sections each of which contains the word "righteous" once. E. Norden pointed out that this is one form of the encomia of the gods in Greek literature.[18] A particularly good illustration of this kind of encomium is Cicero's well-known hymn to Philosophy:

> O Philosophy, thou guide of life, O thou explorer of virtue and expeller of vice! Without thee what could have become not only of me but of the life of man altogether? Thou hast given birth to cities, thou hast called scattered human beings into the bond of social life, thou hast united them first of all in joint habitations, next in wedlock, then in the ties of common literature and speech, thou hast discovered law, thou has been the teacher of morality and order: to thee I fly for refuge, from thee I look for aid, to thee I entrust myself, as once in ample measure, so now wholly and entirely (*Tusc.* 5.5 [King, LCL]).

Wisdom's Efficacy

In light of the tradition of speculation on Wisdom, with its strong individualistic, humanistic, and universalistic orientation, and above all its linkage of divine revelation with the natural order rather than with Sinai, it is easy to understand why our author chose the figure of Wisdom as the ideal mediator of his message to his contemporaries. She was the perfect

---

[17] Cf. *Opif.* 145-46; *QG* 2.60; *Decal.* 41.

[18] See E. Norden, *Agnostos Theos* (5th ed.; Darmstadt: Wissenschaftliche Buchgesellschaft, 1971), 163-65, 223-24. Cf. Acts 7:35-38; Heb 11; CD 2.17-3.12; Lucretius, 1.1-9; Seneca, *Marc.* 20.2; Philo, *Praem.* 11; *Mut.* 149-50; and the Hellenistic aretalogies or hymns of praise discovered in Egypt.

bridge between the exclusive nationalist tradition of Israel and the universalistic philosophical tradition that appealed so strongly to the Jewish youth
of Roman Alexandria. Moreover, for his own use in describing Sophia, the
author very skillfully adapted the Isis aretalogies, a literature that held
great appeal for him in view of his profound empathy with the passionate
religious intensity and mystical intimacy that characterized the Isis
mysteries. The cult of Isis and Sarapis was one of the most popular
Oriental religions in the Roman world from the fourth century BCE to the
fourth century CE, though its peak of popularity was reached in the second
century CE. It should also be noted that the emperor Gaius, who had deco-
rated a room, the *aula Isiaca*, in his palace on the Palatine with paintings
depicting numerous Egyptian religious symbols, had also built a special
temple to Isis and had instituted Isiac mysteries in which he is said to have
participated himself while dressed in female garb (Josephus, *A.J.* 19.30). In
the eyes of our author it was only fitting that he reclaim what in his view
were falsely appropriated ἀρεταί for "her" to whom they truly belonged.

As the divine mind immanent within the universe and guiding and
controlling all its dynamic operations, Wisdom represents the entire range
of the natural sciences: cosmology, physics, astronomy, biology, botany, in
addition to all esoteric knowledge (7:17-21). She is also the teacher of all
human arts and crafts, including shipbuilding and the art of navigation
(7:16; 14:2). She is skilled in ontology ("the unerring knowledge of
existent being"[7:17]) and in the intricacies of logic and rhetoric. Having
unsurpassed experience of both past and present, she also infers the future
and possesses the key to all the divinatory arts (8:8). Moreover, she is the
source of all moral knowledge (8:7), is each individual's counselor and
comforter, bringing rest, cheer, and joy, and bestowing riches and glory on
her own, though her greatest gift is that of immortality (8:9-13). Above all,
as we have already seen, she is synonymous with divine providence,
controlling historical events and in each generation guiding the friends of
God and inspiring his prophets (7:27; 14:3). It is significant that the
author, unlike Ben Sira, nowhere explicitly identifies Wisdom with Torah,
and with the exception of a brief historical reference in 18:9 makes
virtually no mention of the sacrificial cult. His statement that "love for
Wisdom means the keeping of her laws" (6:18) is ambiguous and probably
refers to the statutes of natural law. All we have from him in this regard is
but a passing allusion to Israel's mission of bringing the imperishable light
of the law to the world (18:4).[19] Very likely he believed with Philo that the

---

[19] Cf. *LAB* 11.1-2; 51.3; *T. Levi* 14:4; *Ps.-Orph.* 3; *2 Bar.* 48:40; *4 Ezra* 7:20-24; Philo, *QE*
2.41; *Mos.* 2.36, 44; *Abr.* 98.

teachings of the Torah were tokens of divine Wisdom, and that they were in harmony with the law of the universe and as such implant all the virtues in the human psyche,[20] but when he focuses his attention on Wisdom, it is philosophy, science, and the arts that are uppermost in his mind. He conceives of Wisdom as a direct bearer of revelation, functioning through the workings of the human mind, and supreme arbiter of all values. She is clearly the archetypal Torah, of which the Mosaic law is but an image. When he insists that unless God sends his Wisdom down from on high humanity would not comprehend God's will (9:17), he is certainly implying that the Torah is in need of further interpretation for the disclosure of its true meaning, interpretation that Wisdom alone is able to provide. The author here closely approximates the position of Philo of Alexandria, in whose view, even before the Sinaitic revelation, the Patriarchs were already constituted νόμοι ἔμψυχοι, living embodiments of divine Wisdom. Similarly, in Wisdom 10, Sophia had already served as a personal guide to six righteous heroes who lived before the Sinaitic revelation. An echo of this notion is later found in the statement of R. Avin (fourth century) that the Torah is an incomplete form (נובלת, lit.: the fruit falling prematurely off the tree) or image of the supernal Wisdom (*Gen. Rab.* 17.5; 44.12).[21].

Wisdom and Love of Humanity

Although the substantive φιλανθρωπία never occurs in the book of Wisdom, the adjective φιλάνθρωπος, humane or benevolent, appears thrice. Wisdom is described twice as φιλάνθρωπος (1:6; 7:23), and in 12:19 we are told that God's mercy is a model-lesson for the Israelites, teaching them that the righteous person must be humane. God loves all that exists, loathing nothing that he has created (11:24), and as the lover of all that lives, he spares all, for his imperishable spirit is in all things (11:26; 12:1). We have here a faint intimation of the Middle Stoic doctrine of φιλανθρωπία, which is fully elaborated in the writings of Philo. The special kinship between God and humankind, based on the notion of a divine logos at once immanent and transcendent, led inevitably to the concept of the unity of humanity. The Stoics spoke of the common community of gods and human beings, since they alone make use of reason and live

---

[20] Cf. Josephus, *A.J.* 1. Proem 4:24; *Let. Aris.* 161; 4 Macc 1:16-17; 5:25; Philo, *Opif.* 3; *Mos.* 2.52.
[21] *Midrash Bereshit rabba: Critical Edition with Notes and Commentary* (ed. J. Theodor and Ch. Albeck; 3 vols.; Jerusalem: Wahrman Books, 1965), 1.157, 237.

according to right and law (Cicero, *Nat. d.* 2.154; *SVF* 2.527-28). The early
Stoics, however, still emphasized the dichotomy between the wise and the
foolish, and Zeno insisted that only the wise are capable of concord and
unity (Diogenes Laertius 7.32.3). The Cynics had gone so far as to say that
the nonwise are not human beings (Diogenes Laertius 6.41, 60). It was
only in the Middle Stoa, in the writings of Panaetius and in those of the
stoicizing Antiochus of Ascalon (who professed to be both an Old
Academic and a Stoic), that an all-embracing doctrine of human unity
took shape.[22] Panaetius focused his attention on the ordinary human being
and thus produced an ethical ideal suited to the capacity of all (Seneca, *Ep.*
116.5; Cicero, *Off.* 1.46, 99). Going beyond the negative formulation of
justice that forbids injury to another, he advances the positive definition of
it as an active beneficence that forms the bond of society (Cicero, *Off.* 1.20-
22). The fundamental principles on which this is based are elucidated as
follows:

> We must go more deeply into the basic principles of fellowship and
> association set up by nature among men. The first is to be found in
> the association that links together the entire human race, and the
> bond that creates this is reason and speech, which by teaching and
> learning, by communication, discussion, and decision brings men into
> agreement with each other and joins them in a kind of natural
> fellowship (Cicero, *Off.* 1.50, trans. Baldry).[23]

Following Panaetius, Philo too emphasizes the positive aspect of justice as
an active beneficence (*Virt.* 166-70). This quality is epitomized by him in
the word φιλανθρωπία, a term that apparently came into philosophical
prominence in the writings of Panaetius and Antiochus, and later in those
of Musonius Rufus, and with special emphasis in those of Plutarch. In a
section of his treatise *On the Virtues* devoted to φιλανθρωπία (51-174), Philo
points out that it has εὐσέβεια, "piety," as its sister and twin, for the love of
God involves the love of human beings, inasmuch as the human being,
"the best of living creatures, through that higher part of his being, the
soul, is most nearly akin to heaven ... and also to the Father of the world,
possessing in his mind a closer likeness and copy than anything else on
earth of the eternal and blessed Archetype" (*Decal.* 134). Moreover, in
practicing φιλανθρωπία, the human being is imitating God (*Spec.* 1.294;
4.73). Here we touch upon the formula that constitutes for Philo the best

---

[22] See H. C. Baldry, *The Unity of Mankind in Greek Thought* (Cambridge: Cambridge
University Press, 1965), 177-203.
[23] Cf. Philo, *QG* 2.60; *Decal.* 41, 132-34.

way to describe the τέλος of human life, ὁμοίωσις θεῷ, "imitation of God," and in adopting this Platonic goal, his teaching here fully converged with that of the Jewish tradition.[24]

The Divine-Human Equation in Wisdom and Qumran

The splitting of humanity into two opposing camps constitutes a central teaching in both the Wisdom of Solomon and the Dead Sea Scrolls. An analysis of this theme as it appears in these texts will illuminate the divergent ways in which they describe through subtle shifts of emphasis the nature of the relative autonomy allowed to "dwellers in clay whose origin is dust" (Job 4:19). We read in 1QHᵃ XV, 12-21:

> I know through the understanding which comes from Thee
> that righteousness is not in a hand of flesh,
> that man is not master of his way
> and that it is not in mortals to direct their step.
> I know that the inclination of every spirit is in Thy hand;
> Thou didst establish all its ways before creating it,
> and how can any man change Thy words?
> Thou alone didst create the just
> and establish him from the womb
> for the time of goodwill ...
> But the wicked Thou didst create
> for the time of Thy wrath,
> Thou didst vow them from the womb
> to the Day of Massacre,
> for they walk in the way that is not good.[25]

Similarly, in the book of Wisdom the idea of being worthy either of Death or of Wisdom occurs more than once. In 1:16 we are told that "godless men have summoned Death through word and deed; thinking him a friend they pined for him, and made a pact with him, for they are worthy to be members of his party" (cf. 1QM XIII, 12; XV, 9-10; XVII, 4, where, as Amir has correctly noted, it is stated that the wicked are attached to Belial because "their desire is for him"). We are further told that "it was through the devil's envy that Death entered into the cosmic order, and they who are his own experience him" (2:24). Wisdom, on the other hand, goes

---

[24] For a fuller discussion, see Winston, *Wisdom of Solomon*, 43-46. For Philo's doctrine of εὐσέβεια, see now Gregory E. Sterling, "The Queen of the Virtues: Εὐσέβεια in Philo of Alexandria," (forthcoming).

[25] Trans. from G. Vermes, *The Dead Sea Scrolls in English* (3d ed.; Sheffield: JSOT Press, 1987).

about seeking those who are worthy of her (6:16), and grace and mercy, we are informed, belong to God's chosen (3:9).[26]

As for the question of the origin of this fateful division of humanity, however, the position of Qumran is seen by some to differ radically from that of the book of Wisdom. The scrolls explicitly state that it was God who "has appointed for man two spirits in which to walk until the time of his visitation; the spirits of truth and falsehood" (1QS III, 18, 25). The Wisdom of Solomon, however, according to Yehoshua Amir, locates the source of the split in the free choice of the wicked:

> Do not court death through a deviant way of life
> nor draw down destruction by your own actions.
> For God did not make death,
> nor does he take delight in the destruction of the living;
> he created all things that they might endure.
> All that has come into existence preserves its being,
> and there is no deadly poison in it.
> Death's rulership is not on earth, for justice is immortal.
> (Wis 1:12-15)

But if God did not create Death, where did he come from? He was invited by his confederates (1:16), and it was through the devil's envy that Death came about (2:24). Amir says that the devil, who is mentioned in this verse of Wisdom alone, must be identical with Death, who at the moment of creation stands outside like an exiled monarch who is envious of this happy world being established before his very eyes, but in which he has no share. He cannot by brute force work his way into it, for God has firmly barred his entry; and if no one from within opens up a secret pathway for him, he will forever have to remain on the outside. In fact, however, it turns out that he has his own fifth column within, who through their words and deeds ensure his eventual infiltration. Why such a fifth column exists in the first place is a question that remains outside the author's purview.

Amir thus places the onus for the coming of Death squarely on the shoulders of humanity, who have circumvented God's original intent to exclude that sinister figure from his blissful world. The human creature is no empty tool impotently subordinate to heavenly forces. The world is indeed split into the camps of the righteous and the wicked; the latter belong to the portion of Death, but only those who are worthy of Death are given over to him. This explains the emphasis in the book of Wisdom that God loves all his creatures, for if he had hated anything he would

---

[26] The theme of the predestinarian splitting of humankind into two rival camps of the just and the wicked is also found in rabbinic literature. See *Mek. Pisha* 16; *Gen. Rab.* 3.8, Theodor-Albeck, 23. See Winston, *Wisdom of Solomon*, 56, 113-14, 121-23.

never have fashioned it (11:24); this contrasts with the Dead Sea Scrolls, where it is said that the wicked are hated by the Lord (1QS III, 26). But what of the author's assertion that the Canaanites' "seed was evil and their viciousness innate, and that their mode of thought would in no way vary to the end of time" (XII, 10-11)? The Canaanites are a special case, claims Amir, since the author is clearly referring to their condition of being accursed from the very first as specified in Gen 9:25. As for the Egyptians at the sea, where we are told that a "condign fate drew them on to this denouement and made them forget what had happened, so that they might fill in the one penalty still lacking to their torments, and that your people might accomplish an incredible journey, while their enemies might bring upon themselves a bizarre death" (Wis 19:4-5), here again, says Amir, we have a special case, since scripture specifies that God "had hardened Pharaoh's heart in order to display his signs among them" (Exod 10:1). Indeed the author of the Wisdom of Solomon may have anticipated the interpretation known to us from later times from R. Simeon b. Lakish's comment on Exod 10:1 that "when God warns a man once, twice, and even a third time, and he still does not repent, then does God close his heart against repentance so that he shall exact vengeance from him for his sins" (*Exod. Rab.* 13:3). It is apparently to this that Wisdom refers when it speaks of a "condign fate" (ἀξία ἀνάγκη), that is, a fate that they deserved. We must therefore fully appreciate the book of Wisdom's bold independence in defending humanity's autonomous freedom in spite of the dualistic view common to both it and the scrolls.[27]

The seductive appeal of Amir's interpretation is great, yet in spite of its neatness it seems to me to be considerably forced and to read into the text of Wisdom later concepts of which the author was probably completely unaware. Thus the term "worthy" in the literature of the ancient world often simply refers to those whom God in his infinite wisdom has chosen in advance for their respective roles of righteousness or wickedness. So Philo, for example, can write of Melchizedek: "God has not prefigured any deed of his, but produces him to begin with as such a king, peaceable and worthy of his own priesthood" (*Leg.* 3.79). It is easy to find inconsistencies in these ancient writings where none exists. Helmer Ringgren, for example, sees an inconsistency in 1QHᵃ XV, 13-20 (cited above) inasmuch as this passage gives the impression "that the righteous have indeed been predetermined to a life according to God's will, whereas punishment

---

27   See Y. Amir, "The Wisdom of Solomon and the Literature of Qumran," *Procedings of the 6th World Congress of Jewish Studies* 3 (Jerusalem, 1977): 329-35 (Hebrew); idem, "The Figure of Death in the Book of Wisdom," *JJS* 30 (1979): 254-78.

befalls the wicked because they themselves have done what is evil."[28] The
clause "for they walk in a way that is not good," however, is only meant to
indicate that the punishment they face is appropriate to their wickedness.
The question of why they were chosen for this role in the first place is not
here being addressed, and when it is addressed elsewhere, the only answer
given is that it is in order to demonstrate God's illimitable might and glory.
From the point of view of modern style, there is undoubtedly an unclarity
of expression in the passage referred to, but we must not impose modern
standards on ancient writings, especially one written in the hymnic style. A
similar inconsistency might be seen to exist between Wis 1:4, which implies
that the recipients of Wisdom must already be righteous, and 7:27, which
suggests that it is Wisdom that makes them righteous; John J. Collins,
however, is undoubtedly correct when he suggests that the presence of
Wisdom is simply an identifying mark of the righteous.[29] Once again these
verses do not address the question of why the righteous and the wicked
were chosen for their respective roles, but only indicate that the active
presence of Wisdom in any individual is a guarantee of friendship with
God and is incompatible with fraudulence and wickedness.[30] It should be
clear, then, that for the author of the Wisdom of Solomon, the Canaanites
and the Egyptians are not special cases cited in deference to scripture.
When, for example, he wishes to idealize certain biblical incidents because
their straightforward presentation would mar the effect of his encomiastic
account of the Israelites, he has no scruples in doing so;[31] and when in
12:19-22 he seeks to derive from God's mercy toward the Egyptians and the
Canaanites a model-lesson for Israel, he nonchalantly omits any reference
to the Lord's hardening of Pharaoh's heart, which had robbed him in that
instance even of his relative freedom of choice.[32]

There is, nevertheless, in Qumran a somewhat different approach to the
human condition relative to that of the book of Wisdom. As I have indicated elsewhere,[33] the sectarians of Qumran, like the Stoic philosophers,
accepted the all-regulating hand of an omnipotent providence and tended
to view all things from the divine perspective, thus virtually collapsing the

---

[28] H. Ringgren, *The Faith of Qumran* (Philadelphia: Fortress Press, 1963), 73-4.

[29] J. J. Collins, *Between Athens and Jerusalem* (New York: Crossroad, 1983), 183.

[30] Cf. Philo, *Deus* 3: "For while the soul is illumined by the bright and pure rays of
wisdom, through which the sage sees God and his potencies, none of the messengers of
falsehood has access to the reason, but all are barred from passing the bounds which the
lustral water has consecrated" (Colson, LCL).

[31] See Winston, *Wisdom of Solomon*, on Wis 11:4 and 16:3.

[32] Ibid., 46-58, 243-44.

[33] See ibid., 57.

human pole. Neither wished thereby to deny relative human freedom, but their sharp focus on the divine rather than the human pole made a harsh impression on their contemporaries. The Qumranites were prone to see human spiritual capacities as the sheer gift of divine grace. Thus, even when emphasizing a voluntary human decision, they coupled it with the notion of its complete assimilation to the will of God. The author of Wisdom, in contrast, who wished to give due emphasis to the human part of the divine-human equation, insisted on our active participation in the divine plan and the relative freedom that characterizes our ethical action. He therefore prominently displayed the human role, limited though it be, and our personal responsibility, relative as it is, in introducing Death into the cosmic order.[34] For both him and the Dead Sea Scrolls, however, the ultimate mystery in which the divine scheme for humanity is shrouded remains impervious to any open challenge. What peculiarly distinguishes the position of Qumran is that according to it, the active human partnership with God involves above all the privileged position of a creature fully self-conscious and aware of the role in which it has been cast by the supreme and mysterious divine fiat. D. Dimant put it well when she wrote that in Qumran

> the emphasis has shifted from freedom of action to the mystery of knowledge. The freedom given to man is not to choose where to go but to discover where he is. This can be done only with the aid of divinely-inspired knowledge of the true meaning of the world, of man and of history. This is why the starting point is ignorance, while the final election is marked by a gift of knowledge.[35]

There appears to be an open break, however, between Qumran and the book of Wisdom with regard to the divine attitude toward the righteous and the wicked: according to Qumran, God loves the former while hating the latter; according to the Wisdom of Solomon, God loves all equally. This divergence is nonetheless more apparent than real, for it must be noted that while God has placed eternal hatred between the sons of

---

[34] As for Wisdom's extraordinarily blunt statement that God did not make Death, we may surmise that it undoubtedly signifies (as do Philo's analogous statements that God has no direct contact with the disordered primordial matter, and that we may not ascribe evil human acts to him; *Spec.* 1.329; *Opif.* 72-75) that we may not impute to him any interest in Death as a part of his primary intentionality. Evil is an indirect consequence of God's creative activity and must therefore not be ascribed directly to him, even though he alone is its ultimate source. See Winston, *Logos and Mystical Theology in Philo of Alexandria*, 50.

[35] D. Dimant, "Qumran Sectarian Literature," *Jewish Writings of the Second Temple Period* (ed. M. E. Stone; Assen: Van Gorcum, 1984), 538.

righteousness and the sons of deceit, and while he is said to love the former, when it comes to the latter, it is only asserted that their "counsel" (סוד) he loathes, and all [their] ways he hates forever."[36] We may conclude, then, by saying that although the scrolls do not hypostatize Wisdom, they do, like the author of the book of Wisdom, conceive of it as both immanent and transcendent, thus following a line of thought that induces a sense of mystical intimacy with the divine. Unlike the Wisdom of Solomon, however, which emphasizes the relative autonomy of the human intellect, the scrolls tend to assimilate it fully to the divine mind.

---

[36] Note how carefully he avoids saying, as one would have expected, "the one he loves, the other he loathes." Moreover, even if we were to translate סוד as "assembly," all the text would be saying is that God hates the coming together of the wicked to plan evil.

CHAPTER SEVEN

The Sage as Mystic in the Wisdom of Solomon

The author of the Wisdom of Solomon displays a single-minded intensity in his portrayal of the ideal sage and his concentrated pursuit after wisdom. A mildly ascetic Platonic strain pervades his delineation of the proper life-path that ought to be followed, and although he ultimately allows the enjoyment of external goods, they are at best only tolerated as secondary accessions upon a course of action that demands a narrowly exclusive loyalty of its devotees. The vigorous appreciation for life's amenities that characterizes Ben Sira's writing, which does not exclude even a potential hazard such as feminine beauty (Sir 36:22), is here nowhere in sight.[1] The author's Platonism is austere and lacks the subtle playfulness that pervades the dialogues of the founder of the philosophical school that left so great an imprint on him. There is hardly a trace of humor in his admonitory exhortations, nor any echo of Ben Sira's approval of the enjoyment of good food and wine to the accompaniment of tuneful melodies in congenial company.[2] Missing completely is anything like Sirach's bantering advice to the president-elect of a banquet to ensure the enjoyment of his guests by cutting his speeches short and never interrupting the music (30:21-25, 31:27-31, 32:1-6). Yet, as I shall soon show, the portrait of the ideal sage that emerges from the Wisdom of Solomon has considerable affinity with that found in the Wisdom of Ben Sira.

The Sage's Attributes

From the author's autobiographical sketches of his encounter with Dame Wisdom a composite portrait of his ideal sage can easily be drawn. Fully trusting in the Lord, wise individuals will not seek to test him, nor will they

---

[1] The author of Wisdom of Solomon, or Book of Wisdom, can even say that "it is better to be childless, provided one is virtuous" (4:1), since for him, as for Plato (*Symp.* 208E), it is the life of the soul that is paramount, and if the latter is productive, childlessness is of little moment (cf. 3:13-14).

[2] See A. A. Wieder, "Ben Sira and the Praise of Wine," *JQR* 61 (1970-71): 155-66.

murmur in their hearts, since the latter cancels out whatever good gift or deed accompanies it (Wis 1:2, 10-11; cf. Deut 6:16, Ps 78:18). Filled with a longing for Wisdom (Wis 8:2), they will prefer her to riches and kingship, although she will eventually grant these gifts too (Wis 7:8-12).[3] Wisdom bestows on sages the four cardinal virtues of self-control, intelligence, justice, and courage (Wis 8:7), a classification that goes back to Plato[4] and was taken up by Zeno, founder of the Stoic school, who expressed three of them in terms of the fourth, wisdom.[5] She also confers on them a knowledge of the past and the future, of the rules of logic and the resolution of riddles, and ultimately of all natural phenomena (Wis 7:17-22). The latter is lovingly spelled out in elaborate detail as

> [The] unerring knowledge of existent being,
> ...the structure of the universe and the operation of the elements;
> the beginning, and end, and middle of times,
> the changes of the solstices and the vicissitudes of the seasons;
> the cycles of years and the positions of the stars;
> the natures of living creatures and the tempers of beasts;
> the violent force of spirits and the reasonings of men;
> the species of plants, and the virtues of roots (Wis 7:17-20).[6]

The sage will thus enjoy repute among the masses and honor among the elders, in spite of youth (Wis 8:10). Admired and honored by rulers who will seek the sage's advice, the sage will, in fact, join their ranks as governor of peoples and nations (Wis 8:11-12, 14; 6:20; 10:14). The sage will secure wealth and great renown, will be courageous in war, and will exercise the mastery of elocutionary skill (Wis 8:5, 12, 15, 18). Realizing that wisdom is an inexhaustible treasure for humanity, the sage will freely and

---

[3] There is an echo here of the well-known philosophical debate between the Peripatetics and the Stoics as to the relative importance of external goods for the happy life, such as health, beauty, honor, and wealth. The Stoics had stressed the notion that virtue is self-sufficient for happiness and the only good properly speaking (*SVF* 1.187; 3.29-45, 49-67). The Peripatetic view of the triple good (i.e., external, bodily, psychic; see Aristotle, *Eth. nic.* 1098b; *Rhet.* 1360b; Cicero, *Fin.* 5.84) was explicitly attacked by Philo, who found it symbolized in scripture by Joseph's coat of many colors (*Det.* 6-9). It may be noted that "P[apyrus] Insinger's emphasis is on the need to obtain a minimum for a livelihood, to make it last by living frugally, and not to hanker after wealth"; so M. Lichtheim, *Late Egyptian Wisdom*, 153. For a fuller discussion, see Winston, *Wisdom of Solomon*, 31-32.

[4] *Phaed.* 69C; *Resp.* 427E; *Leg.* 631C.

[5] *SVF* 3.255-61.

[6] Cf. Aeschylus, *Prom.* 436-506, and the striking parallel in Pseudo-Plato, *Ax.* 70B (J. P. Hershbell, *Pseudo-Plato, Axiochus* [Chico: Scholars Press, 1981], 45), where it is argued that it is only through a divine breath in an individual's soul that such knowledge can be attained, and in the light of which immortality is assured.

unstintingly share it with others (Wis 6:23, 7:13).[7] The sage is the stability of the people, and in the ensemble such individuals constitute the salvation of the world (Wis 6:24; cf. 9:18).[8] Finally, becoming a friend and prophet of God and learning the divine pleasure, the sage will have rest, cheer, and joy, and above all the supreme gift of immortality (Wis 7:14, 8:16).[9] In short, occupying the highest rungs of society, the sage will be a leader both at home and abroad, exercising compassion and humanity (Wis 12:19; cf. 1:6, 7:23), and administering the world in holiness and righteousness (Wis 9:3).

A brief comparison with several Jewish writings that exhibit an emphasis on wisdom similar to that in this book will help illuminate the latter's distinctive character. Aside from the books of Proverbs, Job, and Ben Sira, which have clearly influenced this author's portrayal of Wisdom as a female cosmic figure, another important source of inspiration for him was the strong emphasis on wisdom in *1 Enoch*, although that book's insistence on wisdom's supernatural character has been adapted by him to a Platonist philosophical perspective. In the so-called "Apocalypse of Weeks" (chaps. 91-93), Enoch is described as "a skilled scribe and wisest of men" (92:1), and at the close of the seventh "week," we are told that the elect "shall be given sevenfold wisdom and knowledge" (93:10; cf. 91:10, 5:8, 104:12). As to Enoch's eschatological knowledge, it is emphatically stated that it was shown to him in a heavenly vision, that it was an angelic message, and that he had read it from the tablets of heaven (93:2; cf. 103:2-4, 106:19). The "Book of the Watchers" contains a comprehensive picture of the cosmos (chap. 18), but here Enoch's knowledge is based on two cosmic voyages, the second of which culminates in a voyage around the world (chaps. 33-36). In the "Astronomical Book" (chaps. 72-82), it is the angel Uriel who is his source of knowledge. The esoteric nature of Enoch's knowledge is further underlined by his claim that his experience was unique: "And I, Enoch, alone saw the sight, the ends of everything; and no man has seen

---

[7] Cf. Philo, *Prob.* 13-14; Pseudo-Aristotle, *Mund.* 391a17; and Xenophon, *Symp.* 4.43. In the Pseudo-Platonic *Epin.*, a protreptic to the purer and happier life, the author similarly states: "For I have sought this wisdom high and low (ἄνω καὶ κάτω), and so far as it has been revealed to me I will try to render it plain to you" (989A).

[8] For the ideal of εὐστάθεια, or inner calm and stability, see Winston, *Wisdom of Solomon*, 160.

[9] According to the Isis Aretalogy (P.Oxy. XI. 1380), Isis was especially the goddess of immortality, which she conferred upon her husband and brother Osiris and her son Horus. The author of Wisdom skillfully adapted the Isis aretalogies for his description of Sophia; see my *Wisdom of Solomon*, 37. In addition to the literature cited there, see J. S. Kloppenborg, "Isis and Sophia in the Book of Wisdom," *HTR* 75 (1982): 57-84. For Philo's doctrine of immortality see *Fug.* 97; *Abr.* 27; *Post.* 23.

what I have seen" (19:3; cf. 60:10ff.). In any case, the encyclopedic range of
Enoch's knowledge is reminiscent of the similar scope of the sage's
knowledge in the Wisdom of Solomon (7:17-22), though the scientific
character of the latter is sharply opposed to the mythical and fantastic
nature of the former.[10]

Although there is a similar emphasis on knowledge and insight in the
Dead Sea Scrolls, with the phrase "I know" and a large number of knowledge synonyms occurring in them very frequently, God's creative wisdom
(cf. 1QH^a I, 14, 20) is never there personified or hypostatized.[11] Moreover,
in spite of the fact that the scrolls indicate humans come close to God in
relation to wisdom and insight, the Book of Wisdom knows nothing of an
esoteric reading of scripture divinely related to the elect, as in the Qumran
Pesharim. The esoteric character of the mystical knowledge vouchsafed to
the Qumranites is clearly articulated in the following lines from the *Rule of
the Community*: "My eyes have gazed on that which is eternal, on wisdom
concealed from men, on knowledge and wise design (hidden) from the
sons of men" (1QS 5-6).[12] It is a revelation of the supernal realms and their
divine mysteries, and of God's ultimate plan for human salvation, for
which the Qumran psalmist is effusive in expressing thanks.

A much closer connection exists between the Wisdom of Solomon and
Philo of Alexandria, whose conception of the sage and his relationship to
Wisdom is very similar indeed. Both describe *Sophia* (Wisdom) as an
effulgence of God's glory and his agent in creation, whose brightness is
more radiant than the sun.[13] Both employ erotic imagery in connection
with her pursuit, calling her bride or spouse, and speaking of living with
her (συμβιόω) and enjoying kinship (συγγένεια) with her (Wis 8:2-3, 16-17;
Philo, *Congr.* 74; *Contempl.* 68; and *Spec.* 4:14). Wisdom anticipates those
who desire her, and those who seek her will not weary.[14] Without her,
humanity is nothing, and all their words and thoughts are in God's

---

[10] See J. C. VanderKam, *Enoch and the Growth of an Apocalyptic Tradition* (CBQMS 16;
Washington DC: Catholic Biblical Association, 1984), 135-40, 148-51; and I. Gruenwald,
Apocalyptic and Merkavah Mysticism (AGJU 14; Leiden: Brill, 1980), 3-25. For other similari-
ties between *1 Enoch* and Wisdom of Solomon, see Larcher, *Livre de la Sagesse*, 103-12.

[11] See M. Küchler, *Frühjüdische Weisheitstraditionen* (OBO 26; Freiburg, Switzerland:
Universitätsverlag/Göttingen: Vandenhoeck & Ruprecht, 1979), 88-113, esp. 94; and W.
L. Lipscomb and J. A. Sanders, "Wisdom at Qumran," in *Israelite Wisdom* (ed. J. Gammie et
al.; Missoula, Mont.; Scholars Press, 1978), 227-85.

[12] G. Vermes, *The Dead Sea Scrolls in English* (2nd ed.; Harmondsworth: Penguin, 1975),
92.

[13] Wis 7:25-26, 8:4, 9:1-2, 6:12, 7:29; Philo, *Opif.* 30; *Migr.* 40.

[14] Wis 6:13-14; Philo, *Congr.* 122-23; *Deus* 160.

hands.[15] Humans must make their souls a proper abode for her, but the godless, inviting death, conclude a pact with the latter.[16] The doctrine of immortality plays a central role in both. The wise live forever, whereas the godless are spiritually dead even while physically alive.[17] Wisdom must be sought for her own sake, though external goods will follow in due course.[18] Finally, without natural endowments the mind cannot be brought to its fullness, but training with *Sophia* is nonetheless indispensable.[19]

I have already referred to the close affinity between the Book of Wisdom's ideal sage and that of Ben Sira, and now identify the points of contact between them. Wisdom requires strenuous efforts on the part of her would-be devotees (Sir 51:19, 14:20-27), but is swift to anticipate their quest (Sir 15:2). She demands of her followers purity of soul, and holds aloof from fraudulence and arrogance (Sir 15:8, 51:20). She promotes the sage above one's neighbors, granting eloquence and crowning with honor (Sir 15:5-6). Although Ben Sira teaches no doctrine of immortality, he promises the sage that memory of the sage will not die (Sir 39:9). The wise person penetrates the intricacies of parables and knows his or her way among riddles (Sir 39:2-3). Since concealed treasure is of no profit, the sage willingly imparts wisdom to others (Sir 20:30-31), serves rulers and travels widely (Sir 39:4), and is in demand at public discussions (Sir 38:33). Finally, upon attaining wisdom the sage finds rest and joy (Sir 6:28, 51:27).

There are, however, several important differences. The central goal of immortality is missing in Ben Sira, as is also the attainment of mystical intimacy with God and prophecy. Perhaps even more significant is the distinction between their respective conceptions of human knowledge. Whereas the wisdom goal of the Book of Wisdom is one of encyclopedic scope and unlimited range, Ben Sira has a considerably more restricted view of the kind of knowledge that is attainable by humans. In a well-known passage he offers the following advice:

> Seek not (to understand) what is too wonderful for thee,
> And search not out that which is hid from thee.
> Meditate upon that which thou must [or, art permitted to] grasp,
> And be not occupied with that which is hid.
> Have naught to do with that which is beyond thee,
> For more hath been shown to thee than thou canst understand.

---

[15] Wis 9:6, 7:16; Philo, *Post.* 136; *Cher.* 71.

[16] Wis 1:4, 16; Philo, *Somn.* 1.149; *Her.* 45.

[17] Wis 5:15, 1:11, 3:24; Philo, *Ios.* 264; *Det.* 49.

[18] Wis 7:7-11; Philo, *Her.* 285-86.

[19] Wis 8:18; Philo, *Abr.* 52-53. For a more detailed discussion with fuller references, see Winston, *Wisdom of Solomon*, 59-62.

> For many are the conceits of the sons of men,
> And evil imaginations lead astray.
>
> (Sir 3:21-24)[20]

It may well be that in these verses he is referring only to cosmogonic and extraterrestrial speculations, but even if this should be the case, his attitude would still sharply diverge from the audacious and uninhibited confidence that marks the author of the Wisdom of Solomon, who speaks unhesitatingy of his "unerring knowledge of existent being" (7:17). Moreover, in contrast to Ben Sira who alludes to human inability to count "the days of unending time" (1:2), the author of the Book of Wisdom knows "the beginning, and end, and middle of times" (7:17), a phrase with a distinctly cogmogonic ring and one deriving from the Orphic theogony.[21] It may be further noted that Ben Sira refers to Wisdom submitting her disciples to the test before revealing her secrets to them (Sir 4:17-19),[22] whereas in the Wisdom of Solomon there is no hint of any test whatever. In short, the author of the Book of Wisdom appears to be undaunted in his total commitment to the pursuit of the philosophy and science of his age with all its challenges, whereas Sirach's goal in this sphere is more modestly conceived.

The Spiritual Odyssey by which the Aspirant becomes a Sage

In sketching his own spiritual odyssey, the author of the Book of Wisdom confesses to a passion for *Sophia* that had gripped him from his early youth and had led him to the determination to cast his lot with her forever. There is no impression here of a mere literary artifice (although a number of literary models exist; see below); the reader is clearly in the presence of a genuine religious experience that has enveloped the author's mind and soul and has filled them with the divine presence:

---

[20] Translations of Sirach from *APOT*. Cf. Sir 18:6-7. On the phrase "must grasp" in line 22, cf. *1 Enoch* 93-11-14, *4 Ezra* 4, *T. Job* 38:3-4. Wis 9:13-18 expresses similar sentiments, but only in reference to the human condition when it is bereft of divine wisdom, i.e., when individuals fail to activate their higher intuitive intellect.

[21] Kern, *Orphicorum fragmenta*, 91, 201. The same Orphic verse is quoted in the fourth-century-B.C.E Derveni papyrus, and it recurs in the Hellenistic Jewish-Orphic poem. See Winston, *Wisdom of Solomon*, 173-74.

[22] Cf. Philo, *Congr.* 124. A somewhat similar notion is contained in the beautiful parable in the *Zohar* (2:99a-b); see G. G. Scholem, *On the Kabbalah and Its Symbolism* (New York: Schocken Books, 1965), 55-56. There is indeed a striking account of the persecution of the righteous person at the hands of the wicked (Wis 2:12-20) and one's ultimate vindication (5:1-23), but this is quite different from Wisdom's own testing of those who seek her.

Her I loved and sought out from my youth,
and longed to make her my bride,
and I became a lover of her beauty.
She magnifies her noble birth by enjoying intimacy with God,
and the Master of all loved her.
. . . .
I determined, then, to take her to live with me.

(Wis 8:2-3, 9)

The author's unbridled love for Wisdom is even more vividly reflected in his magnificent fivefold description of her essence, in which she is conceived as an eternal emanation of God's power and glory. Here his language becomes luminous and almost lyrical and the reader is quickly borne aloft on the surging waves of the author's mystical passion:

She is an exhalation from the power of God,
a pure effluence from the glory of the Almighty;
therefore nothing tainted insinuates itself into her.
She is an effulgence of everlasting light,
an unblemished mirror of the active power of God,
and an image of his goodness.
. . . .
She is fairer than the sun
and surpasses every constellation;
compared to the light of day she is found more radiant;
for day is superseded by night,
but over Wisdom no evil can prevail.

(Wis 7:25-26, 29-30)

In addition to the concluding poem of Ben Sira (51:13-22), where one finds an artful use of erotic imagery to describe the author's ardent pursuit of Wisdom, there are several Greek models for the personification of Virtue/Wisdom as a beautiful maiden. In the famous parable known as the "Choice of Heracles" and later adapted by Philo (*Sacr.* 21-29), the Sophist Prodicus of Ceos had personified virtue as a fair maiden of high bearing who invited Heracles to choose her (Xenophon, *Mem.* 2:1:21-33). There is also a eulogy that Aristotle wrote after the death of his friend Hermias, cast in the form of a hymn to Arete, Virtue. It begins as follows:

Arete, bringer of toil to the race of mortals, the fairest quarry in life, for the sake of thy maiden beauty is death itself a fate to be prized in Hellas, or the suffering of labours continued and endless. Such imperishable reward dost thou implant in the mind, reward above gold or ancestry or soft-eyed sleep.[23]

---

[23] Translation from Guthrie, *History of Greek Philosophy*, 6:32. For the text see D. L. Page, *Poetae melici graeci* (Oxford: Clarendon, 1962), 444 (or Diogenes Laertius 5.7; or Athenaeus, *Deipn.* 15.696). For commentary see J. Crossett, "Aristotle as Poet: *The Hymn to*

Moreover, in *On the Preliminary Studies*, Philo develops an allegory in which Abraham, the soul, is married to Sarah, who symbolizes Wisdom. The union, however, is unproductive, because the soul is not at first ripe for it, and Sarah is barren. She therefore sends the soul to mate with Hagar the Egyptian, who stands for the preliminary training of the Encyclical or School studies.[24] In time, however, Sarah can bear a child to Abraham, and then Hagar and Ishmael must be cast out. The allegory goes back to Bion of Borysthenes (ca. 325-255 BCE), who is quoted by Pseudo-Plutarch (*Lib. ed.* 7D) as saying that those who, unable to win philosophy, wear themselves out in preliminary learning are like the suitors of Penelope, who when they could not win the mistress contented themselves with the maids.[25]

Wisdom Immanent and Transcendent

In his all-consuming search for Wisdom, the author addresses a very moving prayer to his Lord with the earnest request that the divine throne-companion be graciously dispatched to him from the holy heavens above, so that she may labor at his side and enable him to learn the divine pleasure (Wis 9:1-6, 9-10).[26] It is evident that prayer for the author of the

---

Hermeias," *Philological Quarterly* 46 (1967): 145-55; and Guthrie, *History of Greek Philosophy*, 6:31-34. Chrysippus is reported to have said that Justice was usually represented by the painters and orators of old as "of maidenly form and bearing, with a stern and fearsome countenance, a keen glance of the eye, and a dignity and solemnity which was neither mean nor cruel, but awe-inspiring" (Aulus Gellius, *Noct. att.* 14.4.2 [Rolfe, LCL]). It may be noted that Homer had already personified death, sleep, fear, justice, rumor, fate, and prayers.

[24] Plato had already argued that arithmetic, geometry, astronomy, and harmonics were useful for preparing the guardians for dialectic or pure philosophical reasoning (*Resp.* 524D-31C). By the Middle Ages seven liberal arts and sciences were recognized: the trivium, composed of grammar, rhetoric, and dialectic, and the quadrivium, composed of geometry, arithmetic, music, and astronomy. In one context or another, Philo mentions all these studies, but he "never gives a definitive enumeration of the disciplines which he included in the encyclia"; so A. Mendelson, *Secular Education in Philo of Alexandria* (Cincinnati: Hebrew Union College, 1982), 4. Although the School studies were rejected by the Epicureans and Cynics, and were an object of debate among the early Stoics, in Philo's time the Stoic view of them was probably that expressed by Seneca, that they were indispensable to philosophy (*Ep.* 88.25).

[25] For the use of sexual imagery in describing the intellectual quest, cf. Plato, *Resp.* 490B; and for Philo's skillful adaptation of the Greek allegory, see Y. Amir, "The Transference of Greek Allegories to Biblical Motifs in Philo," *Nourished with Peace: Studies in Hellenistic Judaism in memory of Samuel Sandmel* (ed. F. E. Greenspahn et al.; Chico, CA: Scholars Press, 1984), 15-25. For further discussion see Winston, *Wisdom of Solomon*, 193.

[26] A similar note is struck in Cleanthes' *Hymn to Zeus*: "O Zeus, all bountiful, ... / rescue mankind from wretched / Ignorance, scatter darkness from their minds, / Give them that

Wisdom of Solomon is in no way meant to serve as a substitute for the great effort and stringent training needed in order to attain wisdom. Indeed, far from being perceived as a supernatural modality, turning in prayer to God is seen as nothing but the reflex of God's turning to humans. The mysterious Muslim sage Khadir (or Khidr) put it well:

> Thy calling Allah! was my "Here am I,"
> Thy yearning pain My messenger to thee.[27]

It is clear that training, instruction, and predawn vigilance are prerequisites for the attainment of wisdom.[28] A similar emphasis on the need for prayer is found in Ben Sira, who relates that while still young he sought wisdom in prayer before the temple,[29] and yet insists on formal instruction.[30] The significance of prayer for the attainment of wisdom lies in the sage's firm conviction that all human accomplishments are in reality only the obverse side of effective divine action and that the fundamental error that must be avoided above all is the self-conceit of one who thinks that human power is completely autonomous. Philo encapsulates this sentiment in his own characteristic way: "But I could not exercise it [virtue] shouldest thou not send down the seeds from heaven to cause her to be pregnant" (*Det.* 60).

The helplessness of the human condition in the absence of divine wisdom is strongly emphasized by the author of the Book of Wisdom. It was a notion widely held in the wisdom literature of the ancient Near East, but it is given a Platonic twist in the Wisdom of Solomon and is skillfully integrated into its basic philosophical world view:

> For what man can comprehend the plan of God,
> or who can grasp what the Lord wills?
> The reasonings of mortals are wretched,
> and our devices precarious;
> for a perishable body weighs down the soul,
> and this tent of clay encumbers a mind full of cares.
> We barely make inferences concerning what is on earth,
> and laboriously discover what is at hand;

---

wisdom by which Thou dost steer / All things in justice ..." Translated by F. H. Sandbach, *The Stoics* (Cambridge: Cambridge University, 1975), 111.

[27] See R. A. Nicholson, *The Mystics of Islam* (London: Routledge and Kegan Paul, 1963), 113; cf. A. Schimmel, *Mystical Dimensions in Islam* (Chapel Hill: University of North Carolina, 1975), 81, 165-66: "I call Thee," sang Hallaj, "no, Thou callest me unto Thee!" (*Diwan*, qasida no. 1, v. 2). For Wisdom as both immanent and transcendent, see Winston, *Wisdom of Solomon*, 41.

[28] Wis 6:17, 8:18, 6:14-15.

[29] Sir 51:13-14; cf. 37:15.

[30] Sir 51:16-17, 39:1-3; 6:35-37.

who, then, has tracked out what is in the heavens?
Who was privy to your design, unless you gave him Wisdom,
and sent your holy spirit from on high?
Thus it was that the paths of earthlings were set aright,
and men were taught what pleases you,
and were saved by Wisdom (Wis 9:13-18).

The same idea is eloquently expressed in 1QH[a] IV, 30-32 in almost the same language:

Righteousness, I know, is not of man,
nor is perfection of way of the son of man:
to the Most High God belong all righteous deeds.
The way of man is not established (לא תכון)
except by the spirit which God created for him
to make perfect a way for the children of men.[31]

In its Platonic context this stark recognition of human limitations leads neither to a sense of moral impotence nor to an abject reliance on a supernatural intervention of divine power to adjust the imbalance.[32] From the perspective of the Platonist understanding of reality, the human intellect, far from being eclipsed by divine action, is itself only an extension of it, its earthly image and expression. Hence, the negative intent of the Babylonian wisdom poet's question — "Where have mortals learnt the way of a god?"[33] — is transformed into the positive notion that all one need do is recognize the divine element already lurking within, and by acknowledging its potency allow it to become effectual. The *deus ex machina* has become the God within. The somber plaint of Agur's words, "Who has ascended heaven and come down?" (Prov. 30:4; cf. Ps 115:16), yields to the bold confidence of the Platonist mystic who glories in the heavenly gift of reason.

Purgation

It is clear from various statements of the author that the aspirant after Wisdom will not attain this goal without first purging oneself of certain fundamental flaws and diverse layers of psychic debris that darken the mind and separate one from the ultimate object of desire. The spiritual quest requires replacing doubleheartedness with a singleness of heart, or

---

[31] See D. Flusser, "The Dualism of Flesh and Spirit in the Dead Sea Scrolls," *Tarbiz* 27 (1985): 158-65 (Hebrew); this translation of 1QH[a] is from Vermes, *Dead Sea Scrolls in English,* 163.

[32] For the Platonic background see Winston, *Wisdom of Solomon,* 41 and 207-9.

[33] *Ludlul Bel Nemeqi* 38; see Lambert, *Babylonian Wisdom Literature* , 41.

learning how to be simple (Wis 1:1).[34] This involves ridding oneself of fraudulence, cunning stratagems, and all forms of injustice (Wis 1:4-5). It also requires a trusting heart that does not seek to test the Lord, and avoids every trace of murmuring against him, even while obeying his commandments (Wis 1:2, 10-11). One must become holy by observing God's holy ordinances in holiness (Wis 6:10). The author further warns against the enticements of momentary pleasures,[35] such as those of wine, perfumes, spring blossoms, reveling, and especially illicit sex: "For ... the giddy distraction of desire perverts the guileless mind" (Wis 2:6-9, 3:13-4:6; quotation from 4:12). He further inveighs against blasphemy, arrogance, wealth, and false posturing (Wis 5:8). Above all, however, he points the finger at idolatry, which is born out of a mindless ignorance of God, as being the source of all moral corruption. Following what seems to have been a common Jewish-Hellenistic apologetic tradition, both the author of the Book of Wisdom and Philo draw a sharp distinction between the worship of the natural elements or the celestial bodies, and that of manufactured idols or animals, indicating that the offense of the former is less than that of the latter, although neither is to be excused (Wis 13:6-10; Philo, *Decal.* 66). The utter absurdity of image worship is easily discerned from the fact that it entails the worship of what is soulless or dead by those endowed with soul, and the addressing of prayers to creations inferior to the craftsmen who made them.[36] The author deftly describes the three kinds of false worship in the form of a climax (*klimax, gradatio*; see

---

[34] For doubleheartedness see Ps 12:3 (בלב ולב, Sir 1:28. "Study to be simple," wrote Marcus Aurelius; "a moment and thou wilt be dead; and not even yet art thou simple" (4.26, 37). The fundamental virtue in the *Testaments of the Twelve Patriarchs* is ἁπλότης "simplicity" and it is an equally important theme in Philo (*Opif.* 156; *Migr.* 153; *Plant.* 44-45; *Congr.* 36; and *QG* 4.165). "It is told of rabbi Israel of Kosnitz that he was especially pleased when the 'simple people' came to him. When his disciples asked him the reason for this, he said to them, 'I – all my effort and work is directed toward becoming simple, and they are simple already'." (Martin Buber, *The Origin and Meaning of Hasidism* (N.Y.: Harper Torch Books, 1960), 47. In Zen Buddhism much effort must go into training adepts in effortlessness, and similarly in Taoism, acting must be through not acting. See Winston, *Wisdom of Solomon*, 101. The term "whole-heartedness" (לב שלם) is one of the basic expressions of deuteronomic historiography (1 Kgs 8:61, 11:4, etc.) and was afterward adopted by the Chronicler; see M. Weinfeld, *Deuteronomy and the Deuteronomic School* (Oxford: Clarendon, 1972), 269.

[35] There may be an allusion here to the extreme view of Aristippus of Cyrene (a companion of Socrates), who enjoyed the pleasures that were at hand (τῶν παρόντων), but saw no reason to exert himself to gain pleasures that involved hard work or effort (Diogenes Laertius 2.66)

[36] Wis 15:17, 13:17-19, 14:18-20; Philo, *Decal.* 69.

Quintilian, *Inst.* 9:3:54): the nature worshipers are described as mindless, the idolaters as wretched, and the Egyptian animal worshipers as most foolish of all.[37] The dire results of idolatry are vividly depicted:

> All is confusion — bloody murder, deceitful theft, corruption, treachery, tumult, perjury, ... soul defilement, alteration of generation [i.e. nonprocreative sex, as suggested by L. Williams Countryman in *Dirt Greed and Sex* (Philadelphia: Fortress Press, 1988), 63, or else 'interchange of sex roles', as in my Anchor edition], irregular marriages, adultery, and debauchery. For the worship of the unspeakable idols is the beginning, cause, and end of every evil (Wis 14:25-27).

The author thus drives his main point home, that to know God is the sum of righteousness and to recognize his power is the root of immortality (Wis 15:3).

Goals of the Mystical Quest

In a six-part *sorites* or chain syllogism, the author argues that the desire for Wisdom leads — through love for her and the keeping of her laws — to immortality and nearness to God, and that it is this intimacy with the divine that is the ultimate source of all human sovereignty (Wis 6:17-21).[38] He therefore advises ruling monarchs to honor Wisdom if they wish to reign forever, and those desiring to join their ranks must clearly do likewise. It is undoubtedly significant that Wisdom's intimacy with God is described in virtually the same terms as human intimacy with Wisdom, for this almost certainly implies that the true goal of the pursuit of Wisdom is union with the deity itself, which can only be mediated through union with divine Wisdom.[39] Such union with *Sophia* is possible because of one's kinship with her (Wis 8:17), by virtue of the possession of a mind permeated with her spirit (7:23-24). The author's highly charged language leaves one with the strong impression that he is very likely alluding to his own experience of union with the Wisdom aspect of God. The road to this mystical climax, however, does not in his view demand any special esoteric procedures or disclosures. He is convinced that it is an experience open to all, and along

---

[37] Wis 13:1, 10; 15:4. For further detail, see my commentary, *Wisdom of Solomon,* 248-49.

[38] For a detailed discussion of the *sorites,* see ibid., 154-55. To the many examples given there, add Ahiqar Syriac Berlin 165 no. 55 and Ahiqar Slavonic no. 73; see Lichtheim, *Late Egyptian Wisdom,* 14-17.

[39] See U. Wilckens, "σοφία, σοφός," *TDNT* 7.499; and my commentary, *Wisdom of Solomon,* 41. There is already an incipient movement in this direction in Prov 8:30-31, where Wisdom indicates that just as she was God's joy, so was her own joy with humankind.

with his enthusiastic evocation of Wisdom's exquisite beauties he seeks only to outline the various stages that marked his own passionate search for her, that they may serve as a guide for others. To this end he employs a protreptic or exhortatory discourse in which he offers himself as a living paradigm for others to follow. He is thus not particularly concerned with the transmission of proverbial wisdom, concentrating instead on an attempt to persuade his readers not only that it is *Sophia* who brings her own to ultimate serenity and joy, but that she is openly accessible to all:

> Bright and unfading is Wisdom,
> easily beheld by those who love her,
> and found by those who seek her.
> She is first to make herself known to those who desire her;
> he who anticipates the dawn on her behalf will not grow weary,
> for he will find her seated (πάρεδρον) before his door.
> To set one's mind on her is perfect wisdom,
> and he that is vigilant for her sake will soon be free of care.
> For she herself seeks out those who are worthy of her;
> with gracious good will she appear to them on their path,
> and in every thought comes to meet them.
>
> (Wis 6:12-16)

The Isis Mysteries and Qumran

In detailing his spiritual odyssey, the author of the Book of Wisdom thus strikes a religious chord new to the Hebrew wisdom writings, echoing a type of religiosity that was characteristic of the contemporary Isis mysteries in the pagan world and the earlier Dead Sea sect within the Jewish world. This new chord consisted in an extraordinary sense of mystical intimacy and feelings of ineffable joy in the individual's experience of God. With regard to the Isis cult one catches a glimpse of this passionate religious intensity in the vivid account given by Apuleius of the conversion of the Ass-Man Lucius. Using deliberately veiled language, Lucius describes the heart of his initiation ceremony in the following words.

> I approached the boundary of death and treading on Proserpine's threshold, I was carried through all the elements, after which I returned. At dead of night I saw the sun flashing with bright effulgence. I approached close to the gods above and the gods below and worshiped them face to face.[40]

---

[40] *Metamorphoses* 11.23; translated by J. G. Griffiths, *The Isis-book (Metamorphoses, Book XI)/Apuleius of Madauros* (Leiden: Brill, 1975), 101.

He later addresses Queen Isis as follows:

> Thou in truth art the holy and eternal savior of the human race, ever
> beneficient in helping mortal men, and thou bringest the sweet love
> of a mother to the trials of the unfortunate ... But I am bereft of
> talent in singing thy praises ... indeed a thousand mouths and tongues
> are not enough for the task ... Therefore I shall try to do the only
> thing possible for one who is devoted but indigent; I shall keep for-
> ever, stored in my inmost heart, the memory of thy divine counten-
> ance and most holy godhead.[41]

Finally, when keenly agitated by the divine command to undergo yet a
third initiation, a gracious form enlightens him thus in a prophetic
message by night.

> There is no reason for you to be frightened ... Be filled with gladsome
> joy, rather, because the gods so constantly think you worthy, and
> indeed rejoice that you will achieve three times a boon that is scarcely
> granted to others even once. From this number deservedly conclude
> that you will be happy forever.[42]

As for the Dea Sea Scrolls, the following passage from the *Hodayot*
(*Thanksgiving Hymns*) recalls the impassioned language of the author of
the Book of Wisdom when he speaks of his beloved *Sophia*:

> I give thanks unto Thee, O Lord,
> for Thou hast freed my soul from the pit
> and drawn me up from the slough of hell
> to the crest of the world.
>   So walk I on uplands unbounded
> and know that there is hope
> for that which Thou didst mold out of dust
> to have consort with things eternal.
>   For lo, Thou hast taken a spirit
> distorted by sin,
> and purged it of the taint of much transgression,
> and given it a place
> in the host of the holy beings,
> and brought it into communion
> with the sons of heaven.
> Thou hast made a mere man to share
> the lot of the Spirits of Knowledge,
> to praise Thy name in their chorus.
>
> (1QH^a III, 19-23)[43]

---

[41] Ibid., 102-3; *Metamorphoses* 11.25; cf. Sir 43:27-30.

[42] Ibid., 107; *Metamorphoses* 11.29.

[43] T. H. Gaster, *The Dead Sea Scriptures in English* (Garden City, NY: Doubleday, 1956),
138.

Like the composer of *Hodayot,* the author of the Book of Wisdom experiences the raptures of divine knowledge in his present existence and already enjoys his prize of immortality. On the other hand, as already seen, in contrast both to the Isis mysteries and the Qumran Scrolls, he disdained the path of esotericism, constantly conveying instead the openness of Wisdom's path, which requires neither secret initiations nor entry into the community of a holy elect.

PART FOUR

PHILO OF ALEXANDRIA

CHAPTER EIGHT

Philo's Theory of Eternal Creation: *Prov.* 1.6-9

In his discussion of the origin and duration of the world, Aristotle asserts that all his predecessors held it to have had a beginning (γενόμενον), but some (like Plato) had maintained that having begun it was everlasting, others (such as the Atomists) that it was perishable, and others again (such as Empedocles and Heraclitus) that it was subject to an eternal sequence of cyclic genesis and destruction (*Cael.* 1.10). The Platonic view Aristotle held to be impossible. He was aware, however, that some Platonists interpreted Plato's cosmology differently, though he considered their interpretation to be untrue.

> They claim that what they say about the generation of the world is analogous to the diagrams drawn by mathematicians: their exposition does not mean that the world ever was generated (οὐχ ὡς γενομένου ποτέ), but is used for instructional purposes (διδασκαλίας χάριν), since it makes things easier to understand just as the diagram does for those who see it in process of construction (*Cael.* 279b30).

With the exception of Plutarch and Atticus, this interpretation of Plato's *Timaeus* was steadily maintained by virtually all Platonists down to the time of Plotinus. Moreover, according to Atticus, the motivation for this exegesis was the inability of its authors to resist the Aristotelian argument for the eternity of the universe, while, in their pious devotion to the Master, shrinking from ascribing to him a doctrine considered false by Aristotle (Eusebeus, *Praep. ev..* 15.6.6).[1]

---

[1] The following Platonists interpreted Plato's *Tim.* analytically: Xenocrates, Speusippus, Crantor and his followers, Eudorus of Alexandria, Taurus, Alcinous, Apuleius. See A. E. Taylor, *A Commentary on Plato's Timaeus* (Oxford: Clarendon, 1928), 67-69; J. Pépin, *Théologie cosmique et théologie chrétienne* (Paris: Presses universitaires de France, 1964), 38-43, 86-94; C. Baeumker, "Die Ewigkeit der Welt bei Plato," *Philosophische Monatshefte* 23 (1887): 513-529; A. J. Festugière, *Études de Philosophie Grecque* (Paris: J. Vrin, 1971), 487-506; G. S. Claghorn, *Aristotle's Criticism of Plato's Timaeus* (The Hague: Nijhoff, 1954), 84-98; J. Dillon, *The Middle Platonists* (Ithaca, N. Y.; Cornell University Press, 1977), 7. According to the second century Platonist, Severus, although the cosmos had no temporal origin, it is still periodically destroyed and renewed (Proclus, *in Ti.* 1.289.7-13). See Pépin, *Théologie cosmique,* 94; P. Merlan, in *Cambridge History of Later Greek and Early Medieval Philosophy* (London: Cambridge University Press, 1967), 78-79; Dillon, *Middle Platonists,* 263.

It should be noted, however, that there was some disagreement among the Platonists as to the precise formulation of the Platonic theory of cosmogony. Some were willing to assert that according to Plato the world was in reality ἀγένητος but could, for pedagogical reasons, be characterized as γενητός insofar as it is ultimately derived from higher principles (e.g., the One and the Indefinite Dyad, and secondarily, the Ideas and Mathematicals). Others, however, (such as Crantor and his followers) insisted that according to Plato the world was γενητός, though this was not to be understood in a temporal sense. Proclus, for example, attacks Platonists like Xenocrates and Speusippus for asserting that according to Plato the world was γενητός only κατ' ἐπίνοιαν or was feigned to be so σαφηνείας ἕνεκα διδασκαλικῆς, for Timaeus, he insists, infers the existence of the Maker from the premise that the world is γενητός, and if the premise is merely conceptual, the Demiurge must be so too. It would appear that Proclus' objection rests on semantic considerations. In his view the formulations of Xenocrates and Speusippus and their like are misleading and may result in the branding of their ultimate principles (the One and the Indefinite Dyad)[2] as empty abstractions. Proclus, therefore prefers to say that the world is γενητός, though in the sense that it is ἀεὶ γιγνόμενον καὶ γεγενημένον (in Tim. 290.3-25). This semantic distinction is of some importance for our understanding of Philo's position in this matter, for if our thesis that he taught a doctrine of eternal creation be correct, it would strike one as not a little perverse that he should accept Aristotle's literalist interpretation of Plato's creation doctrine in the Timaeus in preference to that of Xenocrates and Speusippus (Aet. 14-16). He apparently did so, however, in order to substantiate the view that Plato did think that the world was γενητός in the sense that it was the product of a real Demiurgic creativity (cf. Opif. 171), yet at the same time rejecting Aristotle's temporal understanding of it.[3]

---

[2] Merlan has pointed out that disagreement started early among the Platonists as to whether the two higher principles should have absolutely equal status (Merlan, Cambridge History, 17). Hermodorus asserted that according to Plato, the Indefinite Dyad or Matter should not be called a first principle, and later Eudorus of Alexandria posits a supranoetic One above the Monad and Dyad. See A. J. Festugière, La Révélation d'Hermés Trismégiste (4 vols.; Paris: Lecoffre, 1944-54), 4.308-310; Merlan, Cambridge History, 81. On the nature of Speusippus' One, see P. Merlan, From Platonism to Neoplatonism (The Hague: Nijhoff, 1960), 96-140; H. J. Krämer, Der Ursprung der Geistmetaphysik (Amsterdam: Grüner, 1967), 207-218, 351, 358; H. Happ, Hyle (Berlin; New York; de Gruyter, 1971), 208-241; Dillon, Middle Platonists, 12-18; F. Ravaisson-Mollien, "Las Opiniones de Espeusipo acerca de los primeros principios de las cosas examinandas a la luz de los textos aristotelicos," Revista de Estudios clasicos 11 (1967): 28-64.

[3] Philo could have rather endorsed the formulation of Crantor and his followers (if we

In the light of this debate over the meaning of the *Timaeus'* doctrine of creation, we may now examine Philo's discussion of the eternity of the world in *Prov.* 1.6-9.[4] After noting that superficial observation often results in the belief that the world has existed from eternity independent of any creative act (the Aristotelian view), he immediately proceeds to attack the "sophistic" view[5] "elaborated with drawn-out quibbles," that God did not begin to create the world at a certain moment, but was "eternally applying himself to its creation." The intent of this formulation, says Philo, was to avoid imputing to God a most unbecoming inactivity that would otherwise have characterized his pre-creative state.[6] But in this case, the absurdity of

---

follow Proclus' version, *in Tim.* 85a, rather than that of Plutarch, *Mor.* 1.1012D), but he probably preferred not to associate his position with that of the Platonists who coordinated the principle of matter with the One. Moreover, while Eudorus' concept of the One was very close to that of Philo, he not only seems to have employed the ἀγένητος formula which Philo disliked (Plutarch *ib.* 3.1013B), but very likely (under Neopythagorean influence) conceived of the One as emanating both the Monad and the Dyad, a notion which Philo would certainly have rejected (Simplicius, *in Ph.* 181, 10 ff., H. Diels; Alexander of Aphrodisias *Comm. Mete.* 988a 10-11, M. Hayduck; both in *Commentaria in Aristotelem graeca* [23 vol.; Berlin: Reimeri, 1882-1909]).

4   See now Aucher's Latin translations from the Armenian reprinted with a French translation, introduction and notes by Mireille Hadas-Lebel (*De Providentia I et II/Philon d'Alexandrie* [Paris: Éditions du Cerf, 1973]); P. Wendland, *Philo's Schrift über die Vorsehung* (Berlin: Gaertner, 1892); W. Bousset, *Jüdisch-Christlicher Schulbetrieb in Alexandria und Rom* (Göttingen: Vandenhoeck & Ruprecht, 1915), 137ff.; M. Pohlenz, *Kleine Schriften* (Hildesheim: Olms, 1965), 305-83, esp. 313-24; H. Leisegang, "Philo," in PW 20:1, cols. 8-11; S. Lilla, *Clement of Alexandria* (London: Oxford University Press, 1971), 197, n. 2. Bousset finds *Prov.* 1.7-8 hopelessly contradictory ("Kurz hier sind vollendete Widersprüche. Und nach allem, was wir von Philos schriftstellerischer Eigenart kennen, tun wir ihm kein Unrecht, wenn wir annehmen, dass er in 7-8 eine Ausführung, in welcher die platonische Annahme einer vorweltlichen Materie vom Standpunkt der Behauptung der Ewigkeit der Welt aus abgelehnt wurde, gedankenlos und sinnlos in einem Zusammenhang hat stehen lassen, der eine entgegengesetzte Orientierung zeigt" [*Jüdisch-Christlicher Schulbetrieb*, 146]). I believe, however, that in spite of the stylistic gaucherie of these passages (undoubtedly due to the Armenian translator), it is possible to extract from them a consistent Philonic doctrine. (Wendland, *Philo's Schrift*, 184, thought these passages constituted a lost section of Philo's *De Aeternitate Mundi*, and although Bousset was unwilling to go that far, he was inclined to accept Wendland's suggestion that in this section of the *De Providentia* Philo was attempting to fulfill his promise at the end of *Aet.* 150.)

5   Cf. *Aet.* 14: τινὲς δὲ οἴονται σοφιζόμενοι κατὰ Πλάτωνα γενητὸν λέγεσθαι τὸν κόσμον.

6   Cf. *Opif.* 7: τοῦ δὲ θεοῦ πολλὴν ἀπραξίαν ἀνάγνως κατεψεύσαντο; *Aet.* 83: "Moreover if all things are as they say consumed in the conflagration, what will God be doing during that time? Will he do nothing at all?...But if all things are annihilated, inactivity and dire unemployment (ἀργία καὶ ἀπραξία) will render his life unworthy of the name and what could be more monstrous than this? I shrink from saying, for the very thought is a blasphemy, that quiescence will entail as a consequence the death of God." The same argument was employed by the Epicureans. "Moreover I would put to both of you the question," says Velleius the Epicurean, "why did these deities suddenly awake into activity

the hypothesis becomes immediately evident; for those who have espoused it in order to remove a minimal accusation against the deity have actually attached to him a maximal one. Their conception of God's creative act consists, in the last analysis, of the bestowal of order and form on a primordial matter that lacked all previous determination. Is this not equivalent, argues Philo, to making matter into a principle of creation alongside of God? While solicitously clearing God of the accusation of temporary inactivity they have thus nonchalantly overlooked the more genuine threat to his sovereign creative power.

Philo now states his own position:

> God is continuously ordering matter by his thought. His thinking is simultaneous with his acting and there never was a time when he did not act, the ideas themselves existing with him from the beginning. For God's will is not posterior to him, but is always with him, for natural motions never give out. Thus ever thinking he creates, and furnishes to sensible things the principle of their existence, so that one always finds these two processes in conjunction (*Prov.* 1.7).[7]

At first sight this passage seems baffling. Having concluded his denunciation of those who teach a doctrine of eternal creation on the grounds of their converting the Creator into the mere orderer of a primordial principle, Philo now seems to espouse just such a doctrine in turn. God, in Philo's view, is eternally creating inasmuch as he is ever thinking, and his creativity is constituted by nothing more than the meticulously accurate division of a formless matter through his all-incising Logos (cf. *Her.* 134, 137, 140). The solution, however, is not far to seek, if we focus our attention on some important modifications that Philo has introduced into his own theory of eternal creation. In the mystical monotheism of Philo nothing really exists or acts except God;[8] all else is but a shadow reality

---

as world-builders after countless ages of slumber? for though the world did not exist, it does not follow that ages (*saecla*) did not exist ... but from the infinite past there has existed an eternity not measured by limited divisions of time, but of a nature intelligible in terms of extension, since it is inconceivable that there was ever a time when time did not exist. Well then, Balbus, what I ask is, why did your Providence remain idle all through that extent of time of which you speak?" (Cicero *Nat. d.* 1.9.21-22). Cf. Diels, *Doxographi graeci*, 209-301; Lucretius 5.168. A similar argument had already been employed by Parmenides, Diels and Kranz, *Fragmente der Vorsokratiker*, B.8, 9-10: "What need would have made it grow, beginning from non-Being, later or sooner?"

[7] Cf. Spinoza, *Eth.* 1.33, sch. 2: "But since in eternity there is no when nor before nor after, it follows from the perfection of God alone that He neither can decree nor could ever have decreed anything else than that which He has decreed, that is to say, God has not existed before His decrees and can never exist without them."

[8] *Det.* 160: "God alone has veritable being. This is why Moses will say of Him as best he may in human speech, 'I am He that ,' implying that others lesser than He have not being,

ultimately deriving from the truly Existent. Unlike Plato, who was a pluralist, Philo was thus unwilling to allow even for a self-existing void, and therefore made its pattern an eternal idea within the Divine Mind.[9] In Plato's conception of matter, the self-existing Receptable is its most stable and permanent constituent: "It must be called always the same, for it never departs at all from its own character" (*Tim.* 50BC).[10] For Philo, however, not only are the phantasmagoric copies of the ideal four elements indirectly derived from God[11] (whether they are similarly derived for any of the Middle Platonists preceding Philo would depend on whether or not they had anticipated him in making the eternal 'Forms' ideas in the mind of God),[12] but even the virtually non-existent void is but a shadow reflection of an idea in God. Hence what in Philo's view was the crucial defect in the Platonists' doctrine of eternal creation (i.e., the elevation of matter into an autonomous albeit passive principle) has carefully been eliminated from his own version of that theory.[13]

Continuing his argument with the Platonists, Philo now confronts them with what he considers to be an inner contradiction in their doctrine. If, says Philo, one refuses to acknowledge the simultaneity of God's thinking and creating, how can one explain the fact that matter, which existed from all time, was never found in a disordered state? What Philo seems to be arguing is that if one considers matter as an autonomous primordial element, rather than an indirect product of God's thinking, how could it be maintained that it never was in a disordered state? Only if God's thinking is eternally bringing matter into being and simultaneously ordering it can

---

as being indeed is, but exist in semblance only, and are conventionally said to exist." Cf. *Leg.* 2.86; *Cher.* 121; *Her.* 122-124; *Mos.* 1.76. For the theme of human nothingness and utter passivity in Philo, see D. Winston, "Freedom and Determinism in Philo of Alexandria" *in this volume*, 135-50.

[9] See D. Winston, "Philo's Theory of Cosmogony," in *Religious Syncretism in Antiquity*, (ed. B. Pearson: Missoula, Montana, 1975), 157-171. It was probably for this reason that Philo refused explicitly to attribute any motion to primordial matter (ibid., 164, n. 1).

[10] Of Plato's Receptable, J. B. Skempt writes that "it is more real than the 'images' of the Forms which appear in it." ("Hyle and Hypodoche," in *Aristotle and Plato in the Mid-Fourth Century* [ed. I. Düring and G. E. L. Owen; Göteborg, 1960], 207). Cf. Plotinus' concept of matter (ὕλη) as total negativity or absolute evil (*Enn.* 2.4; 1.8).

[11] Winston, "Philo's Theory of Cosmogony."

[12] See A. N. M. Rich, "The Platonic ideas as the Thoughts of God," *Mnemosyne*, ser. 4, v. 7, fasc. 1 (1964): 123-133; W. Theiler, *Die Vorbereitung des Neuplatonismus* (Berlin: Wiedmann, 1964), 1-60; C. J. De Vogel, *Philosophia* (Assen: Van Gorcum, 1969), 1.372-377; J. H. Loenen, "Albinus' Metaphysics. An Attempt at Rehabilitation," *Mnemosyne*, ser. 4, v. 10 (1950): 44-45; Dillon, *Middle Platonists*, 29, 95.

[13] Bousset, (*Jüdisch-Christlicher Schulbetrieb*, 144, n. 1), suggests that Philo may be referring to Jewish opponents who understood the Aristotelian doctrine of the eternity of the world as teaching its eternal creation through God.

one avoid a primordially formless state of matter. But, continues Philo, if there was a time when matter was disordered, then the origin of the world began when order was imposed upon it, and the Platonists can no longer speak of eternal creation.

Philo's theory of eternal creation can now be stated succinctly. Insofar as God is always thinking the intelligible "Forms," he is eternally creating the Intelligible World or Logos, and thereby also indirectly causing its shadow reflection, the sensible world, which he is constantly making to conform as closely as possible to its intelligible counterpart.[14] Corroboration for this interpretation may be found in an oft repeated principle of Philo's theology that God is unchangeable, so that a temporal creation involving as it does a change in God's nature would thus stand in open contradiction to a fundamental assumption of Philo's thought. Nor is it possible to say as St. Thomas later would that God willed freely from eternity that the world should come into existence in time (or have *esse post non-esse*: *Contr. Gent.* 2.31-7; *S.T.* 1.46.1; *De Pot..* 3.17), for Philo has already stated (*Prov.* 1.7) that God's thinking is simultaneous with his acting or creating (cf. *Sacr.* 65; *Mos.* 1.283). In the light of all this we should have to conclude that the many passages in which Philo speaks of creation in temporal terms are not to be taken literally, but only as accommodations to the biblical idiom.[15]

A strangely dissonant note, however, is struck in *Decal.* 58, where it is explicitly stated that "there was a time when the world was not (ἦν ποτε χρόνος, ὅτε οὐκ ἦν). It may be that in a polemical context in which the target is a form of idolatry (worship of the Universe itself: cf. Wis 13:1-9) dangerously attractive even for a Jew if he belonged to the enlightened Hellenistic class, Philo did not hesitate to use locutions that explicitly negated his precise technical position. Moreover, it is not entirely out of keeping with Philo's usual style of exposition to use the phrase ἦν ποτε χρόνος in a context such as this. For analytical purposes, Philo speaks, for example, of the mind's condition as it would have been, had it no connection with the sense-perceptions transmitted to it by bodily sense-organs. Allegorizing the biblical text concerning the creation of Eve, he naturally describes this state of the mind in temporal terms:

> For there was a time (ἦν γάρ ποτε χρόνος) when Mind neither had sense-perception, nor held converse with it ... It was but half the perfect soul, lacking the power whereby it is the nature of bodies to

---

14 Winston, "Philo's Theory of Cosmogony", 170, n. 1.
15 See *Opif.* 16, 19, and *passim*; *Mut.* 27; *Leg.* 2.1-2. For an excellent recent analysis of this controversial issue, with full bibliographical data, see G. E. Sterling, "Creatio Temporalis, Aeterna, vel Continua?", *SPhA* 4 (1992): 15-41.

be perceived, a mere unhappy section bereft of its mate without the support of the sense-perceiving organs ... God, then, wishing to provide the Mind with perception of material as well as immaterial things, thought to complete the soul by weaving into the part first made the other section, which he called by the general name of "woman" and the proper name of "Eve," thus symbolizing sense (*Cher.* 58-60).

We may conclude, then, that it is unnecessary to take the passage in *Decal.* 58 *au pied de la lettre.*[16]

We must now test our interpretation of Philo's creation doctrine by an examination of his theory of miracles to see whether the latter is consistent with the former. One of Philo's favored phrases is πάντα θεῷ δυνατά, a doctrine he never fails to intone as emphatically as he can whenever the opportunity presents itself. According to Philo, God created the heaven only after he had created the earth, so that

> none would suppose that the regular movements of the heavenly bodies are the causes of all things. For he has no need of his heavenly offspring on which he bestowed powers but not independence: for like a charioteer grasping the reins or a pilot the tiller, he guides all things in what direction he pleases as law and right demand, standing in need of no one besides: for all things are possible to God (*Opif.* 46; cf. *QG* 4.51).

This passage makes it clear that the formula "all things are possible to God" does not include what is not κάτα νόμον καὶ δίκην, so that God evidently cannot act arbitrarily, i.e., in a way that might be contrary to his own nature. Nor would it be correct to interpret Philo's position (as Wolfson does)[17] in the light of St. Thomas' view that would allow God to act outside the order of nature:

---

[16] It should also be noted that according to Philo's own analysis of time (*Opif.* 26; *Aet.* 53), it would be absurd to say "there was a time when the world was not," since time and world are for him correlative (cf. Aristotle, *Phys.* 8.1.251b11ff.; Philoponus, *De aeternitate mundi contra Proclum* [ed. H. Rabe; Hildesheim: G. Olms, 1963], 145-147). As to Philo's characterization of God's creative act as one of βούλησις (*Opif.* 16), Wolfson comments: "Following Scripture and Plato, Philo conceives the act of creation as an act of will and design (i.e., not a necessary result of God's nature)" (*Philo*, 1.315). This statement is as incorrect for Plato as it is for Philo, for the Demiurge of the *Timaeus* acts in accordance with his unchangeable nature which is good (or more precisely the source of the good), and Philo is here faithfully following his master. Cf. J. Rist, *Eros and Psyche* (Toronto: University of Toronto Press, 1964), 76: "for although the *Demiourgos* may be said to will creation, he does not choose it as one of two alternatives. He simply wills it because it is good; being good means doing good, and the *Demiourgos* is thus 'beyond' choice."

[17] Wolfson, *Philo*, 1:358.

If we consider the order of things according as it depends on any
secondary causes, God can do something outside such order [e.g.,
produce the effects of secondary causes without them]. For he is not
subject to the order of secondary causes, but, on the contrary, this
order is subject to him, as proceeding from him, not by a natural
necessity, but by the choice of his own will; for he could have created
another order of things.

Moreover,

God fixed a certain order in things in such a way that at the same
,time he reserved to himself whatever he intended to do otherwise
than by a particular cause. So when he acts outside this order, he does
not change (*S.T.* 1.105.6).

Philo, however, gives every indication of explaining God's miraculous acts
within the framework of the existing natural order by simply expanding its
parameters. Since our knowledge of the physical world is extremely
limited, as Philo often emphasizes with a gusto that leads him on occasion
to reproduce the Skeptical tropes (τρόποι or "modes") designed to bring
about suspense of judgment (ἐποχή),[18] we easily mistake the biblically
recorded miracles for events in contravention of the laws of nature. This is
clearly indicated by Philo when he writes of the Israelites' incredulity
concerning the ability of God to rescue them from a seemingly endless
sequence of crises:

For after experiencing strange events outside the customary without
number, they should have ceased to be guided by anything that is
specious and plausible (ὤφειλον ὑπὸ μηδενός ἔτι τῶν εὐλόγων καὶ
πιθανῶν ἄγεσθαι) but should have put their trust in him of whose
unfailing truthfulness they had received the clearest proofs (*Mos.*
1.196).

The speciousness of our perceptions that leads to a narrow-minded view of
what is physically possible is expressed again in the following passage:

To think that after witnessing wonders so many and so great, impos-
sibilities no doubt as judged by what to outward appearance is
credible and reasonable (πρὸς μὲν τὰς πιθανὰς καὶ εὐλόγους φαντασίας
ἀδύνατα πραχθῆναι) but easily accomplished by dispensations of

---

[18] *Ebr.* 166-205; *Ios.* 125-143. Philo omits two of the ten tropes of Aenesidemus as they are
stated by Sextus Empiricus (*Pyr.* 1.36-164) and Diogenes Laertius 9.78-89. See H. von
Arnim, "Quellenstudien zu Philo von Alexandria," (*Philologische Untersuchungen* 11; Berlin:
Weidmann, 1888); C. L. Stough, *Greek Scepticism* (Berkeley: University of California Press,
1969), 67-105; E. Bréhier, *Les Idées philosophiques et religieuses de Philon d'Alexandrie* (3d ed.;
Paris: J. Vrin, 1950), 207-225.

God's providence, they not only doubted, but in their incapacity for
learning actually disbelieved (*Mos.* 2.261).[19]

Although Philo does not explicitly invoke the physical principles
involved in the Stoic theory of *pneuma* in order to explain God's ability to
transform the elements at will, he very likely has this doctrine in the back
of his mind.[20] Nevertheless, one cannot help but feel that in expanding the
natural order to encompass the biblical miracles, Philo has strained it to
the breaking point, and has compromised the credibility of his philosophical position. He had, however, before him a striking example of this
kind of intellectual legerdemain in the attempt of the Stoics to incorporate
divination into their philosophical system. Cicero offers a sharp critique of
the Stoic effort to explain the miracles associated with divination:

> Between that divine system of nature whose great and glorious laws
> pervade all space and regulate all motion what possible connection
> can there be with — I shall not say the gall of a chicken, whose
> entrails, some men assert, give very clear indications of the future, but
> — the liver, heart, and lungs of a sacrificial ox? (*Div.* 2.29)

He especially pokes fun at their explanation of how the sacrificer, in his
search for favorable signs, is able to choose the proper victim by means of
the divine power that pervades the entire universe:

> But even more absurd is that other pronouncement of theirs
> which you adopted: "At the moment of sacrifice a change in the
> entrails takes place; something is added or something taken away;
> for all things are obedient to the Divine Will." Upon my word, no
> old woman is credulous enough now to believe such stuff. Do you
> believe that the same bullock, if chosen by one man, will have a liver
> without a head, and if chosen by another will have a liver with a head?
> ... Upon my word, you Stoics surrender the very city of philosophy
> while defending its outworks! For, by your insistence on the truth of
> soothsaying, you utterly overthrow physiology. There is a head to the
> liver and a heart in the entrails, presto! they will vanish the second
> you have sprinkled them with meal and wine! Aye, some God will

---

[19] See the excellent discussion in Bréhier, *Idées philosophiques*, 182-83. Cf. *Mos.* 1.165,
where the miracle is called "a mighty work of nature" (μεγαλούργημα τῆς φύσεως). See D.
G. Delling, "Wunder, Allegorie, Mythus bei Philo von Alexandreia," *Wissenschaftliche
Zeitschrift der Martin Luther Universtät Halle-Wittenberg* 6.5 (1957): 713-40.

[20] For the Stoic theory of *pneuma*, see Sambursky, *Physics of the Stoics* (Westport, Conn.:
Greenwood Press, 1973), 1-48; D. E. Hahm, *The Origins of Stoic Cosmology* (Columbus,
Ohio: Ohio State University Press, 1977), 153-74; and for their own use of it in explaining
the miracles of divination, see Cicero, *Nat. d.* 3.39.92. (On the complete flexibility of
matter, cf. Diels, *Doxographi graeci*, 307, 22). For its use by Wisdom of Solomon in order to
explain the miracle of the Red Sea, see Winston, "The Book of Wisdom's Theory of
Cosmogony," in this volume 59-77; and idem, *Wisdom of Solomon*, 330-32.

you have sprinkled them with meal and wine! Aye, some God will snatch them away! Some invisible power will destroy them or eat them up! Then the creation and destruction of all things are not due to nature, and there are some things which spring from nothing or suddenly become nothing. Was any such statement ever made by any natural philosopher? (*Div.* 2.35-7)

In the light of this Stoic caper,[21] it is no longer surprising that Philo felt free to exhibit the biblical miracles as emphatically as he did, although he occasionally tried to inject a possible explanation for them that coincided with the normal course of nature (the plague of darkness, says Philo, may have been a total eclipse of the sun: *Mos.* 1.123),[22] and attempted to fit the ten plagues into a neat cosmological pattern. Moreover, just as the Stoics believed that the miracles of divination were included among the causes foreordained by Destiny, so Philo must have considered the biblical miracles as part of the complex patterns of an unchanging and eternal Logos, in which past, present, and future are one.[23] If, nevertheless, Philo's exegetical devices are as unconvincing in this matter as those of the Stoics, we should hasten to point out that his procedure seems to have been to

---

[21] It may well be that Cicero is utilizing the exaggerated version of an overzealous defender of the Stoic theory of divination. The Stoic theory was severely attacked by philosophers like Carneades and Diogenianos. Among the Stoics themselves, however, only Panaetius seems to have dissented (Cicero, *Div.* 1.6).

[22] For other examples see Wolfson, *Philo*, 1:350-54. It may be noted that Philo tells the story of Balaam in *Mos.* 1.269-74 without mentioning the incident of his speaking ass, and in *Cher.* 32-35 he completely allegorizes the story. See Delling, "Wunder, Allegorie", 717.

[23] *Deus* 32. For Philo's concept of time, cf. *Fug.* 57; *Ios.* 146; *Leg.* 3.25; *Mut.* 11; *Sacr.* 76; *Mig.* 139; *Ebr.* 48. See J. Whittaker, *God Time Being* (Oslo: Universitetsforlaget, 1971); S. Lauer, "Philo's Concept of Time," *JJS*, 9 (1958) 39:46. For rabbinic views on pre-cosmic times, see E. Urbach, *Hazal*, 186-87. The tendency to incorporate the biblical miracles into the original order of nature is also found in rabbinic literature (*m. Abot* 5.6; *Gen. Rab.* 5.3. See Wolfson, *Philo*, 1:351, n. 24; Urbach, *Hazal*, 95). Cf. Augustine's doctrine of the *semina* implanted into the cosmos at the time of its creation, which produce the miracles (*De Trin.* 3.8; *De Gen. ad Litt.* 6.14; 9.16-18). See R. Grant, *Miracle and Natural Law*, 218ff. Philo, like the rabbis, emphasized the miraculous and truly marvelous character of the natural order itself, in contrast to the unfamiliar events that amaze us with their strange novelty (*Mos.* 1.212-13. Cf. *Sifra*, Shemini 5.52b; Urbach, *Hazal*, 92-93). The obverse of the tendency to incorporate the miraculous into the order of nature, was the attempt of the Occasionalists to incorporate the order of nature into the category of the miraculous. A Jewish version of this notion was Nahmanides' doctrine of "hidden miracles" (in his comment to Exod 6:3), and the astrological version of Abraham b. Ezra. A midway position was the doctrine of Bahya b. Pakuda and Judah Halevi (*Kuzari*, 109), which blends a hidden natural order within that which is manifest in order to regulate all cosmic events in accordance with the biblical doctrine of divine retribution. Even Maimonides, in his *Treatise on Resurrection*, adopts this doctrine. See G. Scholem, *Ursprung und Anfänge der Kabbala* (Berlin: de Gruyter, 1962), 400-01.

speak to his different audiences on various levels of comprehension, a technique that he projected into the biblical narrative itself.[24] In addressing a general audience, for example, he usually sacrifices philosophical rigor to the larger religious need of preserving the integrity of the biblical tradition in the face of the Greek philosophical challenge without appearing to compromise any essentials on either side. It is the nature of such a pedagogical approach that it renders well-nigh impossible any effort to determine with precision which of the two traditions ultimately has the upper hand when irreconcilable differences between them can no longer be adequately suppressed. In the last analysis, it is the subtle inner flow of Philo's general thought that must guide our interpretation of any particular issue that is obscured by the almost deliberate ambiguity projected by so much of his writing.

---

[24] Cf. *Deus* 53ff.; *Somn.* 1.237; *Fragments of Philo Judaeus* (ed. J. R. Harris; Cambridge: Cambridge University Press, 1886), 8; *QG* 2.54. Johann Mosheim, in his long note on Philo in his Latin translation of R. Cudworth's *True Intellectual System of the Universe* (1773), had already suggested that there were two systems in Philo, the popular religion on the one hand and the more sublime and recondite on the other. See T. H. Billings, *The Platonism of Philo Judaeus* (Chicago: University of Chicago Press, 1919), 6-7. For Philo's very frequent resort to mystery terminology in order to represent the secret level in his theological doctrines, see Lilla, *Clement of Alexandria*, 148-49; V. Nikiprowetzky, *Le Commentaire de l'Écriture chez Philon d'Alexandrie* (Leiden: Brill, 1977), 17-28.

CHAPTER NINE

Theodicy and Creation

One of the central concerns of Philo's philosophy is a consistent effort to deflect all imputation of evil from God. The conviction that God cannot be responsible for evil had already constituted one of the two canons of Plato's theology[1] and had been given strong emphasis by Cleanthes in his well-known *Hymn to Zeus* (*SVF* 1. 537).[2] Fortunately for the Philonic enterprise, it was often the case that the philosophical view of the Hellenic side of Philo's training coincided with that of his Jewish heritage. The present theme is another case in point, for, like Philo, the rabbis insisted that God's name is never associated with evil: "'And God called the light, day' (Gen 1:5). R. Eleazar said: the Holy One, blessed be He, does not link his name with evil, but only with good. Thus it is not written here, 'And God called the light day, and the darkness God called night', but 'And the darkness He called night'" (*Gen. Rab.* 3.5 [T-A: 23]). Moreover, we read in *Sifra, Beḥukkotai* 4.1: "'It has been of your own doing' (Mal. 1:9); evil never proceeds from me, and so it is written, 'It is not at the word of the Most High that weal and woe befall'" (Lam 3:38).[3] A similar formulation is found in *Lam. Rab.* 3.38, (Buber 68a): "'It is not at the word of the Most High that weal and woe befall'. R. Eleazar said: From the time that the Holy One, blessed be He declared to Moses, 'See, I have set before you this day life and good, and death and evil' (Deut 30:15), from that point on it is not at the word of the Most High that weal and woe befall. But do not all goods proceed from the Holy One, blessed be He? Rather, evil does not go forth to those who do good, nor good to those who do evil, but evil goes forth to those who do evil, and good to those who do good; evil to those who do evil, as it is written, 'the Lord reward the evil-doer according to his wickedness' (2 Sam 3:39); good to those who do good, as it is written, 'Do good, O Lord, to the good'" (Ps 125:4).

Although the greater part of Philo's discussions of theodicy are to be

---

[1] *Typoi theologias: Rep.* 379AC; cf. *Rep.* 617E; *Tim.* 42D; 69CD.

[2] Cf. Democritus, DK. 68, B. 175: "But the Gods are the givers of all good things, both in the past and now. They are not, however, the givers of things which are bad, harmful or non-beneficial, either in the past or now, but men themselves fall into these through blindness of mind and lack of sense."

[3] I have followed the reading of the Gaon of Vilna.

found in his treatise *On Providence,* an important aspect of this issue appears in a series of passages scattered through his other treatises in which he deals with the difficulty produced by the fact that Gen 1:26 refers to God's decision to create human beings by using the plural verb "let us make". This embarrassment Philo explains away by insisting that it was not proper for God to be made responsible for the irrational aspect of humanity. In *Opif.* 72-75 he points out that while it was most proper for God to make the stars by himself alone, since they are living creatures that are thoroughly rational and insusceptible of evil, and while it was at least not alien to him to make the plants and animals, since they partake neither of virtue nor of vice, it was in one sense proper and in one sense improper for him to make a human being, a mixed being who is capable of both virtue and vice. Scripture, therefore, ascribes humanity's creation to the joint action of God and some of his subordinates, inasmuch as it was necessary that the Father be blameless of evil toward his offspring. Philo appears to be deliberately vague in this passage as to the precise part played by the divine assistants. He does not say whether it was the irrational part of the human soul that is ascribed to them or whether it was simply the irrational aspect of the rational soul. We shall presently explore the source of Philo's ambiguous formulation.

In *Fug.* 68-72, however, Philo clearly indicates that it is the mortal part of the human soul that is fashioned by the Powers, who imitate God's skill when he was forming the immortal part, since God "deemed it right that by the sovereign should be wrought the sovereign faculty in the soul, the subject part being wrought by subjects." Moreover, God also employed the Powers because the soul of a human being is susceptible of both good and evil, and evil had to be assigned to other makers. Thus, when Scripture uses the article and says "God made the human being" (Gen 1:27), it is referring to the real human being, who is absolutely pure Mind, of whom God alone is the Maker. When it omits the article and employs the plural "let us make a human being," it is referring to the interweaving in humanity of a rational and an irrational nature.

On the other hand, in *Conf.* 168-83, Philo says that it was unfitting for God to be the author of the road to vice within the unreasonable soul (τὴν ἐπὶ κακίαν ὁδὸν ἐν ψυχῇ λογικῇ and he therefore delegated the forming of this part to his inferiors (τοῖς μετ᾽ αὐτόν). "For it was necessary to exhibit the voluntary, constituted as a counterbalance to the involuntary, as having been constructed for the completion of the whole" (179). The meaning of this passage seems to be that since it was not proper to attribute the irrational aspect of humanity's rational soul to God's making, Scripture assigned its formation to his subordinates. There appears to be no talk here of the irrational part of the soul. Nonetheless, even in this passage ambiguity is not absent, for had he wished to be absolutely clear, Philo ought to have said that God had delegated to his inferiors not the forming of this "part" (τούτου τοῦ μέρους) of the soul but rather the forming of this "disposition" (διάθεσις) of the soul. As it stands, one can construe his words to imply that it is the irrational part of the soul that constitutes the "road to vice" within the rational soul.

One further passage dealing with the troublesome plural of Gen 1:26 needs to be considered. In *Mut.* 30-32, we are told that God did not form the soul of the bad, since vice is hateful to him, and "in framing the intermediate soul he was not the sole agent, since such a soul would surely admit like wax the different qualities of noble and base." Hence the plural "let us make," "so that according as the wax received the bad or the noble impress it should appear to be the handiwork of others or of him who is the framer of the noble and the good alone." Again we find a certain degree of ambiguity lurking behind Philo's formulation. Since there is no mention of parts of the soul, one could certainly interpret the passage to mean that it is the irrational aspect or state of the rational soul that is attributed to "others" rather than to God. On the other hand, the language is sufficiently vague to allow the reader, if he or she is so inclined, to attribute the evil impress admitted by the rational soul to the outside action of the irrational part of the soul.

There is thus only one passage (*Fug.* 68-72) that explicitly refers to the irrational part of the soul in dealing with the embarrassing plural of Gen 1:26. In another connection however, Philo does assert that though the irrational soul (ἄλογον) was made by God (ὑπὸ θεοῦ) it was not made through his agency (διὰ θεοῦ), but by that of the reasonable power which rules and holds dominion in the soul (*Leg.* 1.41). Here, I believe, we have the key to Philo's true meaning and a likely explanation for the various degrees of ambiguity in three of the four passages that seek to remove the difficulty generated by the plural of Gen 1:26. Philo's charactization of the role of the rational in *Leg.* 1.41 is considerably amplified elsewhere in his writings. In *Post.* 126-27, for example, he points out that it is the ruling faculty that transmits its powers to the organs of sense: "Nobody of sound mind, at any rate, would say that eyes see, but mind by means of eyes, nor that ears hear, but mind by means of ears, nor that nostrils smell, but the ruling faculty by using them. For this reason it is said in Genesis, 'A fountain rose up out of the earth and watered all the face of the earth' (Gen 2:6). For since nature allotted the face to the senses as the choicest part of the whole body, the fountain arising from the ruling faculty, dividing itself in many directions, sends up something like conduits as far as the face and through them it transmits its powers to each of the sense organs" (*Det.* 168; cf. *Opif.* 67, 117). Moreover, although Philo frequently employs the Stoic enumeration of the various parts of the soul, he adapts it to the Platonic framework which makes a fundamental distinction between the rational and irrational parts of the soul. "The living soul", he writes, "puts forth, as it were, from one root two shoots, one of which has been left whole and undivided and is called 'Mind', while the other by a six-fold division is made into seven growths, five those of the senses and two of two other organs, that of utterance and that of generation. All this herd being irrational is compared to cattle, and by nature's law a herd cannot do without a governor" (*Agr.* 30). When Philo, therefore, wished to give an account of the human tendency to vice, he could do so from two different vantage points. He could either emphasize the irrational part of the soul, which provides both the material and the occasion for the vicious actions initiated by a person's reason, or else he could focus his attention on the rational soul which energizes the irrational faculties in the first place and then falls into error when it allows itself to be overcome by irrational sense-perceptions and emotions.

We may therefore conclude that in *Opif.* 72-75, Philo's fundamental concern is with the basic principle that evil is not to be attributed directly to God, and since a human being alone of all creatures is capable of both good and evil, the creation of the human soul must be seen as the result of a partnership between God and his fellow-workers. The question of the precise location of the evil component in the human soul is simply ignored. In *Conf.* 168-83 and *Mut.* 30-32, Philo does refer to the source of the soul's evil but only in the vaguest terms, since his object again is only to absolve the Deity from blame for human evil, and he is not anxious to become involved in this connection with a detailed explanation of the psychic processes that result in vicious action. His vague formulations in these passages do tend nevertheless to concentrate attention on the rational soul itself as the source of vice. Only in *Fug.* 68-72, where he seeks to approach as closely as he can the Platonic treatment of this issue in *Tim.* 69C, does he direct our attention to the mortal, irrational part of the soul as the fountain of human wickedness. It thus appears that Philo generally prefers to emphasize the role of the rational soul in explaining human vice even while adhering to the Platonic distinction between the *alogon* and the *logikon* as separate parts of the soul. It is only when the language of the *Timaeus* exerts an unusually strong influence on his mode of expression that he reverses the emphasis.[4]

---

[4] For a somewhat different interpretation, see D. T. Runia, *Philo of Alexandria and the*

Some writers have claimed that although Philo attributed the creation of either humanity's rational soul (*Opif., Conf., Mut.*) or the irrational part of the soul (*Fug.*) to God's assistants, he could not have ascribed to the latter the creation of a human body. "Nowhere," writes Runia, "does Philo deny that God creates man's body, on which the Biblical text (Gen 2:7) is quite unambiguous."[5] Moreover, "a vital difference between Plato and the Mosaic account as explained by Philo is that in the former the demiurge *delegates* a large part of the creative task (all the mortal genera, including humanity's irrational soul and body) to the "young gods," whereas in the latter God only *calls in assistance* for the limited task of creating man." Now while it is true that only the creation of the human soul involves a partnership between God and his subordinates, a fact reflected in the plural of Gen 1:26, it is also the case that, according to Philo, the creation of the physical universe may not be ascribed directly to God, since "it was not lawful for the happy and blessed One to touch limitless, chaotic matter. Instead he employed his incorporeal powers, truly designated Forms, so that each genus assume its fitting shape" (*Spec.* 1.329). It is thus Philo's view that the creation of all the mortal genera, including the human body, was delegated, as in Plato's *Timaeus,* to the divine Powers. When Scripture, therefore, speaks of the creation of the mortal genera by God (*Opif.* 62-68), this is to be understood in the light of Philo's distinction between what is done by God (ὑπὸ θεοῦ) though not through his agency (διὰ θεοῦ: *Leg.* 1.41). Similarly, when Scripture tells us that God formed man from the dust of the earth (Gen 2:7), Philo would undoubtedly have understood this in the light of the distinction referred to above. Although the reason given by Philo for God's employment of the Powers or Forms in order to create the mortal genera appears not to be the same as that given by Plato, their meaning may not be very far apart. It is Plato's view that what is directly created by the Demiurge must be eternal and "equal to gods", so that the inferior mortal genera, which must come into being only for the completion of the whole are symbolically delegated to the "younger gods." Similarly, it is Philo's view that it is unlawful for God to handle confused primordial matter directly in his creation of the inferior mortal genera, and he therefore symbolically assigns them to the divine Powers of Forms. There is no doubt whatsoever that what the Powers or the "younger gods" do is actually being affected by God or the Demiurge, and that the ascription of certain actions to subordinates is merely meant to subserve

---

Timaeus of Plato (Philosophia Antiqua 44; Leiden: E.J. Brill, 1986), 242-49.
[5] Runia, *Philo of Alexandria*, 210. Cf. B. A. Pearson, "Philo and Gnositcism", in: *ANRW* II. 21.1 (1984): 324.

the special needs of the Platonic cosmological perspective and provide due emphasis to its characteristic evaluation of the various levels of being.[6]

Runia further believes that there is a substantial difference between Plato's defense of God's goodness and that of Philo. "Mortality", he writes, "is certainly an evil, and the creation of mortal beings is a work unworthy of the demiurgic creator. But it is a weak 'structural' evil, quite different from the active 'volitional' evil perpetrated by man which is Philo's concern."[7] The fact is, however, that Plato's concern is identical with that of Philo, for both assert that the human soul, in contrast to that of the stars, is capable of error or volitional evil, and both insist that this kind of mortal soul had to come into being "for the completion of the universe" (*Tim.* 41B-C; *Conf.* 179). It is true that Plato lumps the irrational soul of humanity together with all the mortal genera when delegating their making to the "younger gods," but it is clear from the context that his chief objective is to account for the irrational part of human beings and justify its inclusion in the plan of creation. Had there been no need for the "All to be truly all", the Demiurge would have contented himself with the creation of the immortal genus alone, and being would have been confined to the perfectly rational souls of the stars. As it is, however, the fulness of the model demands "the weaving of the mortal to the immortal." That it is the irrational component of the human creature that constitutes Plato's major concern is demonstrated by the fact that the only mortal creatures whose making is described in detail in the *Timaeus* are human beings.[8]

In sum, Philo appears to be saying that it is the making of the irrational part of the soul that is to be attributed to the divine assistants, for it is that part that constitutes the first source of human vice. Still, in describing the various tendencies within the human soul, he generally prefers to emphasize the primary role played in these psychic processes by reason. This emphasis, however, must not necessarily be interpreted to mean that it is not the irrational part of the soul that Philo assigns to the divine subordinates. There is no reason to doubt that he follows the basic

---

[6] This readily explains the fact that Plato does not consistently apply the distinction between the Demiurge and the "younger gods." See F. M. Cornford, *Plato's Cosmology* (London: Routledge, 1937; repr., New York: Bobbs Merrill, 1957), 280; L. Tarán, "The Creation Myth in Plato's Timaeus", in *Essays in Ancient Greek Philosophy* (ed. J. P. Anton, and G. L. Kustas; Albany: State University of New York, 1971), 381.

[7] Runia, *Philo of Alexandria*, 247.

[8] "Timaeus' task was at the outset defined as 'ending with the birth of mankind.' Even the plants on which man is to feed are not mentioned till far on at 77A. The lower animals are dealt with briefly at the end (91D) and treated only as degraded forms suitable for the reincarnation of men who have lived unwisely" (Cornford, *Plato's Cosmology*, 141-42).

Platonic psychic dichotomy of rational and irrational which locates the source of vice in the irrational pole, but it is equally evident that he seeks profoundly to implicate the rational pole as well and therefore formulates the ascription of vice to the divine co-workers in terms that stress the involvement of the human mind. Moreover, although he does not mention the fashioning of the human body by the divine subordinates in connection with the plural of Gen 1:26, this must be ascribed to the fact that it is only with regard to the making of the soul that a partnership between God and his assistants is required. It is clear, however, from *Spec.* 1.329, that the fashioning of all bodies, including the human body, is ascribed to the divine Powers. The only deviation from Plato in this regard is Philo's apparent ascription of the making of the bodies of the stars (which must be included in the creation of all bodies referred to in *Spec.* 1.329) to the divine Powers rather than to God himself.[9] As for the making of all the mortal genera, Philo is in full accord with Plato in asigning their making to the divine subordinates.[10]

---

[9] I have argued (*Logos and Mystical Theology of Philo of Alexandria*, 33-34) that Philo did not believe that the stars were entirely without body. His view was rather that they were purely rational, lacking any irrational component whatever, but though they had no earthly bodies, they did possess fiery ones.

[10] When in *Opif.* 73 Philo says that it was not unfitting for God to make the stars by himself alone or that the making of the plants and animals was not alien to him, he means only that no partnership was required in their case, but he is in no way denying that their bodies were made by the divine subordinates.

CHAPTER TEN

Freedom and Determinism in
Philo of Alexandria

The much disputed question of free will owes much of its notoriety to the cloud of semantic ambiguities that has enveloped it since it became an issue between competing philosophical schools. When Philo dealt with it, it already had had a checkered career and a distinctive terminology attached to it.[1] Most discussions of Philo's position, however, unfortunately have not taken adequate account of the philosophical matrix out of which his analysis arises and either have misconstrued his intentions or have accused him of contradictions of which he was not guilty. We shall therefore seek to track the relevant Philonic texts within their immediate philosophical context in an effort to extract their true meaning.

Philo's ideal person would be one who most nearly approaches the πρῶτος ἄνθρωπος described by him in *Opif.* 136ff. The latter had a mind unalloyed (ἄκρατος), able to receive sense impressions in their true reality and encased in a body that God moulded out of the purest and most subtly refined material available in order to serve as a "sacred dwelling-place or Temple of the reasonable soul" (137). Such a mind was in complete control of its sense-perceptions and thus guaranteed inner harmony and wholeness to its possessor. No warring dualities disturbed the stillness of this unperturbed being. "But since no created thing is constant," continues Philo, "and mortal things are necessarily liable to changes and reverses, it could not but be that even the first man should experience some ill-fortune. And woman becomes for him the beginning of the blameworthy life (ἀρχὴ τῆς ὑπαιτίου ζωῆς)" (*Opif.* 151).[2] Overcome by desire and pleasure, "the beginning of wrongs and violation of the law," humanity chose "that fleeting and mortal life, which is not life at all, but a period of time full of misery" (*Opif.* 152). Having abandoned the Creator for the

---

[1] For a brief account of the history of this question in Greek philosophy, see Winston "Freedom and Determinism in Greek Philosophy and Jewish Hellenistic Wisdom" *in this volume*, 44-56.

[2] Translations of Philo's works, unless otherwise noted, are from the Colson et al., LCL. For the meaning of ὑπαίτιος here, see M. Harl, "Adam et les deux arbres du paradis," *RSR* 50 (1962): 340.

created, he forfeited his immortality, and became embroiled in the war of
the passions.[3]

Philo proceeds to analyze humanity's present "fallen" moral life and
attempts to lend to it an air of tragic grandeur. Though second best, it is
nevertheless a life far more elevated than that of the lower animals. Endowed with mind, humanity possesses a unique, divine gift that guarantees
his relative preeminence in the scale of being.[4]

> For it is mind alone [writes Philo], which the Father who begat it
> judged worthy of freedom, and loosening the fetters of necessity,
> suffered it to range as it listed, and of that free will (τοῦ ἑκουσίου)
> which is His most peculiar possession and most worthy of His majesty
> gave it such portion as it was capable of receiving (μοῖραν ἣν ἠδύνατο
> δέξασθαι). For the other living creatures in whose souls the mind, the
> element set apart for liberty, has no place, have been committed
> under yoke and bridle to the service of men, as slaves to a master. But
> man, possessed of a spontaneous and self-determined will (ἐθελουρ-
> γοῦ καὶ αὐτοκελεύστου γνώμης λαχών), whose activities for the most
> part rest on deliberate choice, is with reason blamed for what he does
> wrong with intent, praised when he acts rightly of his own will (ἑκών).
> In the others, the plants and animals, no praise is due if they bear
> well, nor blame if they fare ill: for their movements and changes in
> either direction come to them from no deliberate choice or volition
> of their own. But the soul of man alone has received from God the
> faculty of voluntary movement, and in this way especially is made like
> to Him, and thus being liberated, as far as might be (ὡς οἷόν τε ἦν
> ἐλευθερωθεῖσα) from that hard and ruthless mistress, necessity, may
> justly be charged with guilt, in that it does not honor its Liberator.
> And therefore it will rightly pay the inexorable penalty which is meted
> to ungrateful freedmen (*Deus* 47).

---

[3] Cf. *Opif.* 154: "This description is, I think, intended symbolically rather than literally;
for never yet have trees of life or of understanding appeared on earth, nor is it likely that
they will appear hereafter. No, Moses evidently signifies by the pleasaunce the ruling
power of the soul which is full of countless opinions, as it might be of plants; and by the
tree of life he signifies reverence toward God, the greatest of the virtues, by means of
which the soul attains to immortality; while by the tree that is cognizant of good and evil
things he signifies moral prudence, the virtue that occupies the middle position, and
enables us to distinguish things by nature contrary the one to the other." This would seem
to imply that Adam's sin was to abandon his condition of θεοσέβεια, when he enjoyed
"innocence and simplicity of character" (*Opif.* 170) and an automatic inclination for the
good, for the dubious privilege of a painfully responsible choice between good and evil.
See Harl, "Adam," and Richard Baer, *Philo's Use of the Categories Male and Female* (Leiden:
Brill, 1970), 35-38.

[4] Cf. Plotinus, 3.29.30: "In this way man is a noble creation, as far as he can be noble, and
being woven into the All, has a part which is better than that of other living things, of all,
that is, which live on the earth" (cf. Plotinus, *Enn.* 3.1.8; Philo, *Spec.* 3.83; 4.14).

The first thing to be observed is Philo's emphatic insistence on a person's culpability and responsibility for evil actions, thereby explicitly absolving Deity from any share in the latter.[5] The prime motivation of Philo in this passage is thus very similar to that of Plato when he discusses the laws of reincarnation both in the *Timaeus* and in *Resp.* 10.614ff. The dominant motif is there sounded by the oft-quoted phrase: αἰτία ἑλομένου, θεὸς ἀναίτιος (*Resp.* 10.617E; cf. 10.379B).[6] An analysis of the Platonic passages may therefore help considerably in unravelling the meaning of Philo. It has sometimes been assumed that Plato was somehow attempting to reconcile the laws of destiny with the absolute autonomy of human freedom.[7] The fact is, however, that in the very same dialogue in which Plato seeks to clear the gods of blame for the individual soul's destiny (*Tim.* 42D), he asserts that the soul may very well be plagued by disease due to a defective bodily constitution coupled with bad upbringing, and that this could lead to its being overcome by the passions (*Tim.* 86B). In *Leg.* 644D-E, Plato speaks more bluntly of the ultimately determined character of person's moral nature.

> Let us suppose [says the Athenian] that each of us living creatures is an ingenious puppet of the gods, whether contrived by way of a toy of theirs or for some serious purpose — for as to that we know nothing; but this we do know, that these inward affections of ours, like sinews or cords, drag us along and, being opposed to each other, pull one against the other to opposite actions (Bury, LCL).[8]

It should be abundantly clear, then, that all Plato is asserting by insisting that the blame is that of the soul that chooses, is that the moral career of the latter is not a product of fatality, but a result of the participation in the complex process of choice.[9] That this process is itself ultimately

---

[5] Cf. *Deus.* 49; *Opif.* 149: "He had formed in mortal man the natural ability to reason of his own motion (αὐτοκίνητον), so that He himself might have no share in faulty action."

[6] Cf. Plotinus, *Enn.* 3.2.7; *Corpus Hermeticum* 1:52. According to Justin Martyr (1 *Apol.* 44.1-8 [81B-E]), this dictum was taken by Plato directly from Moses.

[7] Amand, for example, writes: "Platon s'évertue donc, comme nous venons de constater, à maintenir dans toute son ampleur l'idée déterministe de l' εἱμαρμένη et en même temps à sauvegarder pleinement la liberté de la vertu humaine" (D. Amand, *Fatalisme et liberté dans l'antiquité grecque* [Louvain: Bibliothèque de l'Université, 1945], 33). Amand's words are actually ambiguous, and if all he really intended was to ascribe to Plato a concept of relative freedom, we should concur with his analysis.

[8] Cf. *Leg.* 732E, 804B; and Philo, *Fug.* 46; *Opif.* 117; *QG* 3.48

[9] This process is clearly described in *Leg.* 733B: "We desire that pleasure should be ours, but pain we neither choose nor desire; and the neutral state we do not desire in place of pleasure, but we do desire it in exchange for pain; and we desire less pain with more pleasure, but we do not desire less pleasure with more pain; and when the two are evenly

determined is part of the thorny problem of necessary evil which Plato seeks to mitigate elsewhere (*Tim.* 48A and 56C; *Leg.* 896-97; *Phaedr.* 247) by pointing to an ineradicable residue of random motion in the cosmos and an inherent ignorance within the human soul.[10] In any case, the attribution of moral blame or responsibility to humans is fully justified, as far as Plato is concerned, as long as a person's soul is not caught in the web of a fatality that would constrain its actions arbitrarily. By participating in the choice process, a human being becomes willy nilly a moral agent. Thus, for Plato, a concept of "relative" free will is quite sufficient to allow for the notion of moral responsibility.[11]

---

balanced, we are unable to state any clear preference" (Bury, LCL; cf. Aristotle, *Cael.* 295b31). For the Socratic paradox that no one voluntarily does what is wrong, and its distinctively Platonic formulation (*Gorg.* 509E; *Leg.* 731C; 860Cff.), see the excellent discussion of Norman Gulley, *The Philosophy of Socrates* (London: Macmillan, 1968), 75-204. Plato's widening of the class of involuntary actions by defining voluntary as that which one "really" desires, i.e., what one rationally desires, involves him only in a semantic dispute with both Socrates and Aristotle, and as Plato himself notes (*Leg.* 864B): ἡμῖν δὲ οὐκ ἐστὶ τὰ νῦν ὀνομάτων περὶ δύσερις λόγος ("we are not now concerned with a semantic dispute").

[10] Cf. H. Cherniss, "The Sources of Evil According to Plato," *Plato: a Collection of Critical Essays* (ed. G. Vlastos; 2 vols.; Garden City: Anchor Books, 1971), 2.244-58. Plato, moreover, indicates (*Tim.* 41B-C) that mortal creatures came into being so that the Heaven be not imperfect, which it would be if it did not contain all the kinds of living being. Cf. Philo, *Conf.* 179; Spinoza, *Ethics* (New York: Hafner, 1953) 1, Appendix, ad fin.: "But to those who ask why God has not created all men in such a manner that they might be controlled by the dictates of reason alone, I give but this answer: because to Him material was not wanting for the creation of everything down to the very lowest grade of perfection; or to speak more properly, because the laws of His nature were so ample that they sufficed for the production of everything which can be conceived by an infinite intellect." Similarly, Jalal al-Din Rumi writes: "Could He not evil make, He would lack skill" (Nicholson, *The Mystics of Islam*, 99).

[11] Plato, however, makes a sharp distinction between ἄγνοια and ἀμαθία. The former designates a lack of ἐπιστήμη, "a kind of emptiness of habit of the soul" (*Resp.* 585b), which can be filled by νοῦς and τροφή (reason and training). The latter, on the other hand, is a condition of fundamental ignorance produced by ἀπαίδευτος τροφή or improper training, and a πονηράν ἕξιν τοῦ σώματος or a faulty habit of body due to a physiological defect. It is a psychic disorder caused by a pathological condition of the body, as, for example, when the seed in the marrow is copious with overflowing moisture, it causes states of frenzy in which one experiences excessive pleasures and pains (e.g., a state of sexual licentiousness) (*Tim.* 866ff.). In short, Plato is referring here to biological drives whose normal intensities have been rendered abnormal by diseased neurophysiological conditions. In the *Sophist* (228ff.) Plato adds that a state of ἀμαθία can be produced by ἀμετρία by which he apparently means a disproportion between the three parts of the soul. In this case, we have an αἶσχος or deformity (rather than a νόσος or disease), i.e., a structural defect in the soul itself. Cf. Philo, *Virt.* 13. (In *Leg.* 731E-732B, he speaks of an excessive love of self as cause of ἀμαθία . Presumably this may be the result of either νόσος or αἶσχος). Dialectic is a useful treatment both for ἄγνοια and ἀμαθία, but

Returning to Philo, it should now be clear that unless an explicit statement of absolute free will can be confidently extracted from the passage
under consideration, the internal logic of Philo's argumentation does not
demand it and is fully compatible with a relative free will concept. Wolfson,
however, has argued that

> when Philo says that God gave to the human mind a portion "of that
> free will which is His most peculiar possession and most worthy of His
> majesty" and that by this gift of free will the human mind "in this
> respect has been made to resemble Him," it is quite evident that by
> man's free will Philo means an absolutely undetermined freedom like
> that enjoyed by God, who by his power to work miracles can upset the
> laws of nature and the laws of causality which He himself has
> established.[12]

The fact is, however, that Philo is only adapting here for his own use a
typically Stoic notion. Epictetus, for example, writes: "But what says Zeus?
'Epictetus, had it been possible I should have made both this paltry body
and this small estate of thine free and unhampered ... Yet since I could not
give thee this, we have given thee a certain portion of ourself, this faculty
of choice and refusal'..." (*Diatr.* 1.1.10).[13] Now the Stoics held a relative
free will theory of the causal type, and all they meant by saying that God
has given us a portion of himself thereby enabling us to make choices is
that (as A. A. Long has neatly put it) "the logos, the causal principle is
inside the individual man as well as being an external force constraining
him ... This is but a fragment of the whole, however, and its powers are

---

is obviously most effective in the former case, least effective in the latter (*Soph.* 228ff.). In
any case, Plato would apply punishment as a deterrent and rewards as positive
reinforcement in all cases that are judged to be curable to some extent (*Leg.* 862D; 934A;
cf. *Prt.* 324B), but when neither dialectic, nor deterrent punishment, nor the rewards of
positive reinforcement prove effective (i.e., incurable conditions), then the only recourse
is execution cf. *Prot.* 325B; *Resp.* 410A; *Pol.* 309A). Cf. Dodds, *The Greeks and the Irrational*,
207-35; J. J. Walsh, *Aristotle's Conception of Moral Weakness* (New York: Columbia University
Press, 1963), 4-59; Long, "Freedom and Determinism", 174; R. Hackforth, "Moral Evil and
Ignorance in Plato's Ethics," *Classical Quarterly* 40 (1946): 118-20; P. W. Gooch, "Vice is
Ignorance: the Interpretation of *Sophista* 226A-231B," *Phoenix* 25 (1971): 124-33; J. Sten-
gel, "Das Problem der Willensfreiheit im Platonismus," *Die Antike* 4 (1928): 293-313; F.
Guglielmino, "Il problema del libero arbitrio nel sistema platonico," *Archivio di Storia della
Filosofia Italiana* 4 (1935): 197-223; A. W. H. Adkins, *Merit and Responsibility* (Oxford:
Clarendon Press, 1960), 302-8; J. C. B. Gosling, *Plato* (London: Routledge and Kegan Paul,
1973), 82-99.
[12] Wolfson, *Philo*, 1:436.
[13] Cf. Epictetus, *Diatr.* 2.8.11 (Oldfather, LCL): "But you are a being of primary
importance; you are a fragment (ἀπόσπασμα) of God; you have within you a part of Him"
(cf. *Her.* 283; *Opif.* 146; *Somn.* 1.34).

naturally weak, so weak that 'following' rather than 'initiating' events is stressed as its proper function."[14] For the Stoics, a human being is not a mechanical link in the causal chain, but an active though subordinate partner of God. It is this that allows them to shift the responsibility for evil from God to humanity. Cleanthes says as much in his famous *Hymn to Zeus*.[15] According to Long,

> Cleanthes is thinking of God as an absolute power, embracing all things and uniting good and evil. Yet evil actions are not planned by God in his identity as one omnipotent ruler. What he does is to unite all things in a harmonious whole. Can we say that evil actions are ones purposed by certain fragments of his logos? They would bear no more resemblance to God as such than does a brick to the house it helps to form.[16]

Philo's meaning, then, is that in so far as a person shares in God's Logos, he shares to some extent in God's freedom. That this is only a relative freedom is actually emphasized by Philo when he says that God gave humanity such a portion of divine freedom "as man was capable of receiving" and that he was liberated "as far as might be." Yet this relative freedom, in Philo's view, is sufficient for placing the onus of moral responsibility on humanity and clearing God from any blame for a person's sins. It is impossible, then, to locate in our Philonic text an explicit statement of absolute free will. For the sake of the argument, however, let us follow up the logical consequences of an absolute free will doctrine and see how

---

[14] A. A. Long, "Freedom and Determinism," 178-79. Long also correctly notes: "In fact, though he is not explicit on the point, Epictetus' freedom of the Logos seems to be subject to the same qualifications as Chrysippus', and for the same reason."

[15] Nothing occurs on the earth apart from you, O God,
nor in the heavenly regions nor on the sea,
except what bad men do in their folly;
and to harmonize what is dissonant; to you the
alien is akin.
And so you have wrought together into one all
things that are good and bad,
So that there arises one eternal 'logos' of all
things ...

The translation is that of A. A. Long in his *Hellenistic Philosophy* (London: Duckworth, 1974), 181. For Greek text, see J. U. Powell, *Collectanea Alexandrina* (Oxford: Clarendon, 1924), 227-31 (*SVF* 1.537). For a detailed discussion, see A. J. Festugière, *La révélation d'Hermès Trismégiste*, 2.310-30.

[16] Long, *Hellenistic Philosophy*. Cf. W. Theiler, "Tacitus und die antike Schicksalslehre," *Phyllobolia für Peter von der Mühll* (Basel: Helbing & Lichtenhahn, 1946), 54-55 (reprinted in W. Theiler, *Forschungen zum Neuplatonismus* [Berlin: de Gruyter, 1966], 46-103). Cf. Epictetus, *Diatr.* 1.12.

these would chime with Philo's philosophical system as a whole. If absolute free will, for Philo, means that a human being's will is completely autonomous and independent of God, then he would be ascribing to God the ability to do something involving a contradiction.[17] It seems, however, highly unlikely that Philo's formula πάντα θεῷ δυνατά would include the logically absurd. For Philo (as later for Saadia),[18] the latter would signify

---

[17] Briefly stated, the contradiction consists in asserting that God, who alone is self-caused, can create a human will whose moral choices are all self-caused. It is therefore equivalent to saying that God can create another God. Maimonides' comment on this was: "We do not attribute to God incapacity because he is unable to corporify his essence or to create someone like him or to create a square whose diagonal is commensurate with its side" (*Guide* 1.75).

[18] At first blush, it would seem that the same Saadia who refused to attribute the logically absurd to God, insisted nevertheless on God's omniscient foreknowledge coupled with a doctrine of absolute free will (*The Book of Beliefs and Opinions* 4.3ff.). Saadia, however, nowhere speaks of an uncaused volitional action and all he seems to claim is that God's foreknowledge of a person's actions does not preclude the choice process. If God had arbitrarily determined a person's actions by bypassing his deliberative process, we could then speak of humanity's acting out of compulsion rather than freely. When Saadia speaks, for example, of those verses that "describe God's work in shaping man's basic nature," and that are "erroneously believed by some to be tantamount to usurping and influencing man's will" (4.6), he is simply denying that there is any divine irruption that interferes with a person's choice process, for, as he puts it, "what God foreknows is the final denouement of man's activity as it turns out after all his planning, anticipations, and delays" (4.4). The problem emerging out of the fact that the ultimate causes underlying a person's deliberative process must themselves also be attributed by an uncompromising monotheist to God, must be subsumed under a different category, i.e., the question of necessary evil. In 4.2, for example, Saadia raises the question, "Why, with all the distinction accorded to man, did he come to have this feeble frame of a body composed of blood and phlegm and two galls." Hence to tie in the question of why God has ultimately constituted humanity as he has with the question of free will would involve for Saadia, as for many other thinkers, a confusion of categories. In Islam, too, the free will doctrine of the Mu'tazilah does not seem to have implied that God is not the ultimate cause of the deliberative process. Their antagonists, indeed, claimed that the Mu'tazilah's position makes humanity the creator *(khaliq)* of human acts, whereas God alone is creator, but the Mu'tazilah themselves tended to avoid the use of the term *khaliq*. (See 'Ali ibn Isma'il al-Ash'ari, *Die dogmatischen Lehren der Anhänger des Islam*, [ed. Hellmut Ritter; Wiesbaden: Franz Steiner, 1963], 228, lines 4-12; 538, line 5-539, line 10). Moreover, even when they did employ this term, they probably used it (as did Al-Jubba'i) in the restricted sense of "one who acts, or from whom acts proceed, according to a previous determination" (see Watt, *Free Will and Predestination in Early Islam*, 84; and M. Schwarz, "'Acquisition' (Kasb) in Early Kalam," *Islamic Philosophy and the Classical Tradition, Essays Presented by his friends and pupils to Richard Walzer on his Seventieth Birthday* [Columbia: University of South Carolina Press, 1972], 355-87). Furthermore, the Mu'tazilah used the verb *yukhali* ("to leave free") and the verbal noun *takhali* ("permission" or "free access"), in the sense of God's leaving humanity free to act, in opposition to the orthodox *yakhula bain* ("interference" or "intervention") in the sense of God's interposing between a person and his actions (see Morris S. Seale, *Muslim Theology* [London: Luzac, 1964]. 34). The Mu'tazilite doctrine

nothing and it would be meaningless to ascribe it to God's omnipotence. Even Origen would exclude from the general principle that all things are possible to God, things that are contrary to reason (παράλογα) or to God's own character (*Cels.* 5.24).[19]

_____

emerges with greater clarity in 'Abd al-Jabbar's (ca. 935-995) analysis of the free will problem in his *Mughni*. Free choice may be said to take place, according to al-Jabbar, when there are conflicting motives or desires. "God can impose on a person the obligation to perform an action only if and when the person 'has free access *(takhliya)* to the action' and is drawn between opposing motives" (M. Schwarz, "Some Notes on the Notion of ilja' in Mu'tazilite Kalam," *Israel Oriental Studies* 2 [1972]: 422, quoting 'Abd al-Jabbar, *Mughni* 11 [eds. Muhammad 'Ali al-Najjar and 'Abd al-Halun al-Najjar; Cairo, 1965], 393, lines 15-16; cf. al-Ash'ari, *Die dogmatischen Lehren* 230, lines 12-13). In short, when faced by two conflicting motives, a person is not constrained inevitably (*la budda*) to follow automatically the dictates of either one. He must first consider, weigh, and deduce the action to be taken. He is like the person upon whom God has bestowed *lutf* or grace (literally, "kindness" or "gentleness") in contrast to one who acts under constraint. The former deserves reward for his action, while the constrained agent deserves none, because the way in which *lutf* induces a person to act is by urging him to think, consider, and deduce (Schwarz, "Some Notes," 427. If in the contest of motives, one nevertheless chooses to follow the motive that results in an action that is in disobedience to God's commandments, it is because that particular motive has proven to be stronger. But in this case, al-Jabbar refuses to say that the action was due to necessitating causes (*al-'ilala l-mujiba*), but rather that it "follows the motive and is produced according to it (*bi-hasbihi*)" (*Mughni* 6 [ed. G.C. Anawati; Cairo, n.d. (ca. 1966)], pt. 2, p. 88). In sum, when the resulting act is a product of a deliberative process rather than the automatic result of constraint, it may be said that the person has "free access to the action" (*Mughni* 6, pt. 1, p. 7, lines 10-13 as quoted by Schwarz, "Some Notes," 423; cf. G. F. Hourani, *Islamic Rationalism: the Ethics of 'Abd al-Jabbar* [Oxford: Clarendon Press, 1971] 81-102). (I am indebted to Prof. Lawrence Berman of Stanford University for directing my attention to the excellent studies in Islam by Prof. Michael Schwarz of the Hebrew University, and to Prof. Schwarz for kindly sending offprints of his articles dealing with the problem of freedom of the will in Islam.) The only analogue in Arabic philosophy to Alexander of Aphrodisias' doctrine of volition as a product of causeless motion seems to be the argument of Thumama b. Ashras (d. 828) "that generated effects have no author at all" (Fakhry, *A History of Islamic Philosophy*, 67-68, citing Muhammad abn 'Abd al-Karim al-Shahrastani, *Book of the Religious and Philosophical Sects* [ed. W.Cureton; London: Society for the Publications of Oriental Texts, 1842], 49; al-Ash 'ari, *Die dogmatischen Lehren*, 407; 'Abd al-Qahir Ibn Tahir al-Baghdadi, *Kitab al-Farq bayna al-Firaq* [Cairo, 1910], 157).

19 See Winston, "Wisdom's Theory of Cosmogony," 197,n. 33 (in this volume pp. 59-77); cf. Philo, *Abr.* 268: "Though he can do all things, he wills only what is best" (cf. *Opif.* 46; *QG* 4.51). In the light of our analysis, it may be noted in passing that Husik's objection that Judah Halevi's exposition of the free will problem (*Kuzari* 5.20ff.) involves a contradiction inasmuch as he "admits that the will is caused by higher causes ending ultimately in the will of God, and yet maintains in the same breath that the will is not determined," misses the mark, since Halevi's free will doctrine (like Saadia's) does not require him to say that a person's will is uncaused. See I. Husik, *A History of Medieval Jewish Philosophy* (Philadelphia: Jewish Publication Society, 1948), 171-73. Cf. S. Pines' excellent analysis of

Moreover, if as Wolfson believes, absolute free will means that, contrary to the laws of nature, the mind by virtue of its mysteriously free will can miraculously override the effects of the warring potencies of two conflicting drives (ὁρμαί), then we shall be ascribing to Philo the use of vacuous terminology.[20] For the term "will" in this context cannot mean (on the assumptions made)[21] either the predominance of the more potent drive in man or some sort of rational process, but remains a mysterious component never identified. But even if we were to accept the existence of this mysterious entity, it would be difficult to ascribe either merit or blame to humanity for its inexplicable (or uncaused) inclinations now towards the good, now towards the evil. It were as if some alien force lodged in our mind made decisions that we could not account for in any rational manner. One could always argue, of course, either that Philo was unaware of these contradictions and difficulties, or that he consciously suppressed

---

Maimonides' position on this issue in his "abu'l-Barakat's Poetics and Metaphysics," *Scripta Hierosolymitana* 6, Studies in Philosophy (Jerusalem, 1960): Excursus, 195-98; N. Samuelson, "The Problem of Free Will in Maimonides, Gersonides, and Aquinas," *CCAR Journal* 17 (1970): 2-20; Al Altman, "The Religion of the Thinkers: Free Will and Predestination in Saadia, Bahya, and Maimonides," *Religion in a Religious Age* (ed. S. D. Goitein; Cambridge, Mass.: Association for Jewish Studies, 1974), 25-51.

[20] Epicurus had already cautioned against the use of κένοι φθόγγοι or words devoid of meaning (*Ep. Herodotum* 1.38; *Sent.* 37; Cicero, *Fin.* 2.48; *Tusc.* 5.26.73). Cf. Aristotle, *Eth. eud.* 1.8.1217b, 22; Cic., *Tusc.* 1.10.21; Arist., *Metaph.* 991a, 20 (κενολογεῖν); Alexander of Aphrodisias, *Fat.* c. 2; Philo, *Spec.* 1.317; *Corpus Hermeticum* 11.5.15; Plotinus, *Enn.* 2.4.11; Thomas Hobbes, *Leviathan* (ed. A. R. Waller; Cambridge: University Press, 1935), pt. 1, 23-25: "And words whereby we conceive nothing but the sound, are those we call *Absurd, Insignificant,* and *Non-sense.* And therefore if a man should talk to me of a *round Quadrangle,* or *accidents of Bread in Cheese,* or *Immateriall Substances,* or of *A free Subject; A free-Will;* or any *Free,* but free from being hindered by opposition, I should not say he were in an Errour; but that his words were without meaning; that is to say, Absurd ... The seventh [cause of absurd conclusions I ascribe] to names that signifie nothing; but are taken up, and learned by rote from the Schooles, as *hypostatical, transubstantiate, consubstantiate, eternal-Now,* and the like canting of Schoolemen." David Hume, *An Inquiry Concerning Human Understanding,* sect. 2, in *English Philosophers of the Seventeenth and Eighteenth Centuries* (Harvard Classics 37; New York: Collier, 1910), 320: "When we entertain, therefore, any suspicion that a philosophical term is employed without any meaning or idea (as is but too frequent), we need but inquire, from what impression is that supposed idea derived? And if it be impossible to assign any, this will serve to confirm our suspicion."

[21] Wolfson (*Philo,* 1.432) writes: "This power with which the human mind was endowed to choose or not to choose refers not only to the choice of good, but also to the choice of evil, even though the mind is by its very nature rational, for, as says Philo, there are in our mind 'voluntary inclinations (ἑκουσίους τροπάς) to what is wrong' (*Det.* 122). The essential rationality of the mind does not preclude the possibility of its acting, by the mere power of its free will, against the dictates of reason."

them, but in the light of the fact that his discussion of the free will problem is not polemical in tone and that he was undoubtedly acquainted with the subtle and detailed discussions of the Stoics and their adversaries, it does not seem likely that this would be the case.

Finally, Philo explicitly teaches that God "knoweth well the different pieces of his own handiwork, even before he has thoroughly chiselled and consummated them, and the faculties which they are to display at a later time, in a word, their deeds and experiences" (*Leg.* 3.88 ; cf. Seneca, *Ben.* 4.32). It is difficult to believe that Philo would be willing to involve himself in such a palpable contradiction (i.e., maintaining at the same time both one's absolute freedom and God's complete foreknowledge of all of a person's future actions), when he had ready to hand a relative free will theory that could serve all his needs and that had probably already been accepted and adapted by some Jewish Hellenistic and rabbinic writings.[22] Still, it would be hazardous in the extreme to draw any conclusions from this kind of argumentation. Much depends on how one reads the central character of Philo's thought. Wolfson sees Philo as essentially a pious Jew who rarely allows philosophic principle to override the self-evident teachings of Scripture, and thus finds in him a paradigm for much that was characteristic of medieval religious philosophy. It is becoming increasingly clear, however (at least to this writer), that there are numerous hints in Philo's writing that indicate an ambivalence in his manner of philosophical exposition that would seem to place him in the ranks of those whose philosophical convictions run considerably deeper than their adhesion to religious dogma.[23] In any case, our main line of argumentation is in no way involved in the larger controversy concerning Philo's philosophical perspective.

Since many interpreters of Philo had taken his concept of freedom in an absolute sense, they were somewhat puzzled by the fragment from the lost fourth book of his *Legum Allegoriae*, which contains the following homily on Deut 30:15 and 19:

> It is a happy thing for the soul to have the power to choose the better of the two choices put forward by the Creator, but it is happier not for the soul to choose, but for the Creator to bring it over to himself and

[22] See Winston, "Freedom and Determinism in Greek Philosophy and Jewish Hellenistic Wisdom" (in this volume pp. 44-56).

[23] See Winston, "Philo's Theory of Cosmogony." Cf. Isaak Heinemann, *Philons griechische und jüdische Bildung* (Breslau: Marcus, 1932), 542-74; Sandmel, *Philo's Place in Judaism,* 1-29; Walther Völker, *Fortschritt und Vollendung bei Philo von Alexandrien* (Leipzig: Hinrichs, 1938), 1-47; H. Thyen, "Die Probleme der neueren Philoforschung," *TRu* N.F. 23 (1955-56): 230-46.

improve it. For, strictly speaking, the human mind does not choose the good through itself, but in accordance with the thoughtfulness of God, since He bestows the fairest things upon the worthy. For two main principles are with the Lawgiver, namely, that on the one hand God does not govern all things as a man and that on the other hand He trains, and educates us as a man (cf. *Somn.* 1.237; *Deus* 53ff.). Accordingly, when he maintains the second principle, namely, that God acts as man, he introduces that which is in our power as the competence to know something, will, choose, and avoid. But when he affirms the first and better principle, namely, that God acts not as man, he ascribes the powers and causes of all things to God, leaving no work for a created being but showing it to be inactive and passive.[24] He explains this when he says in other words that "God has known those who are His and those who are holy and he has brought them near to himself" (Num 16:5). But if selections and rejections are in strictness made by the one cause, why do you advise me, legislator, to choose life or death, as though we were autocrats of our choice?[25] But he would answer: Of such things hear thou a rather elementary explanation, namely, such things are said to those who have not yet been initiated in the great mysteries about the sovereignty and authority of the Uncreated and the exceeding nothingness of the created.[26]

Having committed himself to ascribing an absolute free will doctrine to Philo, Wolfson is constrained virtually to transform the simple meaning of the above fragment.[27] "In the first place," he writes, "the fragment deals

---

[24] Cf. R. Mordechai Joseph Leiner of Izbica (d. 1854; a disciple of R. Menahem Mendel [Morgenstern] of Kotzk [1787-1859]), according to whose view the signal characteristic of the future world is that in it the illusion of free choice will vanish, and that acts will no longer be ascribed to their human agents but to God, their true author. To substantiate his view, he quotes the following passage from *b. Pesah.* 50a: "The future world is unlike our present world, for in our present world I (God) am written as YHWH but am called Adonai, but in the future world, I shall both be written as YHWH and be called YHWH" (*Mei ha-Shiloah* pt. 1:14b). "Know and understand," he writes elsewhere, "that everything you do is from God and save for him, no one may lift hand or foot to do aught, and you should not boast about your actions ... for all the good which you do you may refer to God, but all the evil you must attribute to yourselves" (128a). See Joseph Weiss, "The Religious Determinism of Joseph Mordecai Lerner [sic] of Izbica," in *Yitzhak F. Baer Jubilee Volume* (ed. S. W. Baron et al.; Jerusalem: Historical Society of Israel, 1960), 447-53 (Hebrew).

[25] Cf. Plato, *Leg.* 9.860E (Bury, LCL): "If this is the state of the case, Stranger [i.e., that all bad men are in all respects unwillingly bad], what counsel do you give us in regard to legislating for the Magnesian State? Shall we legislate or shall we not?' 'Legislate by all means,' I shall reply."

[26] *Fragments of Philo Judaeus* (ed. James Rendel Harris; Cambridge: University Press, 1886), 8. (I have quoted the Drummond-Wolfson translation of this fragment, but have made a number of modifications.) For the two principles 'God is as a man, God is not as a man,' cf. *Deus* 60-68.

[27] Drummond observes that this fragment "reduces the belief in free will to a useful

only with man's choice of the good but makes no mention at all of man's choice of evil." This omission, which "cannot be accidental," can be

> accounted for only by the fact that the point which Philo was going to make in this homily was that only the choice of good was caused by God, but not choice of evil ... In the second place, with regard to the choice of good, we may say at the very outset that such sweeping statements in this passage about the "exceeding nothingness of the created" ... and about the unreality of the presentation of the human mind as being "capable of knowing something, and willing, and choosing, and avoiding" do not in themselves indicate that Philo denied of man the freedom to choose good. Even with his belief in absolute human freedom he could make these statements, in view of the fact that the freedom, as he has said in his extant works, is a gift bestowed upon man by God, a portion of his own proper freedom, whereby he is made to resemble God ... Furthermore, God's direct causation of man's choice of good is described as "the thoughtfulness of God, while he bestows the fairest things upon the worthy." This quite obviously implies that man must first do something to render himself worthy of the bestowal upon him by God of the power to choose good, and this must inevitably refer to some act of free will.

Wolfson thus concludes:

> The cumulative impression of all these statements then is that, while a man is able to choose the better, he will not have to rely upon his own power, that is to say, that power of free will with which God has endowed all men, for, if he proves himself worthy, God will aid him in making that choice by bringing him to himself. The direct intervention of God in man's choice of good dealt with in this fragment must therefore be assumed to refer only to some help lent by God to man in the choice of good, when man proves himself worthy of such help.[28]

Now Wolfson's first argument is easily countered when one remembers that it is a basic principle with Philo not to ascribe evil to God, a principle that he shared both with Plato and the Stoics. Our fragment is assessing a person's actions from the perspective of God, and since in that perspective evil does not really exist, its focus can only be on a person's choice of the good. Wolfson's second argument that since humanity's absolute freedom

---

delusion of the less educated." He concludes, however, that "if this passage has been correctly preserved, it stands alone among Philo's utterances, though not without important points of contact with them, and I must be content to leave it without attempting a reconciliation" (James Drummond, *Philo Judaeus* [reprint, Amsterdam: Philo Press, 1969], 1.347, note). E. Goodenough, on the other hand, has correctly understood Philo's intent (see his *The Theology of Justin Martyr* [reprint, Amsterdam: Philo Press, 1968], 229).

[28] Wolfson, *Philo*, 1:442-46 (I have somewhat abbreviated his remarks).

is itself a gift of God, it is proper to speak of his "exceeding nothingness," falls between two stools. For if God's gift is real (or absolute), then humanity's will is truly sovereign and independent and it would then be improper to speak of his nothingness, and if, on the other hand, it is somehow unreal (or relative), then a person does not indeed possess an absolute freedom of the will. Finally, the third argument revolves around the word "worthy," which according to Wolfson, must imply that a person already possesses some portion of free will. As a matter of fact, however, it need imply no such thing. The "worthy" may simply be those whom God in his infinite wisdom has predetermined to be his chosen ones. Ben Sira, for example, writes: "To fear the Lord is the beginning of wisdom, and with the faithful was she created in the womb" (1:14).

More decisive, however, for the interpretation of the fragment from the *Legum Allegoriae*, is that its plain meaning is fully consonant with the rest of Philo's writings and is actually reinforced by them. The theme of humanity's nothingness and utter passivity runs through much of Philo's works.[29] In *Cher.* 77, for example, he writes:

> What deadlier foe to the soul can there be than he who in his vainglory claims to himself that which belongs to God alone? For it belongs to God to act, and this we may not ascribe to any created being. What belongs to the created is to suffer, and he who accepts this from the first, as a necessity inseparable from his lot, will bear with patience what befalls him, however grievous it may be.[30]

---

[29] Those commentators who find an inconsistency in Plato's ethical determinism naturally find the same inconsistency in Philo's. Billings, for example, writes: "Such passages (which ascribe all human activity to God, including moral progress) are in flat contradiction to the group in which man's freedom and responsibility are asserted, but this inconsistency is one that Philo shares with most determinists. It is in Plato ... There is a similar inconsistency in Stoicism" (Thomas H. Billings, *The Platonism of Philo Judaeus* [Chicago: University of Chicago Press, 1919], 71).

[30] Cf. Cleanthes, *SVF* 1.527: "Guide me, O Zeus, and thou Fate, whither I have been appointed by you. For I will follow freely; and if, grown evil, I prove unwilling I shall follow no less." Chrysippus illustrated this as follows: "Just as a dog tied to a cart follows while being pulled, if it is willing to follow, making its own self-determination comply with necessity; yet it will be in all respects subject to compulsion if it is unwilling to follow. So it is too with men" (*SVF* 2.975). Epictetus quotes Chrysippus: "As long as the consequences are unknown to me, I always hold fast to what is better adapted to secure preferred value, for God himself created me with a faculty of choosing them. Yet if I really knew that it was ordained for me now to be ill, I should wish to be ill; for the foot too, if it had a mind, would wish to get muddy" (*SVF* 3.191). Cf. Epictetus, *Diatr.* 2.10; 3.5.8ff.; 4.1.89ff.; 4.7.19ff.; M. Aurelius 5.8; 4.34; 6.39; 3.16; 7.57; 12.1; 4.23: "All that is in tune with thee, O Universe, is in tune with me! Nothing that is in due time for thee is too early or too late for me!" Seneca, *De Providentia* 5.4ff.: "Good men labor, spend, and are spent, and withall willingly. Fortune does not drag them — they follow her, and match her pace. If they had

Philo's language is occasionally almost identical with that of the Stoics when he wishes to emphasize the relative passivity of humankind's role in the cosmos. He writes, for example, in *Cher*. 128: "For we are the instruments (ὄργανα), wielded in varying degrees of force, through which each particular form of action is produced; the Craftsman it is who brings to bear on the material the impact of our forces, whether of soul or body, even He by whom all things are moved." The Stoics similarly say: "The movements of our minds are nothing more than instruments for carrying out determined decisions since it is necessary that they be performed through us by the agency of Fate."[31] More specifically, Philo insists again and again that a person's virtue is not really his own. "It is necessary," he writes in *Leg*. 3.136, "that the soul should not ascribe to itself its toil for virtue, but that it should take it away from itself and refer it to God, confessing that not its own strength or power acquired nobility, but He

---

known how, they would have outstripped her. Here is another spirited utterance which, I remember, I heard that most valiant man, Demetrius, make: 'Immortal gods,' he said, 'I have this one complaint to make against you, that you did not earlier make known your will to me; for I should have reached the sooner that condition in which, after being summoned, I now am. Do you wish to take my children? — it was for you that I fathered them. Do you wish to take some member of my body? — take it; no great thing am I offering you; very soon I shall leave the whole ... What, then, is my trouble? I should have preferred to offer than to relinquish. What was the need to take it by force? You might have had it as a gift. Yet even now you will not take it by force, because nothing can be wrenched away from a man unless he withholds it'" (Basore, LCL). Licht and Flusser correctly point out that both the philosophical determinism of the Stoics and the predestinarian teaching of Qumran paradoxically emphasize the volitional decision of man. Cf. 1QS 9.24: "In all that he does, he should will it freely, and save for God's will he should have no desire." The difference between this and R. Gamaliel's statement in *Aboth* 2.4 ("Do His will as thou wouldst do thine own will, so that He may do thy will as He does His own will. Set aside thy will in the face of His will, so that He may set aside the will of others before thy will"), as Licht has pointed out, is that here (as in the Stoic statements) there is not the slightest intimation of the reward motif. See J. Licht, "The Concept of *Nedabah* in the Dead Sea Scrolls," *Studies in the Dead Sea Scrolls* (ed. Jacob Liver; Jerusalem: Kiryat Sepher, 1957), 7-84 (Hebrew); idem, *The Rule Scroll; a Scroll from the Wilderness of Judaea* (Jerusalem: Bialik, 1965), 192-93 (Hebrew); David Flusser,"The Pharisees and Stoics According to Josephus." *Iyyun* 14-15 (1963-64): 318-29 (Hebrew).

[31] *SVF* 2.943: "Animorum vero nostrorum motus nihil aliud esse, quam ministeria decretorum fatalium, siquidem necesse sit agi per nos agente fato." Cf. *Her*. 120; *Cher*. 64, 71: "But, if you reform and obtain a portion of the wisdom that you need, you will say that all are God's possessions and not yours, your reflections, your knowledge of every kind, your arts, your conclusions, your reasonings on particular questions, your sense-perceptions, in fact the activities of your soul, whether carried on through the senses or without them." Cf. *Leg*. 2.46; 1.48ff. ("when God sows and plants noble qualities in the soul, the mind that says 'I plant' is guilty of impiety"); *Cher*. 40-52; *Leg*. 2.32; *Mos*. 2.147 (sin is congenital to every created being); *Conf*. 125.

who freely bestowed also the love of it." Indeed, in spite of the fact that, according to Philo, God bestowed some of his own freedom on humanity, only God, says Philo elsewhere, is ἑκούσιον in the absolute sense of the word, since our own existence is ruled by necessity (*Somn.* 2.253). Moreover, terms such as αὐτεξούσιος or αὐτοκράτωρ are never used by Philo to designate humanity's freedom, but refer only to God's sovereign power.[32] Again, Philo's constant use of medical figures in describing the various conditions of the soul and his insistence that at a certain stage its diseased state becomes incurable clearly implies a deterministic scheme.[33] For if the soul were endowed with an absolute freedom it should be able to overcome the natural forces attempting to enslave it. Nor does Philo assert in these frequently recurring passages that God has withdrawn our absolute free will in punishment for our previous choices. Finally, the Stoic terminology to which Philo consistently resorts in his definition of the passions (ἄμετρος καὶ πλεονάζουσα ὁρμή: *Spec.* 4.79; cf. 1.305; 1.8), and his description of the diseased or healthy state of the soul in terms equivalent to the Stoic ἀτονία and εὐτονία [34] (*Conf.* 165-166; *Virt.* 13), lead us once again to some sort of ethical determinism.

It would thus appear that the general tone of Philo's ethical thought is evidently deterministic, inasmuch as it seems to be tied to the notion of an all-penetrating divine Logos that reaches into each person's mind, thus converting it into an extension of the divine mind, albeit a very fragmentary one.[35] In the light of this reading of the human psyche, it should be evident that the relative free will doctrine that characterized much of

---

[32] See M. Harl, "Adam", 377. Cf. *Her.* 201.

[33] See, for example, *Post.* 73; *Det.* 178; *Somn.* 2.195; *Abr.* 115; *Ebr.* 140; *Mut.* 144; *Spec.* 1.281, 2.17, 3.11; *Virt.* 4; *Deus* 89; *Spec.* 4.82; *Decal.* 142; *Virt.* 13; Billings, *Platonism*, 93-95; Völker, *Fortschritt*, 47-95, 115-22.

[34] For the Stoic doctrine of ἀτονία, see *SVF* 3.473, 2.531: J. M. Rist, *Stoic Philosophy*, 87-95. *Conf.* 166: "For when the bonds of the soul which held it fast are loosened, there follows the greatest of disasters even to be abandoned by God who has encircled all things with the adamantine chains of His potencies and willed that thus bound tight and fast they should never be unloosed." See Völker, *Fortschritt*, 93; cf. *Sacr.* 81; *Ebr.* 95,122 (here Philo implies that when the τόνος of the soul is loosened, a person can no longer act voluntarily).

[35] See, for example, *Det.* 90: "How, then, was it likely that the mind of man being so small (cf. Aristotle, *EN* 10.7.7), contained in such small bulks as a brain or a heart, should have room for all the vastness of sky and universe, had it not been an inseparable portion of that divine and blessed soul? For no part of that which is divine cuts itself off and becomes separate, but does but extend itself. The mind, then, having obtained a share of the perfection which is in the whole, when it conceives of the universe, reaches out as widely as the bounds of the whole, and undergoes no severance; for its force is expansive (ὁλκός)." Cf. *Gig.* 27; *Leg.* 1.37; *Corpus Hermeticum* 12.1; Plotinus, *Enn.* 5.2.

classical and Hellenistic Greek thought and had already in its Stoic version left its mark on some Jewish Hellenistic and rabbinic writings, was the most natural option for Philo's thought to take. At any rate, we have found nothing in Philo's writings sufficiently explicit to warrant attributing to him an absolute free will doctrine, and much that would seem to contradict it.

CHAPTER ELEVEN

Was Philo a Mystic?

Introduction

Although it is notoriously difficult to define mysticism, most students of the subject agree that it involves a timeless apprehension of the transcendent through a unifying vision that gives bliss or serenity and normally accrues upon a course of self-mastery and contemplation.[1] This minimal description may serve as an adequate criterion for our analysis of Philo's mystical passages, if in addition to the distinction between complete or undifferentiated identity with the transcendent as opposed to mere union with it, we further distinguish between a union with the ultimate itself and one that is limited to only an aspect of it, for we shall soon see that a human's highest union with God, according to Philo, is limited to the Deity's manifestation as Logos. It is thus in a sense similar to the later mystical notion of the contact or conjunction (*ittisal*) of a human's "acquired" intellect with the transcendent 'active' intellect associated with philosophers such as Ibn Bajjah (d. 1138) and Ibn Rushd (1126-98), and derived from Aristotle's famous commentator Alexander of Aphrodisias (fl. early 3rd cen. CE).[2] This is obviously quite different from the Plotinian absorption into the Ineffable One, which is beyond Intellect, and is described in terms of a "touching" (ἀφή, ἐπαφή, θίξις) or "blending" (συγκρίνω) or the converging centers of circles.[3] Since Philo's barring of the way to God's essence is rooted in his concept of the utter divine transcendence, we shall begin our discussion with an analysis of that concept and its sources.

The Divine Transcendence

It has already been noted that the notion of the absolute transcendence of the supreme First Principle goes back to Speusippus, the successor of Plato

---

[1] See *The Encyclopedia of Philosophy*, s.v. "Mysticism, History of."

[2] See Philip Merlan, *Monopsychism, Mysticism, Metaconsciousness* (The Hague: M. Nijhoff, 1963), 14-29.

[3] See Plotinus, *Enn.* 5.3.17; 6.9. 11. Cf. John Rist, *Plotinus, The Road to Reality* (Cambridge: Cambridge University Press, 1967), 213-30.

as head of the Old Academy, according to whom the primary principle of all things is not identical with any of them, but is prior to them and their attendant qualities (frg. 34).[4] It would appear that this principle was already operative to some extent in early Greek philosophy. Simplicius, for example, explains Anaximander's choice of the ἄπειρον as the ἀρχή in the following manner: "It is clear that, having observed the change of the four elements into one another, he did not think fit to make any one of these the material substratum (ὑποκείμενον), but something else beside these."[5] A similar doctrine to that of Speusippus was propounded by some of the Neopythagoreans, and by the Middle Platonist Eudorus of Alexandria (fl. 25 BCE), with their postulation of a supranoetic First Principle above a pair of opposites: the Monad, representing Form, and the Dyad, representing Matter.[6] In the light of this evidence it should be apparent that Philo's prophetic inheritance, which emphasized the incomparability and unnamability of God, had converged in this instance with his philosophical inheritance to lead him to an emphatic doctrine of divine transcendence. It should be equally clear, however, that (pace Wolfson) it was his philosophic commitment that was the decisive element in his sharp distinction between God's existence and his essence, and his insistence on humanity's total inability to cognize the latter, for the use of such categories of thought was completely alien to both biblical and rabbinic tradition. Many scholars, however, have found Philo's utterances on this subject contradictory, and we must therefore examine his doctrine of transcendence in further detail.

Philo explicitly states on numerous occasions that God is absolutely ἄποιος (*Leg.* 3.36; 1.36, 51; 3.206; *Deus* 55-56; *Cher.* 67), and Drummond and Wolfson have shown that not only does this mean that God is without accidental quality, but that it may be taken to imply also indirectly that in

---

[4] P. Lang, *De Speusippi academici scriptis. Accedunt Fragmenta* (Reprografischer Nachdruck der Ausg. Bonn 1911; Hildesheim: Gg Olm, 1965). See Philip Merlan, *From Platonism to Neoplatonism*, 97, 105; H. J. Krämer, *Der Ursprung der Geistmetaphysik* (2d ed.; Amsterdam: Grüner, 1967), 207-18, 351-58; Happ, *Hyle*, 208 41; John Dillon, "The Transcendence of God in Philo" in *Center For Hermeneutical Studies*, Colloquy 16 (Berkeley: The Center for Hermeneutical Studies in Hellenistic and Modern Cullture, 1975).

[5] Diels and Kranz, *Fragmente der Vorsokratiker*, A.9

[6] Simplicius, *in Ph.* 181, 10-30 (Diels). It is possible that Eudorus was influenced by the first Hypothesis of Plato's *Parmenides*. See E. R. Dodds, "The *Parmenides* of Plato and the Origin of the Neo-Platonic 'One,'" *CQ* 22 (1928): 135-42. Moreover, Philo himself may be referring to the aforementioned philosophers in *Somn.* 1.184: "Others maintain that the Uncreated resembles nothing among created things, but so completely transcends them that even the swiftest understanding falls far short of apprehending Him."

God there is no distinction of genus and species, i.e., He is τὸ γενικώτατον, "the most generic" (*Gig.* 52), and since He belongs to no class, we do not know what He is. Moreover, all the predicates that are predicated of God are strictly speaking "properties" (ἰδιότητες), i.e., they are derivative of His essence, but unlike definitions, do not indicate the essence itself, and unlike qualities are not shared by Him with others. Furthermore, since the essence of God is one and single, whatever belongs to it as a property must be one and single, and Philo therefore reduces all the divine properties to one single property, that of acting (*Cher.* 77).[7] In Philo's hierarchical construction of reality the essence of God, though utterly concealed in its primary being, is nevertheless made manifest on two secondary levels: the intelligible universe or Logos, which is God's image (*Somn.* 1.239; *Conf.* 147-48), and the sensible universe, which in turn is an image of that Logos (*Opif.* 25). Thus, though the essence of God as it is in itself remains forever undisclosed, its effects, images, or shadows (or, to use the Plotinian term, traces: *Enn.* 6.7.17) may be perceived. Philo further attempts to delineate the dynamics of the Logos's activity by defining and describing its two constitutive polar principles: Goodness or the Creative Power (ποιητικὴ δύναμις), and Sovereignty (ἐξουσία) or the Regent Power (βασιλικὴ δύναμις).[8] It is not difficult to recognize in these two powers the ἄπειρον and πέρας or the Unlimited and Limit of Plato's *Philebus* (23C-31A), which reappear in Plotinus's two moments in the emergence of Νοῦς, where we find undefined or unlimited Intelligible Matter proceeding from the One and then turning back to its source for definition.[9] Now, the various positive properties attributed to God by Philo may all be subsumed under either of these two polar forces, and are therefore all expressions of the one Logos that constitutes the manifestation of God as thinking-acting (*Prov.* 1.7; *Sacr.* 65; *Mos.* 1.283). However, since God's essence as it is in itself is beyond any possibility of human experience or cognition, including

---

[7] See James Drummond, *Philo Judaeus*, 2:17-34; Wolfson, *Philo*, 2:94-164. Although Philo generally affirms that God is ἀσώματος and ἄποιος, at *Leg.* 3.206 he asserts that we cannot even make negative statements of God. Cf. Albinus, *Epit.* 10.4 (*Albinus épitomé* [ed. P. Louis; Paris: Les Belles lettres, 1945]), where it is indicated that God is οὔτε ποιόν, οὔτε ἄποιον, i.e., He is beyond such categories altogether; and Proclus, *In Parm.* 7.68-76; *Theol. Plat.* 2.10 (109).

[8] *Cher.* 27-28; *Sacr.* 59; *Her.* 166; *Abr.* 124-25; *QE* 2.68; *Fug.* 95.

[9] *Enn.* 2.4.5; 5.4.2; 6.7.17; cf. Proclus, *Inst.* props. 89-92, 159. A similar triadic configuration reappears in the mysticism of the *Zohar*. The *sefirot* of Wisdom and Intelligence represent the Logos, while those of Love and Stern Judgment are its dynamic polar principles, the Unlimited and Limit which in this case are balanced and anchored in the *sefirah* of Compassion. Cf. Philo, *Her.* 166.

the experience of mystic vision, the only attributes which may be applied to God in His supreme state of concealment are those of the *via negativa* (e.g., ἀγένητος, ἀδέκαστος, ἀκατάληπτος, ἀκατανόμαστος, ἀόρατος, ἀπερίγραφος, ἄρρητος, ἀσύγκριτος),[10] or of the *via eminentiae*. A good example of the latter is found at *Praem.* 39-40.[11]

> The Father and Savior, perceiving the sincerity of his [Jacob's] yearning in pity gave power to the penetration of his eyesight and did not grudge to grant him the vision of Himself in so far as it was possible for mortal and created nature to contain it. Yet the vision only showed that He is, not what He is. For this which is better than the good, more venerable than the monad, purer than the unit, cannot be discerned by anyone else; to God alone is it permitted to apprehend God.[12]

Although at the summit, the powers of the Logos may be grasped as constituting an indivisible unity, at lower levels, there are those who cognize the Logos exclusively as the Creative Power, and those beneath them who cognize it as the Regent Power (*Fug.* 94-105; *Abr.* 124-45). Lower still are those who, sunk in the mire of sensible being, are unable to perceive the intelligible realities with any degree of continuity (*Gig.* 20). At each successively lower level of divine knowledge the image of God's essence is increasingly dimmed or veiled.

---

[10] Wolfson has correctly pointed out that though Philo uses many negative descriptions of God, "he does not say outright that, as a result of the unknowability and ineffability of God, He is to be described by negations. Nor does he apply the principle of negation as an interpretation of those predicates in Scripture that are couched in positive form" (*Studies in the History of Philosophy and Religion* [Cambridge: Harvard University Press, 1973], 117). Philo also hints at another way of predicating of God, i.e., the process of κατ' ἀφαίρεσιν, which consists of depriving the object of knowledge of any sensible attribute (*Deus* 55-56; cf. Albinus, *Epit.* 165.14). See also John Whittaker, "Neopythagoreanism and Negative Theology," *SO* 44 (1969): 109-25; Lilla, *Clement of Alexandria*, 221.

[11] Although Philo's *via eminentiae* put God beyond the good, the beautiful, the One, the ἀρχή, knowledge, blessedness, and happiness, we are nowhere told that He is beyond being (like Plato's Good which is ἐπέκεινα τῆς οὐσίας, *Resp.* 6. 509B). It may be inferred, however, from the fact that God alone is ὄντως ὄν, that his being is of an altogether different order from that of all else. This is made explicit by Philo at *Det.* 160: "For among the virtues, that of God really is, actually existing, inasmuch as God alone has veritable being. That is why Moses will say of Him as best he may in human speech, 'I am He that is' [Exod. 3:14, implying that others lesser than He have not being, as being indeed is, but exist in semblance only, and are conventionally said to exist." (Cf. frag. 2 of the anonymous commentator [Porphyry?] on Plato's *Parmenides*.) See Pierre Hadot, *Porphyre et Victorinus*, (2 vols.; Paris: Études augustiniennes, 1968), 1:119, 2:76.

[12] Cf. *Contempl.* 2; *QE* 2.68; *Leg.* 5; *Opif.* 8; Ibn Khaldun, *Muqaddimah*, (trans. Franz Rosenthal; 3 vols.; New York, 1958), 3:97

Rational Mysticism: Faith, Reason, and Intuition

If we are to determine the function of mystic vision in the philosophy of Philo, we must first clarify his views concerning the relationship between faith, reason, and intuition. Wolfson has claimed that Philo sought to diminish philosophy's stature by reducing it to the status of a bondwoman in contrast to the Torah, which is seen as the mistress, and has argued that when Philo represents philosophy as the bondwoman of wisdom, he thereby indicates that she is the bondwoman of the Torah:

> Philo compares the relation of philosophy, in the sense of Greek philosophy, to "wisdom" in the sense of the revealed Law, to the relation of the "encyclical studies" to philosophy, for he says, "just as the encyclical culture is the bondwoman of philosophy, so also is philosophy the bondwoman of wisdom" (*Congr.* 79) ... This subservience of philosophy to wisdom or the Law is explained by him in a passage in which he says that "philosophy teaches the control of the belly and the control of the parts below the belly," but while all these qualities are desirable in themselves, still they "will assume a grander and loftier aspect if practised for the honor and service of God;" for the service and worship of God, as we have seen, constitutes wisdom, and wisdom is the revealed Law embodied in Scripture. When, therefore, Philo speaks of philosophy as being the bondwoman or handmaid of wisdom, he means thereby that it is the bondwoman or handmaid of Scripture (*Philo,* 1:149-50).

The fact is, however, that a distinction between philosophy and wisdom was quite common among many Stoic thinkers according to Seneca's testimony (*Ep.* 89.4-9), and this distinction probably goes back to the Middle Stoa.[13] It is therefore quite evident that when Philo, following in the footsteps of the Stoa, defines philosophy as "devotion to wisdom" (ἐπιτήδευσις σοφίας) and wisdom as "the knowledge of things divine and human and their causes" (*Congr.* 79),[14] and then concludes that just as the ἐγκύκλια are subservient to philosophy, so philosophy is subservient to wisdom, that by wisdom he means philosophy consummated, which in turn is identical in his scheme of things with the Torah, whose laws are in

---

[13] Seneca writes: "One thing is practically settled, that there is some difference between philosophy and wisdom. Nor indeed is it possible that that which is sought and that which seeks are identical." Other Stoics, he continues, "have maintained the two cannot be sundered" (*Ep.* 89.7, 8 [Gummere, LCL]). Cf. Cicero, *Leg.* 1.22: "And what is more godlike ... than reason, which, once it is full grown and brought to perfection, is rightly called wisdom?" (Keyes, LCL).

[14] Cf. Seneca, *Ep.* 89.4; Cicero, *Off.* 2.25; *Tusc.* 4.25.57; *SVF* 2.36; Diels, *Doxographi Graeci,* 273al3; 4 Macc 1:16.

agreement with the eternal principles of nature.[15] Far from subordinating philosophy to Scripture, Philo is rather identifying the Mosaic Law with the summit of philosophical achievement. Thus, for example, Philo can equate Moses "who had attained philosophy's summit" with Moses "who had been divinely instructed in the greater and most essential part of nature's lore" (*Opif.* 8).[16] Wolfson continues his argument by insisting that "the subordination of philosophy to Scripture means to Philo the subordination of reason to faith. This is clearly expressed by him in his comment on the verses "Abraham believed God and it was counted to him for justice," and "not so my servant Moses; he is faithful in all my house." Commenting on these verses, he says that "it is best to have faith in the immediate knowledge given by God through revelation rather than in the result of our reason."[17] The Philonic passage under discussion (*Leg.* 3.228-29), however, is not contrasting reason and faith, but faulty reason with firm, secure knowledge. Philo employs four emphatic adjectives to draw his sharp distinction between "trust in God" on the one hand, and the use of obscure (ἀσαφέσι), empty (κενοῖς), plausible (πιθανοῖς) arguments, or unreliable conjectures (ἀβεβαίοις εἰκασίαις), on the other. Abraham's faith in God is paradigmatic for Philo of the "unswerving and firm assumption" that is attained when the mind has a vision of the First Cause, the truly Existent.[18] The exuberant variety of physical speculations is frequently the butt of Philo's biting critique,[19] when he wishes to contrast the utter uncertainty of human knowledge of reality with the infinite splendor of the divine wisdom which alone is perfect and self-secure. It is not the denigration of philosophic reason and the attempt to escape into the bosom of divine revelation that motivates Philo's skeptical flights (*Cher.* 65, 113; *Her.* 246; *Somn.* 1.21; *Ebr.* 166-205; *Ios.* 125-43; *Migr.* 134-38), but rather his unshakable conviction that our knowledge of the modal or finite

---

[15] See *Mos.* 2.48,181; *Abr.* 16, 60; *Opif.* 143; *Spec* 1 .31, 155; 2.13; 3.46-47,112,137; 4.204; *Decal.* 132; *Migr.* 128; *Virt.* 132, 18; *Plant.* 49; *Ebr.* 34, 142 (cf. *SVF* 3.613); *Prob.* 160; *Det.* 52; *Agr.* 66; *Q.G.* 4.90; *y. Kil.* 1.7; *b. Qidd.* 39a. Cf. Isaac Heinemann, "Die Lehre vom ungeschriebenen Gesetz im jüdischen Schrifttum," *HUCA* 4 (1927): 149-71.

[16] See Heinemann, *Philons griechische und jüdische Bildung,* 475-78. Cf. *Her.* 213, 182, 179, 301; *Opif.* 53-54; *Post.* 102.

[17] *Philo,* 1:151-52.

[18] For πίστις in Greek philosophy, see Lilla, *Clement of Alexandria,* chap. 4; Rist, *Plotinus,* 231 46; Billings, *Platonism of Philo Judaeus,* 72-75. The opposite of πίστις is called by Philo οἴησις, τυφὸς, κενὴ δόξα, ἀφροσύνη, φιλαυτία (*Mut.* 176; *Spec* 1.10; *Somn.* 1.248-66, 2.162, 192; *Her.* 106). It consists in giving to the senses or to the thought based on them that trust which should be bestowed on God alone. Cf. Plato's denunciations of φιλαυτία in *Leg.* 731D-732.

[19] Cf. Epictetus. frg. 1 (Stobaeus, *Ecl.* 2.1.31).

aspect of reality belongs to the contingent and unabiding, whereas our un-mediated intuition of infinite divinity, limited though it be by the inherent finitude of the human mind, is vastly more effective than discursive reason in affording us a glimpse of the eternally and truly real (*Praem.* 28-30). It is only as a consequence of such an intuitive vision that one begins to read Scripture correctly and in accord with its deeper meaning. Wolfson's attempt, therefore, to foist on Philo "the ancillary conception of philo-sophy that prevailed for many centuries in European philosophy" is essentially misguided.[20]

We must now determine the exact nature of this unmediated intuitive vision in whose praise Philo's efforts are so unflagging. In Philo's philo-sophy, the Logos is the Divine Mind, the Idea of Ideas, the first-begotten Son of the Uncreated Father, eldest and chief of the angels, the man or shadow of God, or even the second God, the pattern of all creation and archetype of human reason.[21] The Logos is God immanent, holding toge-ther and administering the entire chain of creation (*Mos.* 2.134; *Her.* 188), and the human mind is but a tiny fragment of this all-pervading Logos:

> How, then, was it likely that the mind of man being so small (cf. Aristotle, *Eth. nic.* 10.88), contained in such small bulks as a brain or a heart, should have room for all the vastness of sky and universe, had it not been an inseparable portion of that divine and blessed soul? For no part of that which is divine cuts itself off and becomes separate, but does extend itself. The mind, then, having obtained a share of the perfection that is in the whole, when it conceives of the universe, reaches out as widely as the bounds of the whole, and undergoes no severance; for its force is expansive (ὁλκός) (*Det.* 90; cf. *Gig.* 27; *Leg.* 1.37; Pseudo-Plato,. *Ax.* 370B).

To the mind as yet uninitiated into the highest mysteries and still unable to apprehend the Existent alone by itself, but only through its actions, God appears as a triad constituted by himself and his two potencies, the Creative and the Regent. To the purified mind, on the other hand, God appears as One (*Abr.* 119-23). Philo thus distinguishes between the mind that apprehends God through his creation, and the mind that elevates itself beyond the physical universe and perceives the Uncreated One through a clear vision. Following in the footsteps of Plato, Aristotle, and the Stoa,[22] he vividly expounds the teleological proof for God's existence:[23]

---

[20] Cf. Isaac Heinemann, "Philo als Vater dèr mittelalterlichen Philosophie?," *TZ* 6 (1950): 99-116.

[21] See *QE* 2.124; *Conf.* 41; *Migr.* 103; *Conf.* 63, 146; *Deus* 31; *Her.* 205; *Fug.* 112; *Mos.* 2.134; Eusebius, *Praep. ev.* 7.13. 1; *Leg.* 3.96.

[22] See Plato, *Leg.* 886A; *Phileb.* 28E; Aristotle, frg. 12a (*The Works of Aristotle* [ed. W. D.

Anyone entering this world, as it were some vast house or city, and beholding the sky circling round and embracing within it all things, and planets and fixed stars without any variation moving in rhythmical harmony and with advantage to the whole ... will surely argue that these have not been wrought without consummate art, but that the Maker of this whole universe was and is God. Those, who thus base their reasoning on what is before their eyes, apprehend God by means of a shadow cast, discerning the Artificer by means of his works. There is, however, a mind more perfect and more thoroughly cleansed, which has undergone initiation into the great mysteries, a mind which gains its knowledge of the First Cause not from created things ... but lifting its eyes above and beyond creation obtains a clear vision (ἔμφασιν ἐναργῆ) of the uncreated One (cf. Post. 167) so as from him to apprehend both himself and his shadow ... The mind of which I speak is Moses who says, "Manifest Thyself to me, let me see Thee that I may know Thee" [Exod. 33:13], for I would not that Thou shouldst be manifested to me by means of heaven or earth or water or air or any created thing at all ... for the reflections in created things are dissolved, but those in the uncreated will continue abiding and sure and eternal ... Bezalel also has God expressly called, but not in like manner. One receives the clear vision of God directly from the First Cause Himself. The other discerns the Artificer, as it were from a shadow (cf. *b. Ber.* 55a), from created things by virtue of inferential reasoning (ἐπιλογισμός) (*Leg.* 3.97-103). [24]

Elsewhere he speaks of those who have apprehended God through his works as advancing from down to up (κάτωθεν ἄνω) by a sort of heavenly ladder[25] and conjecturing (στοχάζομαι) his existence through plausible inference (εἰκότι λογισμῷ):

But those who have had the power to apprehend him through himself without the cooperation of reasoned inference (λογισμός) to lead them to the sight, must be recorded as holy and genuine worshippers and friends of God in very truth. In their company is he who in the Hebrew is called Israel, but in Greek the Godseer who sees not his real nature, for that, as I said, is impossible — but that He is ... As light is seen by light, so is God too his own brightness and is discerned through himself alone without anything cooperating ...

Ross; Oxford: Clarendon, 1908-1952]); Cicero, *Nat. d.* 2.31-39; Epictetus, *Diatr.* 1.6; Ps. Aristotle, *De Mundo* 6; Xenophon, *Mem.* 1.4.2-19; Albinus, *Epit.* chap. 10; Wis 13.1-9; Rom. 2:20.

[23] For Philo's employment of the cosmological proof, see *Post.* 167; *Fug.* 12; *Mut.* 54; *Post.* 28.

[24] cf. *Praem.* 41; *Spec.* 1. 33-35; 3.187; *QG* 2. 34; *Plant.* 26.

[25] Cf. Plato, *Symp.* 211C: ὥσπερ ἐπαναβασμοῖς χρώμενον. For the history of this image in medieval Arabic and Jewish philosophy, see Alexander Altmann, *Studies in Religious Philosophy and Mysticism* (London, 1969), 41-72; also Beracha Zak, "R. Solomon Alkabetz' Attitude Towards Philosophic Studies ," *'Eshel Be'er-Sheva* 1 (1976): 288-306 (Hebrew).

> The seekers for truth are those who envisaged God through God, light through light (*Praem.* 40-46).[26]

From all this it is quite clear that according to Philo, there is in addition to inferential reason, which provides an indirect mode for the apprehension of God, a direct approach requiring no mediation whatsoever. Wolfson, as well as Lewy, have assumed that Philo is here referring to a direct divine revelation that completely bypasses the powers of human reason and is utterly dependent on God's grace, whose illumination flashes into the human psyche from without. Such an interpretation is, in my opinion, very unlikely. Philo does indeed speak elsewhere of prophetic revelation mediated through divine ecstasy, a theory couched by him in the standard language of Greek theories of divination, but there is no mention of ecstasy or the eviction of the mind at the arrival of the divine Spirit (cf. *Her.* 265) in the passages dealing with the direct vision of God. Instead, Philo speaks of a "purified mind" capable of seeing God through Himself.

Having thus eliminated a revelation that bypasses human reason, we have yet to specify the precise nature of Philo's theory concerning the direct approach to God. The latter can be elucidated, however, by the examination of a well known tradition in the history of philosophy that distinguishes between the cosmological and the ontological proofs for the existence of God. Whereas the former is based upon inferential or deductive reasoning, the latter constitutes an analytical truth and its function is to clarify those propositions which are implied by our definitions. It would appear then that, according to Philo, the concept of God's existence is contained within certain definitions of human reason and needs but an inner illumination to reveal it. It is this inner intuitive illumination, constituting a rational process of an analytical type, that is to be identified with the divine revelation taking shape in the human mind and enabling it to have a direct vision of God. In Philo's figurative language, this experience is expressed as follows: "He in his love for mankind, when the soul came into his presence, did not turn away his face, but came forward to meet him and revealed his nature, so far as the beholder's power of sight allowed" (*Abr.* 79-80). Elsewhere he puts it that "the invisible Deity stamped on the invisible soul the impression of itself, to the end that not even the terrestrial region should be without a share in the image of God ... Having been struck in accord with the Pattern, it entertained ideas not now mortal but immortal" (*Det.* 86-87).[27]

---

[26] Cf. *Post.* 167; Plotinus, *Enn.* 5.3.17; 5.5.10; *Apoc. Ab.* 7: "Yet may God reveal himself to us through himself."

[27] Chroust interprets Philo's direct way of knowing God in the light of Sextus Empiri-

Although Philo does not specify the definitions that in his view contained the concept of God's existence, we may surmise that he is undoubtedly thinking of the various definitions of the *arche* out of which all things arise. Diogenes of Apollonia, for example, explained why the various elements of the cosmos could not be really different from one another in their own nature, so that they must all be modifications of one ἀρχή. "This is obvious," he writes, "for if the things now existing in this cosmos — earth, water, air, fire and all the other things which manifestly exist in this cosmos — if one of these was different from another, different, that is, in its own proper nature, and not the same thing changed and altered in many ways, they could in no way mix with one another, nor affect one another for good or ill."[28] One can easily transpose this into Spinozistic terms: The various elements cannot be ἀρχαί or substances, for substances having different attributes have nothing in common with one another (*Eth.* 1.2), whereas the elements interchange and therefore must have something in common. They therefore constitute but one substance modified in different ways. The immediate origin, however, of Philo's second way of knowing God, is undoubtedly to be found in Plato's well-known remarks at the end of *Resp.* 6 to the effect that dialectical reasoning (νόησις) can arrive at the intuition of a First Principle by "treating its assumptions not as absolute beginnings but literally as hypotheses, underpinnings, footings, and springboards so to speak, to enable it to rise to that which requires no assumption and is the starting-point of all, and after attaining to that again taking hold of the first dependencies from it, so to proceed downward to the conclusion, making no use whatever of any object of sense but only of pure ideas moving on through ideas to ideas and ending with ideas" (511BC; cf. 532AB: "When anyone by dialectics

---

cus's statement (*Math.* 1.20-22) that Aristotle used to say (*De Philosophia*, frg. 12a, [Ross]) that men's thoughts of the gods originated from two sources: the personal experience of the soul and the phenomena of the heavens. "It arose from events which concern the soul because of the inspired states of the soul which occur in sleep and because of prophecies." As we have already indicated, however, Philo says nothing of prophetic inspiration when he discusses the direct approach to God. See A.-H. Chroust, "'Mystical Revelation' and 'Rational Theology' in Aristotle's 'On Philosophy'," *Tijdschrift voor Filosofie* 34 (1972): 500-12. Cf. E. Vanderlinden, "Les divers modes de connaissance de Dieu selon Philon d'Alexandrie," *MScRel* 4 (1947): 285-304; Hans Jonas, "The Problem of the Knowledge of God in the Teaching of Philo of Alexandria," in *Commentationes Judaico-Hellenisticae in Memoriam Johannes Lewy* (Jerusalem, 1949), 75-84 (Hebrew); idem, *Gnosis in spätantiker Geist* (3d ed.; FRLANT 33; 2 vols.; Göttingen: Vandenhoeck & Ruprecht, 1966), 2:70-121. According to Vanderlinden (and also Bréhier, *Idées philosophiques*, 197-205), Philo is referring to a direct mystical contact with the Deity, resulting from a deep longing for Him.

[28]   Diels and Kranz, *Fragmente der Vorsokratiker*, B.2; cf. Philo, *QE* 2.88.

attempts through discourse of reason and apart from all perceptions of sense to find his way to the very essence of each thing and does not desist till he apprehends by thought itself the nature of the good in itself, he arrives at the limit of the intelligible"). The exact nature of this upward-downward dialectical path has been much debated, but the most likely interpretation is that it involves a sudden intuition of the First Principle (cf. *Symp.* 210E; *Ep.* 7.341CD) at the end of a series of analyses of various hypotheses, which then permits a downward series of deductions from that Principle.[29] It may be recalled that Spinoza's third kind of knowledge, *scientia intuitiva*, by means of which a person knows God, is similarly independent of sense perception and deductive reasoning.

Finally, according to the testimony of Cicero (*Nat. d.* 2.12), the Stoics taught that God's existence is imprinted in humanity. Among the many proofs that they adduced there are some that appear to have constituted analytical truths. One series of arguments, for example, revolves around the central notion of the world's perfection, which necessarily includes the highest form of reason. "There is nothing else beside the world that has nothing wanting, but is fully equipped and complete and perfect in all its details and parts" (ibid., 2.37). Since "it embraces all things and since nothing exists that is not within it, it is entirely perfect; how then can it fail to possess that which is best?" (2.38).[30] Although the Stoic arguments cited by Cicero are not quite identical with the ontological argument as classically formulated by thinkers such as St. Anselm, Descartes, and Spinoza, we do have at one point a locution that appears to be an incipient form of St. Anselm's famous "aliquid quo nihil maius cogitari potest" (*Proslogion*, chaps. 2 and 3). The Stoics point out that not only does nothing exist that is superior to the world, but nothing superior can even be conceived (*ne cogitari quidem quicquam melius potest*) (2.18).[31] The ontological proof is essentially constituted by the argument that humans possess the notion of that "than which nothing greater can be conceived," or that which necessarily exists, or that "whose essence involves existence," or a being who exists through his own power, or a being of the highest power or perfection. The Stoic arguments referred to above all endeavor to demonstrate that universal nature is clearly an absolutely perfect being and therefore perfectly intelligent or divine. The human mind thus possesses

---

29 See Richard Robinson, *Plato's Earlier Dialectic* (2d ed.; Oxford: Clarendon, 1953), 156-79.

30 Cf. Sextus Empiricus, *Math.* 9.88-91 where a similar argument is ascribed to Cleanthes; and Aristotle, *De Philosophia*, frg. 16 (Ross).

31 Cf. Seneca, *Nat.* 1.Pref. 13: *qua nihil maius cogitari potest*, Cicero, *Nat.d.* 2.46.

the notion of a being of the highest power or perfection, and may thus be said to have the existence of God engraved within.

It is now clear that the direct vision of God is attributed by Philo to the workings of intuitive reason, and in no way serves as a bypass of humanity's rational faculties. Following Plato's lead, however (*Phaedr.* 249CD), Philo repeatedly asserts that this unmediated vision may at times culminate in an experience of mystical union accompanied by a Bacchic frenzy, an ecstatic condition that shakes the soul to its very foundations. As with most mystics, however, he is convinced that this longed-for experience can only come after long and arduous preparations. We must therefore now turn our attention to a description of that psychic state which in Philo's view is a prerequisite for the mystic experience and the ascetic path leading to it.

Ἀπάθεια and Asceticism

Imitating God, who is completely ἀπαθής,[32] the wise person must achieve a state of ἀπάθεια, i.e., he must convert all his πάθη, "diseased or irrational emotions," into εὐπάθειαι, "rational emotions."[33] Thus, for example, the wise person would never experience the morbid emotion of fear, but only the completely rational feeling of caution or wariness, which requires no further moderation or modification. To grief, on the other hand, he would not be subject in any form, experiencing at most a mental sting or minor soul contractions, which are morally neutral and betray not the slightest trace of irrationality. In his state of ἀπάθεια/εὐπάθεια the σοφός, symbolized for Philo by Isaac, acts out of a fixity of disposition, no longer having to struggle to make rational decisions.[34]

In Philo's view, the body is by no means to be neglected, nor is its well-being deliberately to be compromised in any way. Those who needlessly fast or refuse the bath and oil, or are careless about their clothing and lodging, thinking that they are thereby practicing self-control, are to be pitied for their error. They are similar to those counterfeits who never

---

[32] See *Opif.* 8; *Leg.* 3.2, 81, 203; *Cher.* 44, 46, 86; *Sacr.* 101; *Det.* 54-56; *Post.* 4, 28; *Deus* 7, 22, 52, 56; *Plant.* 35.

[33] There were four generic kinds of πάθη: fear (φόβος), lust (ἐπιθυμία), mental pain (λύπη), mental pleasure (ἡδονή). The three εὐπάθειαι (Lat. *constantiae*) were: wish or well-reasoned appetite (βούλησις), caution or well-reasoned avoidance (εὐλάβεια) joy or well-reasoned elation (χαρά) (Cicero, *Tusc.* 4.14; Diogenes Laertius 7.116; Vergil, *Aen.* 6.733). See especially Sandbach's excellent analysis in F. H. Sandbach, *The Stoics* (London: Chatto & Windus, 1975), 59-68.

[34] See *Abr.* 201-4; *Fug.* 166-67; *Somn.* 1.160; *Sobr.* 8; *Congr.* 36; *Det.* 46; *Mut.* 1. For Moses: *Leg.* 3.128-34 , 140-47; *QG* 4.177; *QE* 1.15; *Migr.* 67.

cease making sacrificial and costly votive offerings in their mistaken belief that piety consists in ritual rather than holiness, and thus attempt to flatter One who cannot be flattered and who abhors all counterfeit approaches (*Det.* 19-21). Moreover, it is a false strategy to oppose irrational desires by taking off in the opposite direction and practicing austerities, "for in this way you will rouse your adversary's spirit and stimulate a more dangerous foe to the contest against you" (*Fug.* 25). Better to indulge in the various pursuits after external goods, but to do so with skillful moderation and self-control. "Begin, then," advises Philo, "by getting some exercise and practice in the business of life both private and public; and when by means of the sister virtues, household-management and statesmanship, you have become masters in each domain, enter now, as more than qualified to do so, on your migration to a different and more excellent way of life" (*Fug.* 36-38). As a matter of fact, even the wise person will indulge in heavy drinking, though in the more moderate manner of the ancients rather than in the style of the moderns who drink "till body and soul are unstrung." For "the countenance of wisdom is not scowling and severe, contracted by deep thought and depression of spirit, but on the contrary cheerful and tranquil, full of joy and gladness" (*Plant.* 167-68).[35]

If the body is thus not to be neglected in any way, neither is it to be allowed to become the central focus of human concern or to usurp the higher dignity reserved for the rational element. Pleasure plays an important role in the life of ensouled creatures, but it must be accepted for what it really is and not elevated into a self-validating principle motivating human behavior. Following the teaching of the Stoics, Philo insists that joy, as well as pleasure, has no intrinsic importance, but is purely adventitious, a supervening aftermath or by-product of virtue (*Det.* 124; *Leg.* 3.80).[36] Moreover, although ἡδονή in the sense of agreeable physical feelings is permitted even to the wise person, this is not the case when it denotes that type of mental pleasure which is accounted a pathos by the Stoics, and is the result of a faulty judgment:[37]

---

[35] For the Stoic debate on whether the wise person will get drunk, see Rist, *Stoic Philosophy*, 18-19. In *Contempl.* 73 and *QG* 2.67, however, Philo suggests that the use of wine is superfluous, and in *Agr.* 35; *Mos.* 2.211; and *Legat.* 42, he warns against effeminate music and the frantic excitement brought on by dancers and the scandalous scenes of mimes.

[36] Cf. Arist. *Eth. nic.* 1147b31-33; Diogenes Laertius 7.94, 86; Arius Didymus, in Stob. 2.53.18; Albinus, *Epit.* 32.7 [Louis]; Plato, *Phileb.* 53C.

[37] See Sandbach, *The Stoics*, 62: "If the pleasantness of experience of touch, sight, taste, smell and hearing was thought to be good and important, a pleasure arose that was passionate and to be censured (Cicero, *Tusc.* 4.20), but the agreeable feelings themselves were not condemned by any Stoic, although there was no agreement on their exact status. Cleanthes denied that they were 'in accord with nature' or had any value in life, Arche-

> The serpent pleasure is bad of itself; and therefore it is not found at
> all in a good man, the bad man getting all the harm of it by himself.
> Quite appropriately therefore does God pronounce the curse without
> giving pleasure an opportunity of defending herself, since she has in
> her no seed from which virtue might spring, but is always and
> everywhere guilty and foul (*Leg.* 3. 68).[38]

The body is for Philo, at best, a necessary evil (*Leg.* 3. 72-73), for it is a
corpse, a shell-like growth, "the dwelling place of endless calamities" (*Conf.*
177), wicked by nature and a plotter against the soul (*Leg.* 3.69). It is the
source both of ἄγνοια and ἀμαθία.[39]

> For souls that are free from flesh and body spend their days in the
> theatre of the universe and with a joy that none can hinder see and
> hear things divine, which they have desired with love insatiable. But
> those which bear the burden of the flesh, oppressed by the grievous
> load, cannot look up to the heavens as they revolve, but with necks
> bowed downwards are constrained to stand rooted to the ground like
> four-footed beasts (*Gig.* 29-31).[40]

Philo quotes with approval Heraclitus's saying "we live their death, and are
dead to their life" (*Leg.* 1.108). The soul that loves God will therefore
disrobe itself of the body and its senses (*Ebr.* 69-70), and, devoting itself to
genuine philosophy, will "from first to last study to die to the life in the
body" (*Gig.* 14).[41]

In sum, like any good Platonist, Philo would much prefer to dispense
with material reality and the human body which constitutes an inseparable
part of it. As a philosophical realist, however, he must accept it and, on
occasion, justify its existence within the divine scheme of things. He consequently never loses track of the body's legitimate needs and functions,
though he is keenly aware of its capacity to entrap and entice the higher
self. He believes that most people must wean themselves away from the
physical aspect of things only very gradually and with the expenditure of
much effort and toil, though he is aware of the psychological contamination that may result from too extended an exposure to bodily concerns. He
is convinced, however, that some, though not many, may ultimately

---

demus thought that they were natural but without value, like the hairs in the armpit, while
Panaetius believed some to be natural and others not." See Sextus Empiricus, *Math.* 11.73.
Cf. Eduard Zeller, *Stoics, Epicureans and Sceptics* (rev. ed.; London: Longmans, Green, &
Co., 1880; reprint ed., New York: Russell & Russell, 1962), 237-38.

[38] Cf. *Leg.* 3.107, where ἡδονή is considered the passion par excellence.

[39] *Gig.* 29-30; *Ebr.* 157-63; cf. Plato, *Resp.* 585B; *Tim.* 86B; *Soph.* 228-30

[40] Cf. Plato, *Phaed.* 66B, 81C; *Tim.* 90A; *Plant.* 16-17; *QG* 4.46

[41] Cf. Plato, *Phaed.* 67E, 64A; Philo, *Her.* 292; *Contempl.* 34; *Conf* 106; *Migr.* 9,16, 204; *Deus*
2; *Her.* 239-40; *Fug.* 91, *Leg.* 1.103.

succeed in focusing their minds much of the time on the eternal realities, while yet going through the motions of somatic activity that will have finally faded away into insignificance.

The Mystical Experience

We are now finally prepared to evaluate the mystical passages in Philo. Like most mystics, Philo is convinced that humanity's goal and ultimate bliss lie in the knowledge or vision of God.[42] Indeed, the mere quest is sufficient of itself to give a foretaste of gladness (*Post.* 20).

> The limit of happiness is the presence of God, which completely fills the whole soul with His whole incorporeal and eternal light. And the limit of misery is His passing on the way ... for the soul to be separated from the contemplation of the Existent One is the most complete of evils (*QG* 4.4).

The soul has a natural longing and love for God and is drawn to him by a surpassing beauty:

> When the mind is mastered by the love of the divine, when it strains its powers to reach the inmost shrine [cf. Plotinus, *Enn.* 6.9.11.18], when it puts forth every effort and ardor on its forward march, under the divine impelling force it forgets all else, forgets itself, and fixes its thoughts and memories on him alone whose attendant and servant it is (*Somn.* 2.232).[43]

The first step leading to God is a person's recognition of his own nothingness, which induces him to depart from himself:

> For when Abraham most knew himself, then most did he despair of himself, in order that he might attain to an exact knowledge of him who in reality is. And this is nature's law; he who has thoroughly comprehended himself, thoroughly despairs of himself, having as a step to this ascertained the nothingness in all respects of created being (*Somn.* 1.60).[44]

At *Her.* 69, Philo writes:

> Therefore, my soul, if thou feelest any yearning to inherit the good things of God, leave not only thy land, that is the body, thy kinsfolk, that is the senses, thy father's house, that is speech, but be a fugitive from thyself also and issue forth from thyself.[45]

---

[42] *Decal.* 81; *Det.* 86; *Abr.* 58; *Praem.* 14.
[43] Cf. *Abr.* 170; *Opif.* 71; *Somn.* 1.71, 165; *Leg.* 3.84; *QG* 4.140; *Deus* 138; *Her.* 68; *Post.* 92.
[44] cf. *Somn.* 1.212; *Sacr.* 55
[45] Cf. *Leg.* 1.82; 3.41-42, 47; *Somn.* 2.232.

Having gone out of himself, the devotee is now asked to attach himself completely to God:

> The mind which has been perfectly cleansed and purified, and which renounces all things pertaining to creation, is acquainted with One alone, and knows but One, even the Uncreate, to whom it has drawn nigh, by whom also it has been taken to Himself. For who is at liberty to say, "God Himself is alone to me," save one who has no welcome for aught that comes after Him? And this is the Levite attitude of mind (*Plant.* 64).[46]

This attachment to God involves the realization that it is God alone who acts, and as long as the mind "supposes itself to be the author of anything it is far away from making room for God" (*Leg.* 1.82). In the fragment from the lost fourth book of his *Legum Allegoria*, Philo writes: "But when [Moses] affirms the first and better principle, namely, that God acts not as man, he ascribes the powers and causes of all things to God, leaving no work for a created being but showing it to be inactive and passive." Those uninitiated, however, "in the great mysteries about the sovereignty and authority of the Uncreated and the exceeding nothingness of the created, do not as yet recognize this truth."[47] Moreover, in abandoning body and sense-perception, the mind is now absorbed in a form of intellectual prayer that is wordless and unencumbered by petition:

> [The reasoning faculty must sever and banish from itself the word of utterance] to the end that the word or thought within the mind may be left behind by itself alone, destitute of utterance in audible speech; for when it has been thus left, it will live a life in harmony with such solitude, and will render, with nothing to mar or disturb it, its glad homage to the Sole Existent (*Fug.* 92).[48]

At *Her.* 71, Philo writes:

> Great indeed was [speech's] audacity, that it should attempt the impossible task to use shadows to point me to substances, words to point me to facts. And, amid all its blunders it chattered and gushed about, unable to present with clear expression those distinctions in things which baffled its vague and general vocabulary.

---

[46] Cf. *Leg.* 3.126; *Post.* 12; *Somn.* 1.243, 252.

[47] Harris, *Fragments of Philo Judaeus,* 8; cf. *Cher.* 77,128.

[48] Cf. *Gig.* 52; *Plant.* 126; *Migr.* 12; *Spec.* 1.272; *Ebr.* 94. For the contemplative mode of prayer in Hasidism see Rivka Shatz-Uffenheimer, *Quietistic Elements in Hasidic Thought* (Jerusalem: Magnes Press, Hebrew University, 1968), 22-31, 95-110 (Hebrew).

The mystic vision of God is a timeless experience that carries the soul to the uttermost bounds of the universe and enables it to gaze upon the Divine Logos:

> Those who serve the Existent ascend in their thoughts to the heavenly height, setting before them Moses, the nature beloved of God, to lead them on the way. For then they shall behold the place (Exod. 24:10: εἶδον τὸν τόπον οὗ εἰστήκει ὁ θεός) which in fact is the Logos, where stands God the never changing, never swerving, and also what lies under his feet like "the work of a brick of sapphire, like the form of the firmament of the heaven," even the world of our senses, which he indicates in this mystery (*Conf.* 95-97).[49]

At *Ebr.* 152 we read:

> What else was meant by the words, "I will pour out my soul" (1 Samuel 1:15) but "I will consecrate it all to Him, I will loosen all the chains that bound it tight, which the empty aims and desires of mortal life had fastened upon it; I will send it abroad, extend and diffuse it, so that it shall touch the bounds of the All, and hasten to that most glorious and loveliest of visions — the Vision of the Uncreated"?[50]

Still, the notion of actual union with God appears in only one passage: "He bids them 'cleave to Him' [Deut 30:20], bringing out by the use of this word how constant and continuous and unbroken is the concord and union (ἕνωσις) that comes through making God our own" (*Post.* 12; cf. *Migr.* 132). In the exceptional case of Moses, however, Philo's language occasionally oversteps its usual restraints and not only describes him as having been resolved into the nature of unity (*QE* 2.29), but also as having been "divinized" by ascending to God (2.40; cf. however, *Det.* 161).

The mystic state is further described by Philo as producing tranquility and stability,[51] and it is sometimes indicated that it supervenes suddenly.[52] It is also frequently described as a condition of sober intoxication, which is invariably depicted in a highly spirited and enthusiastic manner. The best known passage is at *Opif.* 70:

> When on soaring wing it has contemplated the atmosphere and all its phases, it is borne yet higher to the ether and the circuit of heaven, and is whirled round with the dances of planets and fixed stars ... And so, carrying its gaze beyond the confines of all substance discernible

---

49 Cf. *Mos.* 1.158; *Post.* 14.
50 Cf. *Det.* 89, where we are told that the contact with the All is ἄχρονος; *Fug.* 169; Plotinus, *Enn.* 5.1.4.
51 *Gig.* 49; *Deus* 12; *Leg.* 1.16; *Abr.* 58; *Post.* 27-28.
52 *Sacr.* 78-79; *Somn.* 1.71; cf. Plato, *Symp.* 210E; *Ep.* 7.341CD.

by sense, it comes to a point at which it reaches out after the intelligible world, and on descrying in that world sights of surpassing lovelines ... it is seized by a sober intoxication, like those filled with Corybantic frenzy ... Wafted by this to the topmost arch of the things perceptible to mind, it seems to be on its way to the Great King himself; but, amid its longing to see him, pure and untempered rays of concentrated light stream forth like a torrent, so that by its gleams the eye of the understanding is dazzled.[53]

Philo occasionally exhibits a tendency to compare the mystic experience to that of prophetic ecstasy. Addressing his own soul, which yearns to inherit the good things of God, he says:

Like persons possessed and corybants, be filled with inspired frenzy, even as the prophets are inspired. For it is the mind which is under the divine afflatus, and no longer in its own keeping, but is stirred to its depths and maddened by heavenward yearning, drawn by the truly existent and pulled upward thereto, with truth to lead the way and remove all obstacles before its feet ... such is the mind, which has this inheritance (*Her.* 69-70).[54]

Finally, like most mystics, Philo is keenly aware of the inability of humanity to maintain a steady vision of the divine and the consequent ebb and flow which characterizes that type of experience:

---

[53] Cf. *Ebr.* 145; *Fug.* 166; *Leg.* 1.82; 3.82; *Prob.* 13; *Fug.* 32; *Mos.* 1.187; *Contempl.* 89. See Hans Lewy, *Sobria Ebrietas* (Giessen: A. Topelmann, 1929). Cf. the expressions *al-sahw al-thani* "the second sobriety," and *sahwu 'l-jam'* "sobriety of union" of the Sufi mystic Ibn 'al-Farid of Cairo (1182-1235). See R. A. Nicholson, *The Idea of Personality in Sufism* (Cambridge: Cambridge University Press, 1923), 19.

[54] Cf. *Spec.* 3.1; *Plant.* 38-39. In *QG* 3.3, Philo writes that "the heavenly singing does not extend or reach as far as the Creator's earth, as do the rays of the sun, because of his providential care for the human race. For it rouses to madness those who hear it, and produces in the soul an indescribable and unrestrained pleasure. It causes them to despise food and drink and to die an untimely death through hunger in their desire for the song. For did not the singing of the Sirens, as Homer says (*Od.* 12. 39-45), so violently summon listeners that they forgot their country, their home, their friends and necessary foods?" (cf. Plato, *Phaedr.* 259 BC; *Contempl.* 35; *Prob.* 8; Hesiod, [*Scut.*] 395; Plutarch, *Quaest. conv.* 9.14.6). With this we may compare the statement of R. Isaac Napaha that the angel of the Lord opened the ears of Sennacherib's troops who were besieging Jerusalem (2 Kings 19:35) and they heard the song of the *Hayyot* or Heavenly Living Creatures, and died (*b. Sanh.* 95b). See Gershom Scholem, *Jewish Gnosticism, Merkabah Mysticism, and Talmudic Tradition* (2d. rev. ed.; New York: Jewish Theological Seminary of America, 1965), 27. R. A. Nicholson (*The Mystics of Islam* [London: G. Bell & Sons, 1914], 63-64) writes: "Hujwiri gives anecdotes of persons who were thrown into ecstasy on hearing a verse of the Koran or a heavenly voice or poetry or music. Many are said to have died from the emotion thus aroused ... Pythagoras and Plato are responsible for another theory, to which the Sufi poets frequently allude, that music awakens in the soul a memory of celestial harmonies heard in a state of preexistence."

But when the inspiration is stayed, and the strong yearning abates, it hastens back from the divine and becomes a man and meets the human interests which lay waiting in the vestibule ready to seize upon it, should it but show its face for a moment from within (*Somn.* 2.233).[55]

In an autobiographical vein, Philo sometimes describes his own personal experiences, and speaks of an inner voice within his soul that is God-possessed and divines where it does not know (*Cher.* 27). At *Migr.* 34-35, he describes such an experience more spaciously:

I feel no shame in recording my own experience, a thing I know from its having happened to me a thousand times. On some occasions, after making up my mind to follow the usual course of writing on philosophical tracts, and knowing definitely the substance of what I was to set down, I have found my understanding incapable of giving birth to a single idea, and have given it up without accomplishing anything ... On other occasions, I have approached my work empty and suddenly became full, the ideas falling like snow from above and being sown invisibly, so that under the influence of the Divine possession, I have been filled with corybantic frenzy and been unconscious of anything, place, persons present, myself, words spoken, lines written. For I obtained language, ideas, an enjoyment of light, keenest vision, pellucid distinction of object, such as might be received through the eyes as the result of clearest showing.[56]

It is significant that Philo has in this passage assimilated the mind's sudden attainment of clear insight to instances of divine possession and corybantic frenzy, thus providing a further indication that the latter terminology was freely applied by him to all extraordinary experiences of intuitive clarity.[57]

It has been pointed out that one possible motive behind Philo's lyrical descriptions of the mystic condition of the soul is his desire to vindicate prophetic inspiration and thereby authenticate Scripture as inspired writing. Some interpreters of Philo have consequently played down the mystical passages and have regarded them not as a reflection of true mystical experience but rather as a combination of poetic flourishes and clever apologetic. An analogy to this would be the well-known use of "mystery" terminology by many Greek philosophers in order to indicate the more esoteric levels of their teachings.[58] Our detailed examination of

---

[55] cf. *Somn.* 1.115-16,150; *QG* 4.29.

[56] Cf. *Leg.* 2. 85.

[57] Cf. R. T. Wallis, "Nous as Experience," in *The Significance of Neoplatonism*, (ed. R. B. Harris; Norfolk, Va.; International Society for Neoplatonic Studies, Old Dominion University; Albany: State University of New York Press, 1976), 133-35.

[58] See Henry Chadwick, "Philo," in *The Cambridge History of Later Greek and Early Medieval Philosophy* (ed. A. H. Armstrong; Cambridge, 1967), 150-54.

Philo's mystical passages, however, has clearly revealed that they contain most of the characteristic earmarks of mystical experience. These may now be briefly summarized as follows: Knowledge of God is humanity's supreme bliss (with the corollary that separation from God is the greatest of evils); the soul's intense yearning for the divine; recognition of humanity's nothingness and the need to go out of oneself; attachment to God; the realization that it is God alone who acts; a preference for contemplative prayer; a timeless union with the All; the serenity that results from the mystic experience; the suddenness with which the vision appears; the notion of sober intoxication; the ecstatic condition of the soul in the mystic state; and finally the ebb and flow of mystical experience. If this evidence is added to the autobiographical remarks quoted above, it becomes abundantly clear that Philo was at least a "mystical theorist" (if not a "practicing mystic")[59] in the very core of his being and that his philosophical writings cannot be adequately understood if this signal fact is in any way obscured.

---

[59] See E. R. Dodds, *Pagan and Christian*, 70. ("Persons who are of the opinion that [mystical] union is possible I shall call 'mystical theorists'; persons who believe that they have themselves experienced it I shall call 'practising mystics': the first class of persons of course includes the second, but not vice versa.")

CHAPTER TWELVE

Sage and Super-Sage in Philo of Alexandria

Philo's portrait of the sage or wise person (σοφός) is essentially identical with that of the Stoics, faithfully echoing the well-known paradoxes that they had applied to him. In *De Sobrietate* 56 he describes the good person as follows:

> He alone is nobly born, for he has enrolled God as his father and has become by adoption his only son, not merely rich, but exceedingly rich, living luxuriously amid good things only, abundant and genuine, unaged by time, ever renewing their prime; not merely of high repute, but glorious, for he reaps the praise that is never counterfeited by flattery, but confirmed by truth; sole king, for he has received from the All-ruler the unchallenged might of universal sovereignty; sole freeman, for he is released from the most troublesome of mistresses, empty opinion, whom, in view of her excessive pride, God the liberator has deposed from her citadel.[1]

Like the Stoic sage, Philo's wise person achieves simplicity or inner unity: "He whose view is concentrated on one object alone, is simple and unmixed and truly smooth" (*Migr.* 153).[2] Plato had already suggested the ideal of the harmonious soul of a person who has

> brought into tune those three parts, like the terms in the proportion of a musical scale, the highest and lowest notes and the mean between them, with all the intermediate intervals. Only when he has linked these parts together in well-tempered harmony and has made himself one man instead of many, will he be ready to go about whatever he may have to do (*Resp.* 443E).[3]

In the same vein Marcus Aurelius chides: "A moment and thou wilt be dead, and not even yet art thou simple nor unperturbed" (4.37). One of the marks of this inner unity is the harmony of words with deeds, as Philo says: "If man succeed, as if handling a lyre, in bringing all the notes of the

---

[1] My translation. For the Stoic description, see *SVF* 3.591, 594, 599. Translations from Philo, Epictetus, Seneca, Plutarch, and Sextus Empiricus, unless otherwise noted, are from the Loeb Classical Library.

[2] Cf. *Plant.* 44–45; *Congr.* 36; *QG* 3.165.

[3] Plato, *Resp.* 443E (F.M. Cornford [trans.], *The Republic of Plato* [Oxford: Oxford University Press, 1945]). Cf. *Leg.* 961D; *Epin.* 992B6.

thing that is good into tune, bringing speech into harmony with intent, and intent with deed, such a one would be considered perfect and of a truly harmonious character" (*Post.* 88).[4] Seneca similarly writes: "Let us say what we feel, and feel what we say; let speech harmonize with life" (*Ep.* 75.4).[5]

Philo's person of perfection is in need of no external authority but always acts spontaneously and unbidden out of his own inner resources (*Leg.* 3.144). Epictetus similarly writes: "This is the position and character of the philosopher: he looks for all his help or harm from himself" (*Ench.* 48; cf. *Diatr.* 1.9.31–32; cf. Seneca *Ep.* 124.23; 9.3). By the same token, the sage alone is free, since his life is regulated by the law of right reason (Philo, *Prob.* 45–46). He stands defiant and triumphant over all the passions, and no one can compel him, since he has come to despise both pain and death (*Prob.* 21, 30). Philo quotes a saying of Zeno: "Sooner will you sink an inflated bladder than compel any virtuous man to do against his will anything that he does not wish" (*Prob.* 97). The sage, Philo says, is "unbowed by fortune's assaults through advance calculations of its onsets, since the heaviest adversities are lightened by anticipation, when the mind no longer finds anything novel in the events and apprehends them but dully as if they were déjà vues and stale" (*Spec.* 2.46). Seneca expresses this view well:

> The wise man comes to everything with the proviso "if nothing happens to prevent it"; therefore we say that he succeeds in everything and nothing happens contrary to his expectation, because he presupposes that something can intervene to prevent his design (*Ben.* 4.37).[6]

In a flight of grandiloquent rhetoric, Seneca describes the wise man's readiness to embrace Fate:

> Secure, he will view the ground gaping open with its framework broken, even though the regions of the dead are uncovered. Without fear he will stand at the edge of that abyss and perhaps he will jump into the place where he will have to fall (*Nat.* 6.32.4).

---

[4] This is an oft-repeated Philonic theme. See *Spec.* 2.52, 138; *Mos.* 1.29; 2.48. 2.130, and frequently. It is already implied in Democritus's *Tritogeneia*, where the goddess's title is explained as an allegorical reference to right reason, right speaking, and right action (Diels and Kranz, *Die Fragmente der Vorsokratiker*, 68.B2).

[5] Cf. *Ep.* 20.2, 24.19; and frequently; M. Aurelius 10.16; Plato, *Resp.* 498E; Iamb. *VP* 176.

[6] Cf. Seneca, *Tranq.* 13.2–3; *Marc.* 9–11; *Polyb.* 11.1; *Ep.* 63.15, 99.32, 107.3–4; Cicero, *Tusc.* 3.24–34 and 52; where the value of *prolēpsis* is represented as Cyrenaic, in opposition to the Epicurean view that it was futile to dwell on evils beforehand. See C.E. Manning, "Seneca's 98th Letter and the Praemeditatio Futuri Mali," *Mnemosyne* 29.3 (1976): 301–4.

Philo's sage is a cosmopolite whose contemplative mind embraces the cosmos. A superb observer of nature and all that it contains, he investigates earth, sea, air, and heavens, roaming in his thoughts with the circuiting celestial spheres (*Spec.* 2.45). His soul is indeed a replica of heaven, containing within itself pure forms of being, ordered movements, harmonious circuits, divine revolutions, beams of virtue utterly starlike and dazzling, vastly exceeding in number the sensible stars (*Her.* 88–89). Haunting the upper atmosphere and closely examining the divine loveliness, such a mind scoffs at earthly things, considering them to be mere child's play (*Mos.* 1.190).

This contemplative ideal of Philo is a mirror image of that of the Stoics. Posidonius declares that the goal for a person is to live in the contemplation of the truth and ordering of all things and in helping to establish this structure in himself so far as possible (F 186 Kidd). "This study of philosophy," says Seneca,

> is not to be postponed until you have leisure; everything else is to be neglected that we may attend to philosophy, for no amount of time is long enough for it. It makes little difference whether you leave philosophy out altogether or study it intermittently; for it does not stay as it was when you dropped it, but, because its continuity has been broken, it goes back to the position in which it was at the beginning, like things which fly apart when they are stretched taut (*Ep.* 72.3).[7]

Elsewhere he writes:

> The mind possesses the full and complete benefit of its human existence only when it spurns all evil, seeks the lofty and the deep, and enters the innermost secrets of nature. Then as the mind wanders among the very stars it delights in laughing at the mosaic floors of the rich and at the whole earth with all its gold. When the mind looks down upon the earth from above, it says to itself: "Is this that pinpoint which is divided by sword and fire among so many nations? How ridiculous are the boundaries of mortals!" (*Nat.* 1. Pref. 6–9).[8]

Philo says that the wise person is the living embodiment of virtue:

> It is a characteristic mark of the learner that he listens to a voice and to words, since by these only is he taught, whereas he who acquires the good through practice, and not through teaching, fixes his attention not on what is said, but on those who say it, and imitates

---

[7] Cf. m. *'Abot* 2.4: "Say not, 'When I have leisure I will study'—perchance thou wilt have no leisure."

[8] Cf. Cicero, *Resp.* 6.16; Pseudo-Aristotle *De Mundo* 391a. See Dodds, *Pagan and Christian in an Age of Anxiety*, 7–10; A.-J. Festugière, *La Révélation d'Hermes Trismégiste* (4 vols.; Paris: Gabalda, 1949–54) 2:449.

their life as shown in the blamelessness of their successive actions. Thus we read in the case of Jacob, when he was sent to marry into his mother's family, "Jacob heard his father and mother, and went to Mesopotamia" (Gen 28.7). "Heard *them*," it says, not their voice or words, for the practicer must be the imitator of a life, not the hearer of words (*Congr.* 69–70).[9]

Seneca similarly advises: "Let us choose, however, from among the living, not men who pour forth their words with the greatest glibness, turning out commonplaces ... not these, I say, but men who teach us by their lives, men who tell us what we ought to do and then prove it by practice" (*Ep.* 52.8).[10]

Philo tells us that the wise person is no common reality, nor is he easily found by his fellow human beings. He loves solitude, not out of misanthropic sentiments, for he is eminently a lover of people, but because of his hatred of vice, which is welcomed by the multitude:

> For this reason he mostly remains cooped up at home and hardly steps out of doors, or else because of the continuous wave of visitors he leaves town and spends his time at an out-of-the-way farm, finding greater pleasure in having as his companions the cream of the human race, whose bodies time has dissolved but the flame of whose virtues has been quickened by the writings they have left behind in prose or verse, by which the soul is naturally improved (*Abr.* 23; cf. *Spec.* 2.44; *QG* 4.74).

The Stoic view appears to be somewhat less pessimistic than that of Philo. Although, as we have already seen, the Stoic sage may be exempt from public affairs since no actual state is ever worthy of him, and Chrysippus (Plutarch, *Moral.* 1043A–B) has described him as unmeddlesome, retiring, and minding his own business, Seneca generally recommends alternation between solitude and society:

> Moreover, we ought to retire into ourselves very often; for intercourse with those of dissimilar natures disturbs our settled calm, and rouses the passions anew, and aggravates any weakness in the mind that has

---

[9] Cf. *QG* 2.49, and Philo's notion of the Patriarchs and Moses as *nomoi empsychoi* or living embodiments of the Law (*Abr.* 3–6, 34, 61, 275–76; *Prob.* 62; *Virt.* 194; *Mos.* 1.162). See also Aristotle, *EN* 1132a22: The ideal judge is, so to speak, justice personified (*dikaion empsychon*). Cf. also the dictum cited by Moses Hayyim Ephraim of Sudylkov: "The zaddik himself is Law and commandment" (*Degel Maḥane Efrayim* 4a; see Urbach, *The Sages*, 438 n. 20 [Hebrew]).

[10] Cf. *Ep.* 45.65–66, where we are told that Posidonius considered it useful to illustrate each particular virtue, calling this science ethology. Its function is the same as that of precept except that instead of simply giving the precepts of virtue, ethology is virtue's embodiment. In *Ep.* 11.8 Seneca quotes Epicurus's motto: "Cherish some man of high character, and keep him ever before your eyes, living as if he were watching you, and ordering all your actions as is he beheld them." See also Plato, *Leg.* 729C.

not been thoroughly healed. Nevertheless the two things must be combined and resorted to alternately—solitude and the crowd. The one will make us long for men, the other for ourselves, and the one will relieve the other; solitude will cure our aversion to the throng, the throng our weariness of solitude (*Tranq.* 17.3; cf. Epictetus, *Ench.* 33.6).

Epictetus, too, is quick to point out that in living alone, the sage follows the example of Zeus, who, when left alone at the World-Conflagration, communes with himself (*Diatr.* 3.13.4–7; cf. Seneca, *Ep.* 9.16).

For all his prowess, Philo says, the wise person will not court unnecessary danger:

> Surely then such men have lost their wits and gone berserk who eagerly display untimely candor, and at times dare to oppose kings and tyrants in words and deeds. They do not perceive that not only do they have their necks under the yoke like cattle, but that they are so bound with their whole bodies and souls, their helpless wives, children, parents, and the extensive kinship and association of friends and relatives ... And therefore they are branded and scourged and mutilated ... These are the wages of untimely candor, which in the view of sensible judges is not candor at all; rather they are the gifts of foolishness, folly and incurable melancholia ... Who, if he sees a storm at its height, a violent head-wind, a roaring hurricane and a surging sea, sets sail and puts out to sea, when he ought to remain in harbor? (*Somn.* 2.83–85).

Seneca makes precisely the same point: "The wise man will never provoke the anger of those in power; nay, he will even turn his course, precisely as he would turn from a storm if he were steering a ship" (*Ep.* 14.7–8; cf. 28.7).

The wise person will sometimes act in a seemingly vicious manner. At times, as Philo points out,

> because of involuntary occurrences he changes to another kind of form, as in a theatre, for the benefit of the spectators ... And the physician who is skilled in worldly matters does foolish things for a time (but) wisely, and unlasciviously and moderately does lecherous things, and bravely does cowardly things, and righteously does unrighteous things. And sometimes he will speak falsehoods, not being a liar, and he will deceive, not being a deceiver, and he will insult, not being an insulter (*QG* 4.204 cf. *Cher.* 15).

Similarly, the Stoic sage, who possesses knowledge of things true, never speaks falsely, even if he says what is false,

> because he does not utter it from an evil but from a cultivated disposition. For just as the doctor who says something false respecting the cure of his patient ... is not lying though he says something false ...

and just as the best commanders, when, as often, they concoct
messages from allied states for the encouragement of the soldiers
under their command, say what is false yet are not liars because they
do not do this with a bad intention—and just as the grammarian,
although when giving an example of a solecism he utters a solecism, is
not guilty of bad grammar ... so also the Sage ... will at times say
something false but will never lie because his mental disposition is not
assenting to what is false (*SVF* 3.132 = Sextus, *Math.* 7.42–44).[11]

Finally, Philo characterizes the sage as divine: "For the self-taught kind is
new and higher than [discursive] reasoning,[12] and truly divine, arising by
no human will or purpose but by a God-inspired frenzy" (*Fug.* 168). More
striking is the reference to Moses in *Quod Omnis Probus Liber Sit* 43:

The legislator of the Jews in a bolder spirit went to a further extreme
and in the practice of his "naked" philosophy, as they call it, ventured
to speak of him who was possessed by love of the divine and
worshiped the Self-Existent only, as having passed from a man into a
god [Exod 7:1],[13] though, indeed, a god to men, not to the different
parts of nature, thus leaving to the father of all the place of King and
God of gods (cf. *QE* 2.40).

The wise person follows God or nature, and his actions are nothing else
than the words of God (*Migr.* 128–30).[14] The Stoic sage is similarly
declared to be godlike (θεῖος) for he has something divine within him"
(Diogenes Laertius 7.119). According to Seneca, he differs from God in
the element of time only; he is God's pupil, his imitator,[15] and true

---

[11] Cf. *SVF* 3.554, 177; and Plato, *Resp.* 389B; Saul Lieberman, *Greek in Jewish Palestine*, 142–43; and A.A. Long, "Language and Thought in Stoicism," *Problems in Stoicism* (ed. A.A. Long; London: University of London, 1987) 98.

[12] *Kreitton logou* may mean, as Esther Starobinsky-Safran suggests (French translation, Les Oeuvres de Philon d'Alexandrie [ed. R. Arnaldez, J. Pouilloux, and G. Mondesert; 35 vols.; Paris: du Cerf, 1961 ff.] 17:229 n.9), "beyond verbal expression."

[13] Cf. *Det.* 161–62: "The wise man is said to be 'god' of the fool, while in reality he is not a god at all, any more than a counterfeit tetradrachma is really a tetradrachma." See the excellent discussion in C. R. Holladay, *Theios Aner in Hellenistic Judaism* (Missoula, Mont.: Scholars Press, 1977) 103–98.

[14] Cf. *Post.* 101–2; Seneca, *Vit. beat.* 15.6: *deum sequere*; *Prov.* 5.6; *Ep.* 90.34; M. Aurelius 3.16.2, 12.27.

[15] Cf. Philo, *Fug.* 63; Epictetus, *Diatr.* 2.13.11–13: "Next we must learn what the gods are like; for whatever their character is discovered to be, the man who is going to please and obey them must endeavor as best he can to resemble them. If the Deity is faithful, he also must be faithful; if free, he also must be free; if beneficent, he also must be beneficent; if high-minded, he also must be high-minded, and so forth; therefore, in every thing he says and does, he must act as an imitator of God;" *Mekilta Shirta* 3, Lauterbach 2.25: "Abba Saul says: O be like Him! Just as He is gracious and merciful so be thou also gracious and merciful" (*b. Šabb.* 113b; *Sota* 14a). See Marmorstein, *Studies in Jewish Theology*, 106–21; Schechter, *Some Aspects of Rabbinic Theology*, 199ff.

offspring (cf. Philo, *Sobr.* 56). It is impossible to injure or benefit the wise person, since that which is divine does not need to be helped, and cannot be hurt, and the wise person is next-door neighbor to the gods and like a god in all save his immortality" (Seneca, *Const.* 8.1–2). Epictetus declares more boldly:

> Let one of you show me the soul of a man who wishes to be of one mind with God, and never again to blame either god or man ... to be free from anger, envy and jealousy—but why use circumlocutions?—a man who has set his heart upon changing from a man into a god, and although he is in this paltry body of death, does none-the-less have his purpose set upon fellowship with Zeus (2.19.26–27).[16]

Occasionally, however, the exuberance of the Stoic description of the wise person transgresses the bounds that restrain Philo's own expression in this matter. According to Plutarch, Chrysippus says in the third book concerning nature:

> As it befits Zeus to glory in himself and in his way of life and to be haughty and, if it must be said, to carry his head high and plume himself and boast, since he lives in a way worth boasting about, so does this befit all good men, since they are in no wise surpassed by Zeus (*Mor.* 1038C).

Seneca goes even further:

> The wise man surveys and scorns all the possessions of others as calmly as does Jupiter, and regards himself with the greater esteem, because, while Jupiter cannot make use of them, he, the wise man, does not wish to do so (*Ep.* 73.14; cf. Philo, *Prov.* 6.6).[17]

The Philonic sage has thus far appeared before us in the guise of the Stoic wise person. In depicting Moses, however, Philo's description transcends the established parameters of Stoic theory. Moses is Philo's supreme paradigm of the sage and is described as superior even to the patriarchs. The seventh from Abraham, he does not, like those before him, haunt the outer court of the Holy Place as one seeking initiation, but as a mystagogue

---

[16] The wise person is said in no way to fall short of the virtue and happiness of Zeus (Plutarch, *Mor.* 1076A). Contrast *Mut.* 49–51, where Philo says that complete virtue is impossible for a human, and *Mut.* 181–85, where he asserts that lifelong virtue is impossible. Cf., however, *QG* 4.92, and *Virt.* 177.

[17] In *Ep.* 120.14, however, Seneca asserts that the perfect person is inferior only to the mind of God, from whom a part flows down even into this heart of a mortal, and in *Ep.* 109, he concedes that the wise person is not all-knowing and will therefore need to communicate with other wise people for the knowledge of certain facts.

has his abode in the sanctuary (*Post.* 173).[18] The highest point of wisdom reached by Abraham is the initial course in Moses' training (*Post.* 174).[19] As prophet and friend of God, he was a partner in God's possessions, so that the entire cosmos was placed in his hands, each of its elements submitting to his sovereignty (*Mos.* 1.55–56). He was named god and king of the whole nation, and entered into the darkness where God was, namely into the unseen, invisible, incorporeal and archetypal essence of existing things. Bringing himself into public view like a picture excellently wrought, he set himself up as a model for those willing to copy it (*Mos.* 1.158).[20]

Although both Isaac and Moses exemplify soul-types that achieve perfect virtue without toil, Moses presumably represents for Philo a higher type than does Isaac, since he is ultimately translated to an even higher station than that of the latter by being placed beside God himself, above genus and species alike (*Sacr.* 8).[21] Isaac thus symbolizes the wise person whose psyche generates only εὐπάθειαι or rational emotions.[22] Moses, on the other hand, would appear to symbolize the god-like person, "given as a loan to earthlings" (i.e., he belongs to that category of rational souls that

---

[18] Cf. Maimonides' famous parable in *Guide of the Perplexed* 3.51: "If you have understood the natural things, you must have entered the habitation and are walking in the ante-chambers. If, however, you have achieved perfection in the natural things and have understood divine science, you have entered in the ruler's place into the inner court and are with him in one habitation."

[19] This is reminiscent of the axiom cited by the thirteenth century Kabbalist R. Isaac of Acre in the name of R. Moses of Burgos: "the standing place of their [the philosophers'] heads, is the place of our feet" (see Gershom Scholem, *The Kabbalah in Gerona* [ed. Joseph Ben-Shlomo; Jerusalem: Hebrew University, 1964] 112 [Hebrew]. In *Deus* 109–10, Philo says that Noah represents only a copy of the supreme wisdom shown in Moses, and that God grants grace to Noah only via his powers, whereas to Moses he does so directly.

[20] Moses' mystic vision of intelligible reality is, as Holladay (*Theios Aner*, 126) has suggested, in line with the Platonic notion of the ideal philosopher-king who alone has grasped the Idea of the Good and is therefore uniquely qualified to govern the ideal state.

[21] See also *Ebr.* 94, where Moses is ranked above Isaac.

[22] For the Stoic theory of *pathē* and *eupatheiai*, see Sandbach, *The Stoics*, 59–63; Pohlenz, *Die Stoa*, 151–58; David Winston, "Philo's Ethical Theory," *Aufstieg und Niedergang der römischen Welt II: 21.1* (Berlin: de Gruyter, 1984), 400–405. The one difference between Isaac and the Stoic sage is that Isaac, like Moses, achieves this level without toil, being *automathēs* or self-taught (i.e. taught directly by God; cf. *Od.* 22.347), whereas the Stoic sage has had to struggle to attain it. This apparent difference, however, is probably not very significant, since Seneca would say that some are so blessed with natural endowments (*euphyia*) that they seemed to have attained wisdom virtually without effort (*Ep.* 95.36). Philo's intent is undoubtedly the same. Isaac and Moses both require training, but their natural *euphyia* is such that their acquisition of wisdom is virtually automatic. As Philo notes with regard to Moses: "His happy natural gifts anticipated his teachers' instruction, so that it seemed to be a case of recollection rather than of learning, and he himself further devised conundrums for them" (*Mos.* 1.21–22).

ordinarily never leave the supernal spheres for embodiment below), who has achieved an absolute state of ἀπάθεια or absence of passion and is no longer affected in any way by human feelings, living as it were in the disembodied realm of pure νοῦς. In *Legum Allegoriae* 3.129, Philo says that Aaron, who is inferior to Moses, being only a προκόπτων or one who is making gradual moral progress, merely curbs and controls the spirited element, thus practicing μετριοπάθεια, moderation of passion, whereas Moses cut it out entirely, thus achieving complete ἀπάθεια. In *De Migratione Abrahami* 67, however, it is stated more specifically that Moses purges every form of desire, and completely removes the warlike *thymos*, "so that the better portion of the soul that is left, the rational element, may employ its truly free and noble-minded impulses towards all things beautiful, with nothing tugging at it any longer and diverting it." In this passage Philo is clearly employing the Platonic tripartite division of the soul, so that Moses' excision (ἐκτέτμηται of ἐπιθυμία and θυμός signifies his excision of all lower desires and the entire range of spirited feelings, with the result that his λογιστικόν or reason operates in a sort of emotional vacuum. Moses therefore appears to consist solely of body and rational soul, his bodily sensations producing none of the lower impulses in his single-tiered psyche to which his reason must give or withhold assent.

Philo has thus provided us with the extraordinary phenomenon of a super-sage,[23] whose perfected reason does not need to generate rational impulses, but simply computes its body's true needs and proceeds to satisfy them in the only way it knows how, which is with perfect rationality. Moses' mind thus lives in lower impulse-free conjunction with his body, and with the sole exception of joy (χαρά), is unaccompanied by the ordinary sage's rational emotions. The Mosaic mind is accordingly the closest possible approximation to the divine mind, since neither of them is characterized by the usual rational emotions. As I have indicated elsewhere,[24] it is very

---

[23] It is no wonder, then, that in *Mos.* 1.27–29, Philo attributes the following sentiments to Moses' contemporaries: "Naturally, then, his disciples and everyone else were astonished, struck with amazement as at a novel spectacle, and investigated the nature of the mind which dwelt enshrined like an image in his body, whether it was human or divine or a blend of both, since it contained nothing resembling the multitude, transcending them and exalted to a more splendid height." Cf. Aristotle, *On the Pythagoreans*: "The following division was preserved by the Pythagoreans as one of their greatest secrets—of rational living creatures, some are gods, some men, and some beings like Pythagoras" (F 192R³; trans. Barnes, *The Complete Works of Aristotle*, 2441). Cf. Iamblichus *VP*. "... whether he [Pythagoras] was a god, a daemon, or a divine man." See Louis Delatte, *Études sur la littérature pythagoricienne* (Paris: Librairie Ancienne Honoré, Édouard Champion; 1915), 120; E.R. Goodenough, *The Politics of Philo Judaeus* (repr. Hildesheim: Olms, 1967), 98.

[24] See my article, "Philo's Conception of the Divine Nature," *Neoplatonism and Jewish*

likely that the only rational emotion Philo allows God is joy, provided it is applied to him analogically, inasmuch as the divine joy differs from that of the sage or wise person in its not involving any elation. Here, at last, the Mosaic mind falls short of the Divine, since unlike the latter's eternal and elationless joy, that of Moses is constituted by the expansion of his psychic pneuma upon his arrival at maturity and wisdom.

Further corroboration for our interpretation of Moses' unique status may perhaps be found in *De Gigantibus* 55, where it is said that Moses, unlike others, "has ever the divine spirit at his side leading him in every right way." Moreover, in *De Vita Mosis* 2.192, he is called "holiest of all men yet born," and in *De virtutibus* 177, it is hinted that he was sinless, as only a divine person could possibly be.[25] Philo clearly did not regard the Patriarchs as sinless (*Abr.* 6), and in *De Mutatione Nominum* 50, he asserts that the "complete acquisition of the virtues is impossible for man as we know him."[26] Finally, Holladay[27] has suggested that when Philo writes of the prophetic mind of Moses, he means that Moses' mind in its generic sense, including both the irrational and rational parts of the soul [28] becomes in prophetic experience completely rational: "When it becomes divinely inspired and filled with God, it becomes like the monad, not being at all mixed with any of those things associated with duality ... so that such men become kin to God and truly divine" (*QE* 2.29). Since according to Philo Moses' prophetic state was virtually continuous, inasmuch as the divine spirit was ever with him, he must have had no irrational component in his soul. If my interpretation of the evidence is correct, it becomes immediately evident that Philo is here continuing his game of "one-upmanship"[29] by adding to his insistence that Moses was the Father of Greek Philosophy[30] the further claim that he was also the greatest of all sages, greater even than the rare and supremely idealized species of wise person depicted by the Stoics.

Tradition (ed. L.E. Goodman; New York: State University of New York Press, 1992), 21–42, esp. 24–30.

[25] Holladay (*Theios Aner*, 176) insists that the *theios anēr* in *Virt.* 177 "is and must remain anonymous," but it is especially characteristic of Philo to avoid explicitness in sensitive areas. He generally prefers in such instances to lead the reader to the brink of whatever it is he is about, in the hope that he will prove sagacious enough to take the final step himself. A good example is his refusal to designate the Logos explicitly as a divine emanation. See Winston, *Wisdom of Solomon*, 185–86.

[26] Cf. Philo, *QG* 4.203, *Mos.* 2.147, *Spec.* 1.252, *Deus* 75–76, *Sacr.* 15.

[27] Holladay, *Theios Aner*, 155–60.

[28] Cf. Philo, *Leg.* 2.23.

[29] See John Dillon, *The Middle Platonists*, 38, 120.

[30] See Philo, *Leg.* 1.108; *QG* 3.5; 4.152, 167; *Her.* 214; *Prob.* 57; *Aet.* 18–19; *Spec.* 4.60–61.

CHAPTER THIRTEEN

Judaism and Hellenism:
Hidden tensions in Philo's thought

Few writings have provoked so great a diversity of interpretation as the vast literary legacy of Philo of Alexandria. Yet in spite of the huge number of studies that it has engendered, rarely has it been studied for its own sake. Although faint echoes of Philo's teachings can be found in several rabbinic dicta, his name appears nowhere in the extensive rabbinic corpus, and were it not for the preservation of his works by the Church, they would surely have perished. While it is not impossible that the rabbis had some oral knowledge of his teachings and made occasional use of them, it is very unlikely that they ever studied his writings. This is hardly surprising, since the rabbis had evinced little interest in philosophical speculation, and there can be little doubt that a Jewish intellectual of the Philonic stamp would have been regarded with some suspicion by the Palestinian religious leadership. This virtual neglect of Philo by the Jewish world continued through the medieval period, since Greek remained inaccessible to the major Jewish thinkers of that age, and a Syriac or Arabic translation was apparently available, if at all, for only a small portion of his works. In short, it is likely that it was only in the Hellenistic Jewish diaspora, and especially in his native Alexandria, the hub of Greco-Roman civilization, that Philo had a sympathetic and eager audience.

Philo does not resurface in Jewish literature before the sixteenth century, when Azariah dei Rossi, the most influential forerunner of the modern science of Judaism, outlined a number of his characteristic doctrines in the third part of his treatise *Me'or 'Einayim* (Mantua, 1573-75). According to dei Rossi, some of his contemporaries, such as the Provenzali brothers, had championed the case of Philo, "setting a golden crown on his head," but although he himself greatly appreciated Philo's ability, his own attitude towards him was clearly ambivalent. His most serious criticisms revolved around Philo's ignorance of Hebrew and Aramaic, his belief in the eternity of matter, his allegorization of scripture, and his deviations from the Palestinian halakha. As a result, he refused to decide whether Philo's work was, as he put it, "pure or impure," and although he would not refer to him as Rabbi or *hakham,* neither would he condemn him as a heretic, but called him instead Yedidyah the Alexandrian, a felicitous Hebrew equivalent of his Greek name, and treated him merely as one of the sages of the non-Jewish world. On the other hand, dei Rossi's friend and mentor, R. Judah Moscato, the father of the modern Jewish sermon, who makes several references to Philo in his writings, was pleased to call him "Rabbi Yedidyah." In the seventeenth century, the Venetian rabbi Simone Luzzatto, in his Italian *Discorso* of 1638 on the Jews of Venice, much admired Philo, whom he cited from a Latin version, and suggested that his motive for allegorizing the Scriptures was for the purpose of attracting his pagan audience. Wistfully, he wishes that Philo had educated contemporary Jews instead of writing for the Greeks. "Had Philo put his mind to teaching the Jews," he writes, "rather than to converting the Greeks, perhaps he would have reaped greater fruit from his labor, honored the nation more and gained greater praise than he found among the Greeks – for his brethren were already disposed to the apprehension of his doctrine.'[1] Finally, and paradoxically, the Jewish evaluation of Philo comes full circle in a quaint and little known volume, *Qol ha-Nevuah, The Voice of Prophecy*, published by R. David Cohen in 1970. The so-called Rav Ha-Nazir, a disciple of Rav Kook, acclaimed Philo as "the giant of ancient Jewish philosophy." In contrast to Greek philosophy, which is conceptual and contemplative, Cohen characterized Judaism as auditory. In Judaism, a person is summoned by the cosmic voice not to see God which is impossible, but to understand and listen to him. According to the Nazir, it was the eclipse of Philo that misled medieval Jewish philosophers into adopting a Hellenistic mode that Philo knew how to resist with his doctrine of the *Ma'amar*, the Logos. Only the Kabbalah remained faithful to Philo.[2] Ironically, Cohen's basic dictum that "hearing is greater than seeing" would have greatly displeased Philo, and the key biblical verse "Hear, O Israel !" (Deut. 6:4), upon which it is based, is strangely never explicitly cited by him. The aberrant view of the Nazir apart, it must be acknowledged that the one Jewish thinker who possessed a direct and unmediated knowledge of a Stoicizing and Pythagorizing Platonism, and had attempted to adapt it to

[1] See R. Marcus, "A Sixteenth Century Hebrew Critique of Philo," *HUCA* 21 (1948):29-71; J. Weinberg, "The Quest for Philo in Sixteenth-Century Jewish Historiography," in *Jewish History: Essays in Honour of Chimen Abramsky* (ed. A. Rapoport-Albert, S. J. Zipperstein; London: Peter Halban, 1988), 163-87; B. Septimus, "Biblical Religion and Political Rationality in Simone Luzzatto, Maimonides and Spinoza,"in *Jewish Thought in the Seventeenth Century* (ed. I. Twersky, B. Septimus; Harvard Judaic Texts and Studies 6; Cambridge MA: Harvard University Press, 1987), 399-433.
[2] See A. Neher, "Les références à Philon d'Alexandrie dans l'œuvre du Rav Hanazir, disciple du Rav Kook," in *Hellenica et Judaica: Hommage à Valentin Nikiprowetzky* (ed. A. Caquot, M. Hadas-Lebel et J. Riaud; Leuven-Paris: Peeters, 1986), 385-90.

Jewish thought by way of a detailed allegorical biblical commentary, left hardly a mark on mainstream Judaism.

It must be emphasized, however, that it is in the nature of so vast an enterprise of conceptual adaptation, that inner tensions must inevitably work their way ever so subtly to the surface, thus creating elements of stress that only an exposition employing systematic ambiguity could contain. It is my intention here to examine several fundamental themes that will illustrate the inherent ambiguity that permeates Philo's commentary on Scripture. The roots of this ambivalence lie in the fact that Philo seeks assiduously to retain the terminology and idiom of his biblical text in the very process of transposing its teaching into a philosophical key. The reader constantly finds Greek philosophical terms mingling freely with biblical locutions, and is thus deftly beguiled into discovering philosophical doctrine beneath the shell of the scriptural narrative. No philosophical view seems to be too abstruse to be able to withstand the subtle interweaving of traditions represented by Philo's characteristic blend of divergent outlooks. In a number of important instances, however, the Jewish component in the Philonic mix resists total integration, and in spite of some minor modifications that are intended to diminish the jarring effect, what is peculiarly Jewish cannot be given up.

In short, although much in Philo's thought represents a highly successful fusion of Judaism and Hellenism, a virtual restructuring of biblical thought through the categories of Greek philosophy, there are a number of important issues, where fusion has seemingly been replaced by a rough conjunction or coexistence of ideas, and where one can clearly see the seams joining the disparate conceptions as they have emerged from Philo's multilayered mind. A consideration of such highly sensitive Philonic themes as repentance, the divine nature, Moses as sage, and Moses as prophet, will, I hope, enable us to discover Philo's inner mind and allow his true philosophical portrait to emerge.

Repentance

I begin with a Jewish religious ideal that seems to have been virtually nonexistent or at best only marginal in the Greek world. Greek philosophy generally had little interest in the feelings of regret or remorse that may at times lead an individual to a fundamental reassessment of his former life path. The single favorable statement in classical Greek literature on μεταμέλεια or remorse is the statement of Democritus: "Remorse for shameful deeds is salvation in life" (DK 68.B43). According to Eduard Norden, "either this saying is not by Democritus, or, if it is genuine, it must have anticipated future development of the concept by centuries."[3] Aristotle does indeed note that there is no cure for one who does not regret his error (ἀμεταμέλητος, *Eth. nic.* 7.1150a23), but not only does he nowhere say that repentance is a virtue, but further asserts that the good person "knows no regrets" (ἀμεταμέλητος, 1166a29), whereas bad people "are full of regrets (1166b25). Following in Aristotle's footsteps, the Stoics declare: "The philosopher surmises nothing, repents of nothing, is never wrong, and never changes his opinion" (Cicero, *Mur.* 61).

From the polemic of the Stoics against repentance, however, Werner Jaeger had already surmised "the widespread existence of a type of ethics in which it had high value."[4] A faint echo of such a religious tradition has been detected by Rudolf Pfeiffer. The statue of the Delian Apollo held the graces in his right hand and bow and arrow in his left. This gave rise to an allegorical-ethical interpretation, namely, that the god holds the bow in his left hand, "because he is slower to chastise if man repents" (Callimachus, *Aet.* fr. 114.8-17, Pfeiffer). Pfeiffer noted that a copy of an inscription from the Delphic temple was found at the beginning of this century in Miletopolis in Asia Minor. In this new inscription, not to be dated much later than 300 BCE, we read amongst the other precepts: "repent when you did wrong (μετανόει ἁμαρτών)". "How very different," writes Pfeiffer, "appears this Apollo from the terrible god who at the opening of our *Iliad* shoots his deadly arrows immediately after his wronged priest's prayer for revenge, leaving no time for repentance."[5]

Although Philo knew this interesting Apolline tradition (*Legat.* 95; cf. *Leg.* 3.105-06), and there was a close rabbinic parallel to it (*Sifre, Pinhas* 134), he was certainly aware that it could not easily be harmonized with Greek philosophical thought. Yet the centrality of the doctrine of repentance in Hebrew prophetic literature and in the Palestinian traditions of Philo's own day was such that he could not only not ignore it but felt impelled to give it a prominent place in his writings (a separate segment of his treatise *On Virtues* is devoted to it). He thus reads it into the scriptural text even when it is not there, after the manner of a similar Palestinian tradition. In response to the question "why, after their entering the ark, did seven days pass, after which came the Flood," he answers that it was to grant them repentance of sins (*QG* 2.13; cf. *Mek. Shirta* 5; *QG* 1.91; *Tg. Ps.-J.* on Gen.6:3). Moreover, in contrast to the Stoics who denied that the wise

---

[3] Norden, *Agnostos Theos*, 136.

[4] W. Jaeger, *Göttingsche gelehrte Anzeigen* 175 (1913):590.

[5] R. Pfeiffer, *Ausgewählte Schriften* (München, 1960), 55-71.

person would ever repent, Philo asserts that "to do no sin is peculiar to God; to repent, to the wise man" (*Fug.* 157; cf. *Virt.* 177; *Leg.* 2.60), and, like the Greek version of Sir. 44:16, he finds in Enoch a paradigm of the penitent (*Abr.* 17; *Praem.* 15; *QG* 1.82-86).

The effects of repentance are such that sin is expunged, "the old reprehensible life is blotted out and disappears and is no more found, as though it had never been at all" (*Abr.* 19). This was also the prophetic view and was emphatically repeated by the rabbis (*Pesik. de Rav Kahana* 120). The efficacy of repentance, however, clearly depends on its sincerity: "The man who, lying against the truth, maintains while still doing wrong that he has repented," says Philo, "is a madman" (*Fug.* 160). A sure sign of sincere repentance is that it is marked by bitterness, weeping, sighing, and groaning (*QE* 1.15). The *Pesikta Rabbati* similarly remarks: "Propitiation requires confession, supplication, and tears" (*Piska* 50, Braude 847)

So far, we have found nothing in Philo's account of repentance that differs from Jewish tradition. In analyzing the process of repentance, however, Philo appears to introduce a philosophical mode of description. In an allegorical interpretation of Exod. 12:9a, he tells us that "those who change by the principle of knowledge and are hardened as though by the force of fire have acquired a stable and unmoving usefulness" (*QE* 1.16). More revealing is his description of repentance in *Fug.* 159 as a "restricted and slow and tarrying thing." In contrast, the rabbis emphasize the instantaneousness of the process of repentance (*Pesik.R.* 44, *Pesik. de Rav Kahana* 24.12). Elsewhere, however, Philo does describe repentance as being "suddenly possessed with an ardent yearning for betterment" (*Praem.* 15), and speaks of the proselytes as acquiring all the virtues at once (*Virt.* 182). We may reconcile these apparently conflicting passages by distinguishing between the psychological events that ultimately lead up to a complete change in the individual's psyche, which usually constitute a slow, lengthy process, and the moment of conversion itself to wisdom. The Stoics, for example, believed that the transition of the person who is making moral progress to the state of perfected wisdom is instantaneous, supervening suddenly upon a long course of self-mastery without the individual being conscious of it (*SVF* 3.539-42, 637-70). Philo was fully aware of this Stoic teaching.[6]

Finally, in assessing the relative rank of the penitent and the person who is perfect, Philo gives the palm to the latter. "Repentance," he says, "holds the second place to perfection, just as a change from sickness to health is second to a body free from disease" (*Abr.* 26). The unbroken perfection of

---

[6] Cf. *Agr.* 161; *Somn.* 2.270.

virtues stands nearest to the divine power, and "the perfect person" (i.e. Noah) is complete from the first. Furthermore, in *Aet.* 40, Philo reports the view that repentance is a *pathos* or distemper of the soul, and although this passage probably derives from Aristotle's lost treatise *On Philosophy* (fr. 19c Ross), there is not the slightest hint here that Philo would disagree with his formulation. Moreover, in *Spec.* 1.103, he points out that "in the souls of the repentant there remain, in spite of all, the scars and prints of their old misdeeds." The rabbis, too, however, debated the question of the relative merit of the penitent and the person of perfection. "R. Hiyya b. Abba said in the name of R. Yohanan: All the prophets prophesied only on behalf of penitents; but as for the wholly righteous, "Eye hath not seen, oh God, beside Thee." He differs in this from R. Abbahu, who said: In the place where penitents stand even the wholly righteous cannot stand" (*b. Ber.* 34b). We may compare the similar sentiment in Luke 15:7, "There will be more joy in heaven over one sinner who repents than over 99 righteous persons who need no repentance." Moreover, Philo's assertion that the scars of old misdeeds cannot be effaced also appears to be paralleled in the Talmud. On the other hand, Philo's assertion that repentance is an irrational emotion naturally finds no echo in rabbinic literature, though it must be noted that that assertion is found in one of his purely philosophical treatises and in another context.

In sum, although Philo has not succeeded completely in assimilating the concept of repentance to his philosophical thought, he does nevertheless emphasize its secondary rank in the hierarchy of virtue, explicitly refers to the scars of old misdeeds, and clearly indicates the lengthy intellectual process that precedes conversion to a better life. Even more revealing, however, is his casual reference to repentance as an irrational emotion. It should be noted, however, that Philo was probably aware of a Neopythagorean preoccupation with self-examination that was taken up by the Roman Stoa, and this may have made it easier for him to incorporate the Jewish emphasis on repentance into his own writings in the manner that he did.[7]

The Divine Nature

From human repentance, we move on to the even more problematical notion of divine repentance and Philo's vacillating conception of the

---

[7] Epictetus 3.10.2; Seneca *Ira* 3.36.1-4; *Ep.* 28.9-10; M. Aurelius 1.7; cf. *Tabula of Cebes* 10.4.

divine nature. In reinterpreting popular myth, the Stoics were constrained to criticize both anthropomorphic and anthropopathic descriptions of the divine (Cicero, *Nat. d.* 2.70). As an exegete of Scripture, Philo faced a similar problem. He took great pains to neutralize biblical verses that appeared to contradict his philosophical convictions about the divine nature, but his efforts in this direction were considerably facilitated by the Stoic doctrine of εὐπάθειαι, wholesome or rational emotions. This aspect of the Stoic theory of the emotions will help us to understand Philo's readiness to ascribe certain emotions to God.

According to the Stoics, impulses of various kinds are generated in the commanding faculty of an individual as a result of the stimulus of various impressions conducted to it from the excited sense organs by way of tensile motion. If the commanding faculty is in a healthy state, i.e., in a condition of right reason, the impulses released through its acts of assent will be rational or wholesome εὐπάθειαι and express correct judgments (*SVF* 3.169-77). If, on the other hand, the commanding faculty is diseased or irrational, the impulses released will be excessive and will constitute πάθη or erroneous judgments. The sage's perfect commanding faculty spontaneously and unerringly makes correct judgments, thus wholly eliminating the πάθη or passions and generating instead only εὐπάθειαι, purely rational impulses.

The three canonical εὐπάθειαι are βούλησις (wishing, or rational desire), εὐλάβεια, (watchfulness or caution), and χαρά (joy), and it seems that Philo was in no way embarrassed to apply at least two of them to God. He thus frequently employs the verb βούλομαι and the noun βούλημα of God, and if the reports of Diogenes Laertius and Plutarch are accurate, it would appear that even the Old Stoa spoke of "the will (βούλησις) of him who orders the universe" (Diogenes Laertius 7.88, Plutarch *Comm. not.* 1076E). Similarly Philo had no difficulty in describing God not only as beneficent but also as benevolent and kind (*Opif.* 81, *Mut.* 129, *Abr.* 137). For benevolence (εὔνοια) was classified by the Stoics as a variety of βούλησις. Antipater of Tarsus characterizes God as beneficent (εὐποιητικόν), though not benevolent. But Seneca adds that the gods are "ever gentle and kindly (*placidi ac propitii*), and bear with the errors of our feeble spirits" (*Ira* 7.31.4; cf. 2.27.1). Joy, too, was accounted a rational emotion by the Stoics. So it comes as no surprise that this attribute also was ascribed by Philo to God (*QG* 4.188). The wise person's joy, however, is not the equal of God's, for the limited capacity of finite creatures denies us the unbroken continuity that marks the divine archetype of our happiness (*Abr.* 201-07). It is not clear, however, how the Philonic attribution of joy to God is related to the Stoic position. For the earliest explicit testimony for the

Stoic assignment of joy to God is found in Seneca, who attributes to the Deity and to those who imitate it unceasing joy (*Ep.* 59.16, 18). Like Cleanthes, he must have believed that once a person becomes wise, he has achieved a state of uninterrupted virtue, so that the rational elation of joy attendant on his exercise of virtue (D. L. 7.94) continues at least to his death. God, whose rationality is unchanging, must forever be in a state of joy, his πνεῦμα presumably characterized by the perfect tension (εὐτονία, *SVF* 3.47) that the wise person's psyche attains or expands into only on his conversion to the life of virtue. It is not inconceivable, therefore, although there is no explicit evidence for it, that the early Stoa also held that the perfect rationality of God was continuously accompanied by a steady state of joy. While agreeing with Seneca that God may be characterized as being in a state of continuous joy, Philo diverges from him and appears to approximate the position of Chrysippus in denying a like condition to the sage.

The rational emotion of watchfulness or caution, is never ascribed by Philo to God directly, although there may have been no theoretical difficulty in his doing so. Watchfulness is the rational avoidance of evil (Cicero *Tusc.* 4.15; Plutarch *Stoic. rep.* 1037F; cf. Philo *Det.* 45; *Somn.* 2.82), and it could be said that the Divine Logos is continuously characterized by such a spontaneous avoidance. Indeed, the Stoics come very close to saying as much when they state that the Deity is a living being "admitting nothing evil into itself" (κακοῦ παντὸς ἀνεπίδεκτον, Diogenes Laertius 7.147; cf. *Opif.* 73). For Philo, God's watchfulness could readily be subsumed under the βασιλικὴ δύναμις, God's Royal Power, by which he rejects and punishes evil.

Joy, however, is considered by Philo to be the best of the rational emotions (*Mut.* 131; *Congr.* 36; *Praem.* 31), and it is quite possible that, like the early Stoics, he would have shrunk from ascribing either wishing or watchfulness explicitly to God, since, strictly speaking, the Deity could not be characterized by want of any kind. Joy, as an ἐπιγέννημα or byproduct, (D. L. 7.94; cf. Aristotle *Eth. nic.* 10.1174b32), was exceptional in that it involved no imputation of want to its subject and was therefore designated by Philo as the best of the rational emotions. As for Philo's use of terms like βούλημα and βούλομαι in relation to God, this can readily be seen as a concession to ordinary linguistic usage. But since joy in relation to God does not involve an elation, it should not strictly be called a rational emotion at all. That term accurately describes a psychic state only in man. In enjoying χαρά God may be said to be characterized by a state which in humanity is designated as a rational emotion, that is, the rational emotion of joy is assigned to God only analogically. If the above interpretation is correct, we should have to conclude that Philo ascribes to God neither passions (with the possible exception of pity) nor rational emotions, but only a perfect εὐδαιμονία, his objective state, and a subjective joy, which in view of the fact that in God it involves no change whatever, is strictly not accounted a rational emotion.

Turning from the rational emotions to the passions proper, we find Philo in complete accord with the Stoics in rejecting anger (θυμός) as a feeling that is inapplicable to God (cf. *Let. Arist.* 254). He is quite willing to stand Scripture on its head in order to avert such an attribution. After indicating that the description of God as wrathful was necessary for the duller folk who need to be schooled by fear (*Deus* 51-68), he offers a considerably forced interpretation of the troublesome verse in Gen 6:7, "I was wroth in that I made them," and then goes on to find in the statement that Noah had found grace with God, a pointed teaching concerning God's saving mercy (σωτήριον ἔλεον). Were God's judgment not tempered by mercy, we should find, he says, that the human race could not endure, since sin is unavoidable (*Deus* 74-76).

In thus ascribing pity (ἔλεος) to God, Philo decisively parts company with the Stoics, who had classified pity as a species of λύπη or distress, one of the four primary passions (*SVF* 1.213; 3.394, 413-16; cf. Seneca *Clem.* 2.4ff). He might have avoided the overt break without yielding too much on the issue of God's mercy, had he simply substituted the terms φιλανθρωπία (humaneness) and ἐπιείκεια (equity) for ἔλεος. Thus Seneca sharply distinguishes *misericordia*, "pity" from *clementia*, "mercy". He recommends the latter as the action of "an unruffled mind and a countenance under control" (*Clem.* 2.6.2-3). The Old Stoa had made no such distinction. But the Middle Stoa may have modified the Old Stoic view of ἐπιείκεια in the direction of Seneca's theory. We know from Cicero (*Tusc.* 4.56) and Seneca (*Clem.* 2.5.2) that the Stoics, it seems, were attacked for their severity in rejecting pity as a vice, and may have been compelled to emend their unpopular position.[8]

In the light of the later Stoic doctrine of *clementia*, it may be asked why Philo did not see fit to restrict himself to the Middle Stoic φιλανθρωπία/ἐπιείκεια formula in his description of God's mercy. Had Greek possessed a word precisely equivalent to *clementia*, Philo might well have been happy to have adopted it as a substitute for ἔλεος. But in the absence of such a convenience, he undoubtedly felt constrained by the stress laid upon God's attribute of mercy in Jewish tradition. It seemed incumbent to

---

[8] See M. T. Griffin, *Seneca, A Philosopher in Politics* (Oxford, 1976), 129-71. Cf. Maimonides, *Guide* 1.54, p. 126 Pines; Nietzsche, *Fröhliche Wissenschaft* 44.338; M. Buber, *Hasidism and Modern Man* (New York 1958), 120-21.

ascribe ἔλεος not only to the wise person (*Sacr.* 12; cf. *Ios.* 82; *Spec.* 2.115, 138; *Virt.* 144), but also to God. There is an occasional slip in Seneca (*Vit. beat.* 24.1; *Ben.* 6.29.1; cf. M. Aurelius 2.13), but Philo's frequent indulgence in the ascription of pity to God and on occasion even anger (*Somn.* 2.179; *Opif.* 156), which he had labored so mightily to remove from him in *Deus* 70-73, is considerably more jarring. We may conclude that it was the frequent application of ἔλεος to God in the Septuagint, Philo's canonical text, that made it so difficult for him to avoid the philosophically problematic attribution. Yet in ascribing ἔλεος to God, he undoubtedly had in mind a rational form of the emotion, like Seneca's *clementia.*

Moses as Sage

From the perfection of the divine nature, we now turn to Philo's concept of human perfection, which is exemplified for him by Moses. Although Philo's portrait of the sage is essentially identical with that of the Stoics, in depicting Moses his description transcends the established parameters of Stoic theory. Moses is Philo's supreme paradigm of the sage, and is described as superior even to the Patriarchs. The seventh from Abraham, he does not, like those before him, haunt the outer court of the Holy Place as one seeking initiation, but as a mystagogue he has his abode within the sanctuary (*Post.* 173.). The highest point of wisdom reached by Abraham is the initial course in Moses' training (*ibid.* 174). As prophet and friend of God, he is a partner in God's possessions, so that the entire cosmos was placed in his hands, each of its elements submitting to his sovereignty (*Mos.* 1.155-56). He was named god and king of the whole nation, and entered into the darkness where God was, namely into the unseen, invisible, incorporeal and archetypal essence of existing things. Although both Isaac and Moses exemplify soul-types that achieve perfect virtue without toil, Moses presumably represents for Philo a higher type than does Isaac, since he is ultimately translated to an even higher station than that of the latter by being placed beside God, above genus and species alike (*Sacr.* 8; cf. *Ebr.* 94, where Moses is ranked above Isaac). Isaac thus symbolizes the wise person whose psyche generates only rational emotions. Moses, on the other hand, would appear to symbolize the god-like person, "given as a loan to earthlings" (*Sacr.* 8) (i.e., he belongs to that category of rational souls that ordinarily never leave the supernal spheres for embodiment below), and having achieved an absolute ἀπάθεια is no longer affected in any way by human feelings, living as it were in the disembodied realm of pure νοῦς.

In *Leg.* 3.129, we are told that Aaron, who is inferior to Moses, being only a προκόπτων or one who is making gradual moral progress, merely curbs
and controls the spirited element, thus practicing μετριοπάθεια (moderation of passion), whereas Moses cuts it out entirely, thus achieving complete
ἀπάθεια or absence of passion. In *Migr.* 67, however, it is stated more specifically that Moses purges every form of desire, and completely removes the
warlike θυμός, "so that the better portion of the soul that is left, the rational element, may employ its truly free and noble-minded impulses towards
all things beautiful, with nothing tugging at it any longer and diverting it."
In this passage Philo is clearly employing the Platonic tripartite division of
the soul, so that Moses' excision (ἐκτέτμηται) of ἐπιθυμία and θυμός
signifies his excision of all lower desires and the entire range of spirited
feelings, with the result that his reason operates in a sort of emotional
vacuum. Moses therefore appears to consist solely of body and rational
soul, his bodily sensations producing none of the lower impulses in his
single-tiered psyche to which his reason need give or withhold assent.

Philo has thus provided us with the extraordinary phenomenon of a
super-sage, whose perfected reason need not generate rational impulses,
but simply computes its true bodily needs and proceeds to satisfy them in
the only way it knows how, i.e. with perfect rationality. Moses' mind thus
lives in lower impulse-free conjunction with his body, and with the sole
exception of joy, is unaccompanied by the ordinary sage's rational emotions. The Mosaic mind is accordingly the closest possible approximation
to the Divine Mind, since neither of them is characterized by the usual
rational emotions. As I have indicated above, it is very likely that the only
rational emotion Philo allows God is joy, provided that it is applied to him
analogically, inasmuch as the divine joy differs from that of the sage in its
not involving any elation. Here, at last, the Mosaic mind falls short of the
Divine, since, unlike the latter's eternal and elationless joy, that of Moses is
constituted by the expansion of his psychic πνεῦμα upon his arrival at
maturity and wisdom.

If my interpretation of the evidence is correct, it becomes immediately
evident that Philo is here continuing his game of "one-upmanship" by
adding to his insistence that Moses was the father of Greek philosophy the
further claim that he was also the greatest of all sages, greater even than
that rare and supremely idealized species of wise person depicted by the
Stoics. The object of this adulation, however, is not Moses the recipient of
a special and parochial divine revelation, but Moses the philosopher, the
perfect exemplar of rational intuitive thought. We are thus led to the most
complex of our illustrations of Philo's inner ambivalences, his conception
of Mosaic prophecy.

Moses as Prophet

In *Mos.* 2.188, Philo enumerates three kinds of divine oracles: the special laws, spoken by God in his own person (ἐκ προσώπου τοῦ θεοῦ)[9] with his prophet as interpreter; revelation through question and answer, in which the prophet asks questions of God about matters on which he has been seeking knowledge, and God replies and instructs him; and predictive prophecies, spoken by Moses in his own person, "when inspired and of himself possessed." Philo's description of the first and third categories of oracles yields two types of prophecy, ecstatic and hermeneutical or noetic (since, although Philo makes a clear distinction between ἑρμηνεία and προφητεία in *Mos.* 2.191, elsewhere he employs these terms synonymously). The one is mediated through possession, the other through the prophet's noetic response to the divine voice, which is regarded by Philo as a figure for rational soul. As for the second category of oracles, inasmuch as there is no clear indication by Philo that the ἐνθουσιασμός of Moses when he poses his questions to the Deity involves the kind of possession that displaces his own mind, it would seem that, *contra* Wolfson,[10] both question and answer in the four cases cited by Philo are exemplifications of noetic prophecy in which, as we shall soon see, the prophet's mind is not only not preempted, but actually appears to seize the initiative. Although Philo has very likely deliberately refrained from drawing out the full implications of the two distinctively different modes of Mosaic prophecy referred to by him, his idiosyncratic bifurcation of the prophetic personality is of fundamental significance for a proper understanding of his concept of divine revelation. Philo's momentary restriction of the use of the term "prophecy" to the predictive model of inspiration conveniently enables him to focus the reader's gaze almost exclusively on ecstatic prophecy, and thus allows him to deal with the noetic type with almost casual unconcern. We are driven to a distant but singular passage in *Decal.* 32-35, if we wish to seek out his understanding of the latter form of prophecy. Philo's descriptions of ecstatic possession are rhetorically elaborated in a series of passages in which it is emphatically asserted that in that state the prophet's sovereign mind is entirely preempted by the Divine Spirit, so that he becomes a passive "medium" for the Deity's message, a conductor, as it were, for a higher source of energy.

A closer look at ecstatic prophecy in the ancient Greek tradition is now essential if we are properly to gauge the precise form of this prophetic

---

[9] Cf. Justin Martyr *Apol.* 1.37.1; 1.38.1; *Dial.* 25.1; 42.2.
[10] Wolfson, *Philo,* 2:33.

mode which Philo has attributed to Moses. It goes without saying that the biblical picture of Mosaic prophecy is generally non-ecstatic (the one exception is recorded in Num 11), and that Philo's ascription of a series of eight instances of ecstatic prophecies to the great lawgiver must be seen as deriving from the Hellenic side of his training. Philo was undoubtedly aware of two diverse conceptions of ecstatic prophecy in Greek thought: the one radical, the other considerably milder. The nature of the Pythia's ecstasy at Delphi, the best known example of this mantic form, is unfortunately enveloped in controversy. The usual description of it derives from a source as late as a passage from bk. 5 (165-74) of Lucan's *Civil War* (first century CE), where we have a clear example of psychic invasion, and a portrayal of the Pythia as the god's medium. As Fontenrose has stated, however, "Lucan is not only describing an unhistorical consultation, but he also had no knowledge of Delphi .... It is Aeneas' visit to the Sibyl of Cumae in *Aeneid* 6.9-158 that lies behind Lucan's account of Appius' visit to Delphi, as Amandry and others have pointed out."[11] In his own portrayal of ecstatic prophecy, however, Philo was probably following in the footsteps of his favorite philosopher, Plato, who does indeed speak of the Pythia's madness, connecting μαντική with μανική (*Phaedr.* 244A-245C), and who, in *Tim.* 71E, says that no one achieves true divination in his right mind (ἔννους). Elsewhere he indicates that the poets, like the prophets, say many fine things, but know none of the things they say (*Apol.* 22C, *Meno* 99C), and that "God takes away the mind of these men and uses them as his ministers just as he does soothsayers and godly seers, in order that we who hear them may know that it is not they who utter these words of great price, when they are out of their wits, but it is God himself who speaks and addressses us through them" (*Ion* 543C, trans. Lamb).

A milder form of ecstatic prophecy is advanced by Plutarch in *The Obsolescence of Oracles* 431B-438. After explicitly rejecting the notion that "the god himself after the manner of 'belly-talkers'" (ἐγγαστρίμυθοι) enters into the bodies of his prophets and prompts their utterances, employing their mouths and voices as instruments (414E), he attempts to explain prophetic oracles by means of the following theory put into the mouth of Lamprias. The soul is inherently prophetic, although its mantic element is an imaginative faculty (φανταστικὴ δύναμις), irrational and indeterminate in itself, like a blank writing tablet, but receptive of impressions. When a prophetic breath or current, emanating from the earth or streams, enters the body it creates in the soul an unusual temperament (κρᾶσις) that heats it up and opens up certain passages through which impressions of the

---

[11]   J. Fontenrose, *The Delphic Oracle* (Berkeley: University of California Press, 1978), 210.

future are transmitted (cf. [Arist.] *Pr.* 954a). In this heated condition, the soul succeeds in relaxing the reasoning element and prevents it from diverting and extinguishing the inspiration (432F).

Clearly, Plutarch's theory of ecstatic prophecy envisages no displacement or dissociation of the human mind, though it does provide for its tranquilization. Nor is his theory without antecedents, for we learn from Cicero's *On Divination* 1.113, that the frenzied soul (*furibunda mens*) spurns the body and flies abroad, inflamed and aroused by various kinds of influences, such as groves and forests, and subterranean vapors. In all these cases it sees the things it foretells in its prophecies, as Cassandra did. Now a close examination of Philo's description of predictive prophecy reveals that while he has adopted the more radical form of Greek ecstatic prophecy as his model with regard to the prophecies of Abraham and Balaam (*Her.* 264-66; *Mos.* 1.274-91), this is not the case with the predictive prophecies of Moses. Here there is no explicit reference to the displacement of the prophet's mind, to his ignorance of his own prophetic words, or to the fact that God prompts the words that he speaks. Moreover, in two instances we are told that under the divine inspiration, Moses sees certain visions. In one case, he has a vision (φαντασίαν λαμβάνω) of the Egyptians dead, in the other, he "sees the earth opened and vast chasms yawning wide, great bands of kinsfolk (i.e., Korah and his ilk) perishing and living men descending into Hades" (*Mos.* 2.252, 281). Philo does indeed say that the divinely possessed Moses "was no longer in himself" (οὔκετ᾽ ὢν ἐν ἑαυτῷ: *Mos.* 2.250) and this expression is sometimes used of one whose mind is displaced (Plato, *Ion* 534B; *QG* 3.9; cf. *Her.* 264), but it is also used of the state of philosophic frenzy, and may simply indicate that the mind is completely absorbed in the Deity (e.g., *Her.* 70). In short, to adopt Aune's terminology, the ecstatic predictive prophecies of Moses may best be characterized as products of "vision trance" rather than "possession trance."[12]

If my interpretation is correct, it would readily fit the pattern of uniqueness that frames Philo's portrait of Moses, for it is now evident that not only is Moses' legislative prophecy unique, but even his predictive prophecy, a gift he otherwise shares with Noah and the Patriarchs (*Her.* 260-61), is likewise unique in character, since it is not as with the latter, a product of psychic invasion and displacement.

In sharp contrast to ecstatic prophecy, divine voice or noetic prophecy does not render its recipient passive. Although no separate account is given by Philo of this mode of Mosaic prophecy, we may discern its nature

---

[12]   D. E. Aune, *Prophecy in Early Christianity and the Ancient Mediterranean World* (Grand Rapids: Eerdmans, 1983), 19, 32-34, 147-52, and 348, n. 8.

from his description of the giving of the Decalogue, which must serve us as the paradigm for prophecy through the divine voice. God, we are there told, is not as a human being needing mouth, tongue, and windpipe (cf. *Deus* 83; *Migr.* 47-52; *Sacr.* 78). Rather He created a rational soul full of clearness and distinctness that shaped the air around it into a flaming fire, sounding forth an articulate voice. This miraculous voice was activated by the power of God which created in the souls of all another kind of hearing far superior to that of the physical organ. The latter is but a sluggish sense, inactive until aroused by the impact of the air, but the hearing of the mind possessed by God (ἐνθέου διανοίας) makes the first advance and goes out to meet the conveyed meanings (φθάνει προϋπαντῶσα τοῖς λεγομένοις) with the swiftest speed (*Decal.* 35). It is clear from this description that the inspired mind that perceives this special rational soul created by God, far from being preempted or rendered passive, is rather extraordinarily quickened and sharpened.

For the notion of a mind to mind communication in order to explain the divine voice at Sinai, Philo was undoubtedly indebted to the Middle Platonic tradition. The Platonists had been exercised by the need to explain the nature of Socrates' famous δαιμόνιον or sign, and one of the interpretations recorded by Plutarch is very similar to that adopted by Philo to explain the Divine utterance at Sinai:

> It occurred to us [says Simmias in Plutarch's *On the Sign of Socrates*] as we examined the question in private among ourselves, to surmise that Socrates' sign was perhaps no vision, but rather the perception of a voice or else the mental apprehension of language that reached him in some strange way ... Socrates had an understanding which, being pure and free from passion, and commingling with the body but little, for necessary ends, was so sensitive and delicate as to respond at once to what reached him. What reached him, one would conjecture, was not spoken language, but the unuttered words of a daemon, making voiceless contact with his intelligence by their sense alone (*Gen. Socr.* 588D).

It is essential to note that Philo invokes the notion of ecstatic possession only to explain the ability of the prophet to predict the future, a talent clearly requiring the exclusive services of the divine *pneuma*, since no finite mind could enjoy such a power (cf. *Mos.* 2.6, 187; *Her.* 261). Moses' promulgation of the special laws, however, communicated to him by the divine voice (*Mos.* 2.188), is understood to involve the active participation of the prophet's mind. The same is true of the "ten Words" which summarize the entire Law and which required the quickened perception of the entire Israelite nation. In the light of the general thrust of Philo's philosophic thought, it is very likely that he understands "noetic" prophecy to refer to the activation of humanity's higher mind or intuitive intellect, by means of which he grasps the fundamental principles of universal being viewed as a unified whole. Wolfson has noted the fact that Philo does not resort to the Platonic doctrine of the recollection of Ideas in order to account for the mind's knowledge of the intelligible realities, but his assertion that the latter form of knowledge was based upon prophetic revelation taken in its literal sense is unconvincing. Philo did not need the Platonic doctrine of recollection, since for him the human mind was an inseparable fragment of the Divine Logos, and all that it required in order to attain to the intelligible Forms was the initial stimulus of sense-perception which formed a kind of gateway into them (*Somn.* 1.187-88). Presumably the formation of sensible images and the ideas derived from them activated the mind's dormant access to the world of incorporeal Forms (cf. *Her.* 111). The unified vision of the world of intelligible Forms thus constitutes an inherent characteristic of the human mind, though for most people much effort is ordinarily required to actualize it. When it does occur, however, a human achieves direct knowledge of the divine. Philo therefore undoubtedly understood the prophetic revelation through which Moses attained to his understanding of the Law, as an intuitive grasp of the fundamental principles of being and the natural laws that constitute its structure.

In support of our interpretation of Philo's theory of noetic prophecy we turn now to several key passages from *The Migration of Abraham.* At *Migr.* 80, Philo notes that thoughts are nothing else than God's words or speech, "for without the prompter (τοῦ ὑποβολέως) speech will give forth no utterance, and mind is the prompter of speech, as God is of mind." Moreover, interpreting the verse in Exodus 4.10 ("from the time thou hast begun to speak to thy servant"), he speaks of God's flashing into Moses the light of truth by means of the undying words of absolute Knowledge and Wisdom (ἐπιστήμης καὶ σοφίας αὐτῆς, *Migr.* 76). The divine illumination of Moses' mind is thus mediated through a vision of the eternal Forms. Moreover, according to Philo "the true priest is necessarily a prophet, advanced to the service of the truly Existent by virtue rather than by birth, and to the prophet nothing is unknown since he has within him a spiritual sun and unclouded rays to give him a full and clear apprehension (κατάληψιν) of things unseen by sense but apprehended by the understanding" (*Spec.* 4.192, trans. Colson). That this description of prophecy cannot apply to the ecstatic prophet goes without saying, since the latter "has no power of apprehension when he speaks but serves as the channel for the insistent words of Another's prompting" (*Spec.* 1.65, trans. Colson; cf. 4.49). More significant, however, is the insistence here that the prophet is illuminated by an internal sun for the clear apprehension of intelligible truth.

In Philo's mystical thought, true prophetic power is rooted in the special intellectual capacities that God has graciously bestowed on his chosen ones, and of the latter Moses stands out as a unique exemplar of unsurpassed excellence. The fact that at Sinai it was the entire Israelite people that had attained an unmediated intellectual vision of the ten Words should not surprise us, for in Philo's allegorical code Israel is nothing but a symbol of "the man who sees God," the initiate into the highest divine mysteries. Philo's insistence on the infallibility of prophetic inspiration, in contrast to the ordinary processes of reason, must therefore be seen as a reflection of his conviction that the former is a product of the intuitive reason of one whose mind has a virtual lock on the ultimate divine truths by virtue of a congenital divine endowment. His conservatism, however, has naturally led him to preserve much of the scriptural idiom of divine interventionism in preference to the integrationist approach of the philosopher, though this ought not deflect the astute reader from a correct assessment of his true intentions.

Ecstatic and Noetic Prophecy and Mystic Vision

A final word must be added with regard to Philo's view of the relationship between ecstatic prophecy and mystic vision, and between the latter and noetic prophecy. Although many of the characteristic terms employed by Philo for ecstatic prophecy recur in his descriptions of philosophical mystical vision, a sharp distinction must be drawn between these two spiritual states, for while the former represents a psychic invasion, the latter refers to a psychic ascent. Both are nevertheless characterized by an inspired frenzy like that of Corybants and Bacchants, a going out and forgetfulness of one's self, sudden seizure, and bodily transformation. In spite of these similarities, it is the source of the initiative that primarily differentiates the ecstatic from the mystic. In the former, the initiative lies with the Deity, whereas in the latter it is seen as lying in the hands of a human being. Moreover, in ecstasy the frenzy is the essential element mediating the prophecy, whereas in mystic vision it is only an accompaniment of the culmination of the noetic ascent. The question now remaining before us, is whether there is any significant difference between the mystic vision and the noetic form of prophecy exemplified by Moses in his legislative capacity. Inasmuch as there is no reference to a state of frenzy in our paradigm for noetic prophecy, it is very likely that this prophetic state is characterized by total calm and serenity. Commenting on the verse, "But you stand here with me" (Deut. 5:31), Philo says that this oracle indicates that God gives the person of virtue a share in his own nature, which is repose (ἠρεμία). Similarly, citing Moses' words "And I stood between the Lord and you" (Deut. 5:5), he notes that this verse indicates that the "mind of the Sage, released from storms and wars, with calm still weather and profound peace around it (νηνέμῳ δε γαλήνῃ καὶ βαθείᾳ εἰρήνῃ), is superior to human beings, but less than God" (*Somn.* 2.229; cf. *Fug.* 174; *Deus* 10-12). It would seem, then, that once again, true to his delineation of the Mosaic paradigm as entirely unique, Philo has placed his noetic prophecy at the apogee of the human ascension to God and has granted it superiority even over the mystic vision of all other members of the philosophical elite. The Mosaic summit of spirituality is thus marked by a state of absolutely serene joy, inferior only to that of the Deity itself.

Conclusion

We may thus conclude that a subtle and deliberate ambiguity shapes the expression of Philo's philosophical vision whenever a clash between the twin traditions that he seeks so devoutly to unite becomes unavoidable. In such cases, although he allows the Jewish side of his thought the dominant place in his presentation, he invariably tones it down by introducing some philosophical twist and by allowing the perceptive reader a glimpse of his true position. The more the issue cuts into the heart of his essential world view, the greater and more complex becomes his effort to divert the attention of his uninitiated audience from the deeper levels of his thought, while yet maintaining a narrow opening to his authentic views for his intellectually sophisticated reader. The philosophical portrait of Philo that thus emerges is that of a mind fully committed to a mystical form of Platonism. At the same time, it is the mind of a Jew who has remained loyal to his native religious tradition and has convinced himself that it was entirely possible to accommodate the Biblical text to his philosophical convictions. To this task he devoted the greatest part of his literary efforts, and were it not for the fact that the Alexandrian Jewish community in which he lived and wrote soon disappeared from the historical stage, his remarkable synthesis of Judaism and Hellenism would undoubtedly have become an integral part of the Jewish spiritual heritage.

CHAPTER FOURTEEN

Philo and the Rabbis on Sex and the Body

Amid the spate of recent scholarship on ancient views about the body, sexuality, and gender, one of the more persistent themes that has emerged has been the difference — and for some scholars, the virtual opposition — between Greco-Roman attitudes and those represented in the literature of ancient Judaism. Not surprisingly, given his critical location between these two ancient traditions, much of this scholarship has focused on Philo and his allegorical exegesis with its attempt to reconcile Scripture with philosophy. Thus, R. Howard Bloch locates the beginning of the tradition of misogyny in Western culture in Philo's interpretation of the Genesis account of the creation of woman. According to Bloch's reading of Philo,

> woman is by definition a derivation of man, who, as the direct creation of God, remains both chronologically antecedent and ontologically prior. This is at any rate, how Philo understood things (*Leg.* 2.4-5) ... Woman is conceived from the beginning to be secondary, a supplement. Here the act of naming takes on added significance. For the imposition of names and the creation of woman are not only simultaneous but analogous gestures thoroughly implicated in each other. Just as words are the supplements of things, which are supposedly brought nameless to Adam, so woman is the supplement to, the "helper" of man.[1]

The Fall, according to Philo as read by Bloch, is thus merely the logical conclusion of what is implicit in Eve's creation.

In his classic study "The Image of the Androgyne," Wayne Meeks has similarly characterized Philo as representing in the Judaism of the Hellenistic era a "pocket of real misogyny," principally on the basis of his using male and female as symbols of reason and sense perception and his associating with woman an extraordinary number of pejorative expressions.[2] Tikva Frymer-Kensky repeats the misogyny charge, though she softens it by referring to it as "symbolic."[3] "Greek philosophy," she writes in a vast generalization, "portrayed females as inherently and essentially different

---

[1] R. H. Bloch, "Medieval Misogyny," *Representations* 20 (1987): 10.
[2] W. A. Meeks, "The Image of the Androgyne," *HR* 13 (1974): 176.
[3] T. Frymer-Kensky, *In the Wake of Goddesses* (New York: Free Press, 1992), 210.

from men, and fundamentally less valued. The male-female distinction was one of the great polarities of the Greek dualistic system."[4] Even Dorothy Sly, who in her generally well-balanced analysis of Philo's perception of women assiduously avoids the term "misogyny,"[5] emphasizes nevertheless Philo's strong conviction that male supremacy is in accordance with natural law; she shows how Philo handles the biblical text in such a way as to avoid lauding woman's independent action, and how he views woman's life-purpose in a restricted way as derivative from that of the male.

An even more ambitious attempt to ground Philo's "misogyny" in Greek philosophical principle is to be found in Daniel Boyarin's fascinating book *Carnal Israel: Reading Sex in Talmudic Culture*, in which he characterizes Philo's attitude toward female sexuality as the polar opposite of that of the rabbis.[6] Much of Boyarin's argumentation rests on the sharp body-soul dichotomy inherent in Platonic thought, which he sees as leading "to a severe downgrading at best of the role of the body" (31). He thus consistently contrasts Philo's Platonic dualism with the monistic anthropology of the rabbis, citing as a demonstration of the latter the blessing Jews are enjoined to pronounce after urinating or defecating. Although the rabbis were a part of the Hellenistic world, their conception of the body marked a significant departure from views that had been assimilated by other Jews of that period, such as Philo, Josephus, Paul, and the Qumran community (34-35). Indeed, for Boyarin Rabbinic Judaism operates primarily as a sort of resistance movement against Hellenism. Whereas the rabbis greatly valued the flesh and controlled women and sexuality as highly prized

---

[4] Frymer-Kensky, *In the Wake of Goddesses*, 203. She does, however, candidly remark that she does "not speak from primary sources" (276, n. 4). For a nuanced survey of Greek philosophical attitudes toward women, see J. M. Rist, *Human Value* (Leiden: E. J. Brill, 1982), 132-41. A timely admonition against such oversimplifications is sounded by D. E. Aune ("Human Nature and Ethics in Hellenistic Philosophical Traditions and Paul: Some Issues and Problems," in *Paul in His Hellenistic Context* [ed. T. Engberg-Pedersen; Minneapolis: Fortress, 1995], 295): "Refutations of proposals that Hellenistic conceptions of human nature influenced Paul's own views have frequently been based on caricatures of 'the Greek view,' often based on an oversimplified understanding of classical sources coupled with a superficial understanding of Hellenistic paradigms of human nature." Cf. also D. Biale: "In reality, there were many Hellenisms, just as there were many Judaisms in late antiquity. By taking the most extreme expressions from the ancient world as yardsticks against which to measure rabbinic culture, one risks misunderstanding the Rabbis' position" (*Eros and the Jews* [New York: Basic Books, 1992], 37).

[5] Sly notes that Philo "would not have understood the charge of misogyny. He uses the word *misogynaios* only once, and in that instance it signifies men who tire of their wives and try to get rid of them by making false accusations of infidelity (*Special Laws* 3.79-82)" (*Philo's Perception of Women* [Atlanta: Scholars Press, 1990], 58, n. 22).

[6] D. Boyarin, *Carnal Israel: Reading Sex in Talmudic Culture* (Berkeley: University of California Press, 1993).

essentials, Hellenized Jews, by contrast, abhorred the flesh and feared women and sexuality. Boyarin thus sees the rabbinic movement as largely a rejectionist movement against the Hellenization of much of first century Judaism, including that of Palestine (77).

Here again, though, Philo is the key figure insofar as his allegorical procedure establishes the basic system of oppositions that ground both body politics and meaning. According to Boyarin,

> the allegorical reading of Philo and Paul and their intellectual descendants is founded on a binary opposition in which meaning exists as a disembodied substance prior to its incarnation in language, that is, in a dualistic system in which spirit precedes and is primary over body, thus allowing for the disavowal of sexuality (6, 9).

Boyarin's argument is powerfully stated but it is insufficiently nuanced and at times even rooted in misunderstanding. For example, Boyarin's critique of the Philonic allegoresis of the Adam and Eve narrative in Genesis is sharpened by his unfounded claim "that the creation of sense-perception (Eve) in the state of sleep (Gen 2:21), while recognized by Philo as a necessity, is profoundly and explicitly unwelcome to him." In support of this, Boyarin cites Philo's statement that "as it is, the change is actually repugnant to me, and many a time when wishing to entertain some fitting thought, I am drenched by a flood of unfitting matters pouring over me" (*Leg.* 2.31-32).[7] But what is repugnant to Philo is very clearly not "the creation of sense-perception and its effects on what was formerly pure mind," but only the fact that, at times, at the very moment that he seeks to concentrate on some fitting thought (i.e., the intelligibles proper to the mind), he is flooded by an influx of matters unfitting. Conversely he is grateful for God's coming to his rescue when he is on the verge of admitting something vile into his mind. To attribute to Philo, as Boyarin does, the view that God's creation of woman/sense-perception is unwelcome to him would stand on its head Philo's firm and confident conviction that all that God has created, without exception, is evidence of His absolute perfection and excellence.[8]

---

[7] D. Boyarin, *A Radical Jew* (Berkeley: University of California Press, 1994), 20-21.

[8] Boyarin's is virtually a Gnostic reading of Philo. A common Gnostic theme is that "woman is created by the demiurge in an attempt to distract man so that he will not become aware of the spiritual elements within him that make him superior to his creator. See R. Gershenzon and E. Slomovic, "A Second Century Jewish-Gnostic Debate: R. Jose b. Halafta and the Matrona," *JSJ* (1985): 21-22. In *Leg.* 3.67, Philo notes that "sense-perception belongs to things neither good nor bad, but is an intermediate thing and common to wise man and fool alike, and when found in a fool is bad, when found in a virtuous man good." Cf. *Sacr.* 105-06.

Similar problems inform Boyarin's treatment of rabbinic attitudes. According to Boyarin, Rabbinic Judaism, in contrast to Philo, "defined the human being as an animated body and not as a soul trapped or even housed in a body."[9] To elaborate on this last point, Boyarin cites the remarks of Alon Goshen-Gottstein that though

> there may be an existential confrontation, metaphysically soul and body form a whole rather than a polarity. Crudely put — the soul is like a battery that operates an electronic gadget. However, the difference is not one of essence. It may be of heavenly origin ... but it is not Divine ... More significant, the gadget and its power source ultimately belong together, rather than separately.[10]

To bolster Goshen-Gottstein's claim, Boyarin cites a passage in *Genesis Rabbah* 34.10, that likens the soul to salt that preserves meat.[11] It should be noted that this analogy derives from Stoic sources where, however, it refers not to the human soul but to that of animals.[12] Chrysippus says that the pig is given a soul to serve as salt and keep it from putrefaction, a witticism that is also picked up by Cicero and developed by Philo himself.[13]

Now, in the exchange between Antoninus and R. Judah the Patriarch, the salt analogy is applied to the fetus whose status was debated by many ancient thinkers, whether Iranian, Chinese, or Greek.[14] Plato and the Stoics thought that the fetus was endowed with a sentient soul only at the moment of birth, although for Plato, who classified plants as ζῷα or living creatures, the fetus could nevertheless be considered a ζῷον since it did possess a nutritive soul, whereas the Stoics, who also assigned the fetus a

---

[9] Boyarin, *Carnal Israel*, 33.

[10] Boyarin, *Carnal Israel*, 33-34. A. Goshen-Gottstein, "The Body as Image of God in Rabbinic Literature," *HTR* 87 (1992): 171-95.

[11] Theodor and Albeck 320-21 (cf. *b. Sanh.* 91b). The full text reads: "[Antoninus asked Rabbi:] 'At which stage is the soul instilled in a human being?' Said Rabbi to him: 'As soon as he leaves his mother's womb'. He replied: 'Leave meat without salt for three days, will it not become putrid?' The answer must be: From the moment that he [the child] is commanded to [come into existence]. And Rabbi admitted to him that Scripture also supports him: 'As long as my breath is in me and the spirit of God is in my nostrils (Job 27:3) and Thy command hath preserved my spirit' (Job 10:12) — when didst Thou give me the soul? From the moment that Thou didst command me." (translation in Urbach, *The Sages*, 220).

[12] R. Meyer, *Hellenistisches in der Rabbinischen Anthropologie* (BWANT 4.17-22; Stuttgart: W. Kohlhammer, 1937), 26.

[13] Cicero, *Nat. d.* 2.160; *Fin.* 5.38; Philo, *Opif.* 66. Translations from Cicero, Epictetus, and Philo (unless otherwise indicated) are from the Loeb Classical Library.

[14] For a good recent survey of the scholarly literature dealing with Antoninus and Rabbi on the soul, see S. Newmeyer, "Antoninus and Rabbi On the Soul: Stoic Elements of a Puzzling Encounter," *Koroth* 9 (1988): 108-23.

growth principle (their equivalent of the Aristotelian nutritive soul), but denied that plants were ζῷα, considered the fetus only as a part of the mother's womb (μέρος τῆς γαστρός).[15] For Plato, consequently, feticide is one of the regular institutions of the ideal state. Whenever the parents are beyond that age which he thinks best for the begetting of children, the embryo should be destroyed (*Resp.* 5.461C; *Leg.* 5.740D).[16] Aristotle distinguished between three stages of fetal development: the fetus was endowed in successive stages with a nutritive or plant soul (θρεπτική), a sentient or animal soul (αἰσθητική), and a rational soul (διανοητική) (*Gen. an.* 2.736a33-b30), and in *Politica* 7.1335b25, he advocates that abortion should be performed before the fetus has attained animal life.[17] The Pythagoreans, on the other hand, held that the embryo possessed a sentient soul from the moment of conception, and hence rejected abortion unconditionally. It thus appears that when the Patriarch agrees with Antoninus that it must be "from the moment [the child] is commanded to come into existence" that the fetus is endowed with a soul, he is undoubtedly not thinking of either the sentient or rational soul but rather of the nutritive soul, which merely preserves the embryo from putrefaction. This readily explains the rabbinic ruling that until the fetus emerges from its mother's womb it is not yet considered a separate person.

Boyarin's assumption that the rabbis' use of the salt analogy characterizes their conception of the body-soul relationship as such is therefore unwarranted. Other problems attend Boyarin and Goshen-Gottstein's shared view that the primary distinction between the hellenic and rabbinic conceptions of body and soul is that for the Platonist, and even for the Stoic, the soul is a fragment of divinity, whereas for the rabbis, the soul may indeed derive from the heavenly realm but is by no means itself divine. To this two things must be said. First, the distance between these two forms of

---

[15] Diels 425; Von Arnim 2.806; Philo, *Spec.* 3.117.

[16] See L. Edelstein, *The Hippocratic Oath* (Bulletin of the History of Medicine, supplements no. 1; Baltimore: Johns Hopkins University Press, 1943), 16; Winston, "The Iranian Component in the Bible," 202, n. 52; and W. Deuse, *Untersuchungen zur mittleplatonischen und neuplatonischen Seelenlehre* (Wiesbaden: Franz Steiner, 1983), 174-82. The Rabbis were evidently aware of the Stoic view that the fetus was "a part of the mother's womb," since some of them used the equivalent expression, 'ubar yerek 'imô (*b. Hul.* 58a; *Git.* 23b). (Philo mentions the Stoic view in *Spec.* 3.117). It is therefore likely that they were also aware of the Stoic view that the fetus was endowed only with a nutritive principle. According to Urbach, "among the Tannaim we do not find anyone who upholds, in the field of Halakha, the view that the embryo, while still in its mother's womb, is a separate body, and regards it as a living being" (*The Sages*, 243).

[17] Although Aristotle is willing to say that plants are alive, he is unwilling to call them ζῷα, living creatures, a term he reserves only for sentient beings (*De an.* 2.2.413b1-4).

dualism is not as great or as sharply delineated as it might appear, and the boundaries between them are at times somewhat blurred, although never explicitly transgressed.[18] Second, and perhaps more important, the mere fact of the divinization of the human soul does not in and of itself lead inevitably to a greater measure of asceticism, or to a more negative evaluation of the body.

To support the first statement about dualism, let me turn to some well-known rabbinic passages that reveal the polarities in the body-soul compound. The heavenly creatures, says R. Simai, derive both body and soul from heaven, the earthly ones from the earth, with the exception of the human being, whose soul is from heaven and his body from earth. Doing God's will assimilates one to the heavenly beings, whereas disobedience to it assimilates one to earthly beings.[19] In *Genesis Rabbah* 8.11 (Theodor and Albeck 64-65) it is said that the human creature eats and drinks like a beast, propagates like a beast, relieves itself like a beast, and dies like a beast. On the other hand, it stands erect like the ministering angels, speaks like them, sees like them, and like them possesses understanding (cf. *b. Ḥag.* 16a; *Gen. Rab.* 8.11 [Theodor and Albeck 66]). In King David's five-fold repetition of the words "Bless the Lord, O my soul" (Pss. 103-04), the rabbis find an allusion to five ways in which the soul resembles the Holy One. Both respectively fill and feed the whole world, see and are not seen, are pure and abide in the innermost precincts. "Let that which has these five qualities come and praise Him who has these five qualities" (*b. Ber.* 10a).[20] Finally there is the statement of R. Eleazar: "Let a man

---

[18] Although, for example, Goshen-Gottstein's remark that for the rabbis "the gadget and its power source ultimately belong together rather than separately" is basically correct, a very different view appears to inspire Hillel's response to his disciples that "the pitiful soul is nothing but a guest (*xenos*) in the body, here today and gone tomorrow" (*Lev Rab.* 34.3 [M. Margulies, *Midrash Wayyikra Rabbah* [Jerusalem: Wahrmann, 1972]], 777]. See Bergmann, "Die stoische Philosophie und die jüdische Frömmigkeit," 162 and 165; Meyer, *Hellenistisches in der rabbinischen Anthropologie*, 49. A similar notion is found in Seneca *Ep.* 102.24; 120.14 (cf. Cicero *Sen.* 84); 34.11. If Meiri's text is original (*echthes 'atya' we-sēmeron 'azla'*), as M. Margulies has suggested (*Midrash Wayyikra Rabbah*), the Greek origin of Hillel's statement becomes immediately self-evident. We may also compare the partially similar sentiment expressed in Hadrian's famous address to his soul: *animula vagula blandula,/hospes comesque corporis/quae nunc abibis in loca/pallidula rigida nudula?/nec ut soles dabis iocos* (W. Morel, ed., *Fragmenta poetarum latinorum epicorum et lyricorum* [Leipzig: Teubner, 1927], 136). This is rendered by A. O'Brien-Moore as follows: "O blithe little soul, thou, flitting away,/Guest and comrade of this my clay,/Whither now goest thou, to what place/Bare and ghostly and without grace?/Nor, as thy wont was, joke and play" (In Magie 1961-67, 1: 79).

[19] *Sipre Deut.* 306 (L. Finkelstein, *Sifre on Deuteronomy* [New York: Jewish Theological Seminary of America, 1969 {1939}], 340-41).

[20] Compare with *Lev. Rab.* 48 (Margulies 96, where eight points of comparison are

always consider himself as if the Holy One dwells within him" (*b. Ta'an.* 11a-b).

The clear implication of these rabbinic passages is that the human soul is a heavenly or angelic entity joined to an earthly frame. This is not so different from what Plato, in an influential passage of the *Timaeus* (90a), said when he identified the rational part of the soul as the daemon of each person, and later Platonism made no very clear distinction between daemons and angels. What Greek philosophers call daemons, says Philo, Moses is accustomed to call "angels" (*Gig.* 6-7). The soul is thus a divine component (τὸ θεῖον) superior in rank to its bodily partner, and the human task and goal is to become assimilated to it. The rabbinic formulation of the body-soul synergy does not much differ from the Platonist conception of the daemon as the part "that lifts us from earth towards our celestial affinity, like a plant whose roots are not in earth, but in the heavens" (trans. Cornford).[21] It must be admitted, however, that the rabbis never made bold explicitly to declare that the human soul was a "divine" entity, much less to make a statement equivalent to that recorded by Cicero: "Know, then, (says the ghost of Scipio Africanus to the younger Scipio) that you are a god, if a god is that which lives, feels, remembers, and foresees, and which rules, governs, and moves the body over which it is set, just as the God above us rules this universe."[22]

Nonetheless, the body-soul relationship is sometimes described in basically similar terms by both the rabbis and Philo, except that Philo speaks in terms of the relationship between the rational soul and the irrational parts of the soul, which are directly related to bodily functions. "Were a man," says Philo, "to do away with the mind, the eighth and ruling part of the soul (the seven irrational parts are the five senses, speech, and generation), he will disable the seven also" (*Det.* 168). Somewhat analogously, in a *baraita* cited in *b. Niddah* 31a, we are told that the father and mother and the Holy One are partners in the creation of the

---

provided); Philo *Migr.* 186; *Leg.* 1.91; *Opif.* 69; Diogenes of Babylon in Von Arnim 3.217; Seneca *Ep.* 65.24. See Winston, *The Wisdom of Solomon*, 252.

[21] See Meyer, *Hellenistisches in der Rabbinischen Anthropologie*, 32 n. 3.

[22] Cicero, *Resp.* 6.26 (*Somnium Scipionis*). Compare with Aristotle *Protr.* F 61 R³, Barnes 2416: "For mind is the god in us and mortal life contains a portion of some god;" Cicero, *Tusc.* 1.65: "The soul is, as I say, divine, as Euripides dares to say, God." For a more guarded formulation, see *Tusc.* 5.38. In *QG* 2.62, Philo asserts that assimilation to God cannot proceed beyond a certain level of transcendence. Cf. D. T. Runia, *Philo and the Timaeus of Plato* (Leiden: E. J. Brill, 1986), 343. For Philo's characterizations of the human mind, see my discussion in Winston, *Logos and Mystical Theology in Philo of Alexandria*, 28-30. See also J. Guttmann, *Philosophies of Judaism* (New York: Rinehart and Winston, 1964), 35.

human embryo, the former two being responsible for five components each, while the divine contribution is double that number,[23] and apparently includes those components that were designated by the Greeks as the nutritive soul, the sentient soul (רוח ונשמה *ruah> u-neshamah*), and the rational soul (דעת בינה והשכל *da'at, binah, we-haskel*, knowledge, understanding, and discernment). When one's time to depart from the world approaches, the Blessed Holy One takes away his share and leaves the shares of the father and mother with them. It is this, observes R. Papa, that people have in mind when they say, "shake off the salt, and throw the flesh to the dog."[24] Moreover, citing *b. Aboda Zara* 27b, "Happy are you Ben Dama, for you were pure in body and your soul left you in purity," Nissan Rubin notes that the body can be termed pure by the rabbis in the same way that soul is termed pure.[25] Here again, Philo is able to say of the seven irrational parts of the soul, which are directly associated with bodily functions, that in the wise person they are found to be pure and undefiled and herein deserving of honor, whereas in the soul of the foolish they are unclean and polluted (*Det.* 169). Indeed, in Philo's usage, the terms "body" and "flesh" (cf. *Gig.* 29-31) often serve to designate the irrational component of the human psyche.

We can now turn to the second weakness in Boyarin's attempt to set Philo and the Rabbis in opposition, namely, his claim that Philo's divinization of the soul necessarily leads to a great degree of asceticism. It is true that Philo speaks of the body as "wicked and a plotter against the soul," as "a cadaver and always dead," and claims that "the chief cause of ignorance is the flesh and our affinity for it." But this Platonic rhetoric, in which Philo sometimes revels, does not necessarily commit him to a severe downgrading or hatred of the body as such. That this is so can readily be seen from his description of Adam's body. The earth-born founder of our race, says Philo, was made most excellently both in body and in soul. In the first place, the newly formed earth out of which God had fashioned him was pure and free from admixture, and also elastic and easy to work. Second, God selected its purest and most thoroughly filtered part in fashioning a

---

[23] In *y. Kil.* 8.4, 31c, each of the three partners contributes three components.

[24] The parallel version in *Qoh. Rab.* 5.13 adds that "the father and mother thereupon weep and say before Him: So long as your portion mingled with ours, our portion was preserved from maggots and worms." R. Papa's remark is clearly made in light of Antoninus' well-known salt analogy, and he is himself either referring only to the nutritive soul component or else, if he was unaware of the Greek background of that analogy, which may well be the case, he is mistakenly applying it to the soul as such.

[25] N. Rubin, "The Sages' Conception of the Body and Soul," in *Essays in the Social Scientific Study of Judaism and Jewish Society* (ed. S. Fishbane and J. N. Lightstone; New York: Ktav, 1989), 47-103.

sacred shrine or dwelling-place for the rational soul that a human was to carry as a holy image (cf. *Decal.* 133, and a similar image in Plato's *Leg.* 969B). Third, and most important, in addition to the perfect symmetry of its parts, God bestowed on the body goodly flesh (εὐσαρκία) and embellished it with an exquisite complexion, desiring the first man to be as fair as could be to behold (*Opif.* 136-38).[26]

Furthermore, in his exegesis of Deut 7:16, Philo justifies God's promise of freedom from bodily disease on the ground that a healthy body is indispensable for the proper functioning of the mind that is devoted to wisdom and feasts on holy thoughts and doctrines, a mind in which the Deity walks as in a palace and house of God (*Praem.*119-23). Nor does Philo think that true self-control consists of mortification of the flesh and neglect of the body, whose well-being must not be compromised in any way (*Det.* 19-21). The wise person will even indulge in heavy drinking, though in the more moderate way of the ancients, "for the countenance of wisdom is not scowling and severe ... but full of joy and gladness."[27]

David Runia has noted that a similarly positive attitude towards the body is evident in the following comment of Philo on Gen 27:8-10:[28]

> If Isaac, as an old man, succeeded in eating two kids, how much more when he was young! This he did not through insatiableness, for he was continent as no one else has ever been found to be, but because of his wonderful structure. For it was fitting that he who was so great in virtue and the founder of so great a nation should have a formidable and wonderful greatness of body (*QG* 4.200).

Runia has pointed out, however, that although gymnastics are part of a sound education at *Spec.* 2.230, it is significantly missing in the ideal education enjoyed by Moses (*Mos.* 1.20-29).[29] Furthermore, he compares Plato's advocacy of bodily exercise and his ideal of symmetry between body and soul in the *Timaeus* (87B-89D) with Philo's approving references to the great spiritual athletes who despise bodily training (*Abr.* 48) and the philosophers who pay no regard to the cadaver-like body (*Leg.* 3.72; cf. *Agr.* 119; *Leg.* 3.190). Runia suggests that it may be unwise to attach too much significance to a few scattered passages in Philo, and correctly concludes that "the double attitude towards the body is just as markedly present in Philo as it is in Plato," whose pessimistic view of the body in the *Phaedo* is counterbalanced by the stress on its relative perfection in the *Timaeus*. To

---

26 For the combination of inward and external beauty, cf. Plato *Resp.* 3.402D; 7.535A.
27 *Plant.* 160, 166-67; see Von Arnim, *Quellenstudien zu Philo von Alexandrien*, 101-40.
28 Runia, *Philo and the* Timaeus *of Plato*, 321-22.
29 Ibid.

this I would add that, as a matter of fact, the few Philonic statements that apparently denigrate bodily training all occur in passages contrasting the unholy contests that the Greek states held in their triennial festivals with the truly sacred contests for the winning of virtue and take up a motif made popular by the Cynic/Stoic diatribe. The position of Heracles as the paradigm of the moral athlete in that tradition is occupied in Philo in the first place by the patriarchs, although Moses too is a wrestler for virtue (*Mos.* 1.48), as are also Joseph (*Leg.* 3.242), Enoch (*Praem.* 15), Noah (*Abr.* 35), and the children of Israel (*Praem.* 4-6; *Congr.* 164-65). The Cynic polemic against the folly of the national games emphasized the priority of the psychic over bodily ἄσκησις and the need to transfer the purely physical exercise to the intellectual level before ascribing to it any moral value. It is only natural, then, that in employing this popular Cynic/Stoic theme, Philo would not merely emphasize the superiority of the moral ἄσκησις but at the same time would tend to disparage its somatic counterpart.[30]

The heaping of pejoratives in describing the body and the claim that "in this life itself, what constitutes our self in each of us is nothing other than the soul" (*Leg.* 12.959b; cf. Aristotle, *Eth. nic.* 10.7.1178a2) is not an exclusively Platonic preserve. It is equally characteristic of Stoic references to the body, as many sources testify.[31]

Nonetheless, as Bonhöffer writes, the Stoics "did not understand the body's nothingness metaphysically as Plato did, but only ethically, and not absolutely but only relatively, insofar as the interest of the body was in competition with that of the soul."[32] If perfection is not achieved within the bodily existence, it is clearly the fault of the soul. Far from seeing the aspirant to wisdom as hampered by the chains of the flesh, Epictetus finds in his capacity, "while still in this paltry body of death" (ἐν σώματι τούτῳ τῷ νεκρῷ, cf. Seneca *Ep.* 24.19; 1 Cor. 15:31) to set his purpose nonetheless on fellowship with Zeus, a sign of humanity's triumphant freedom of the spirit.

Thus, for Epictetus, the body may be worthless as compared to the mind, but it too is ultimately a product of Deity, for

> from God have descended the seeds of being (τὰ σπέρματα) ... to all
> things that are begotten and grow upon earth, and chiefly to rational

---

[30] See P. Wendland, *Philo und die Kynische-Stoische Diatribe* (Berlin: Georg Reimer, 1895), 43-44 and V. C. Pitzner, *Paul and the Agon Motif* (Leiden: E. J. Brill, 1967), 23-75.

[31] Epictetus, *Diatr.* 3.22.41; 1.20.17; 1.1.11; 3.1.40; 3.13.17; 1.9.12.16; M. Aurelius 4.41; 3.3; 8.37; 10.38; 7.68; Seneca *Ep.* 41.4; 65.15-24.

[32] A. Bonhöffer, *Epictet und die Stoa* (Stuttgart: Ferdinand Enker, 1890), 34.

beings, seeing that by nature it is theirs alone to have communion in the society of God (*Diatr.* 1.9.4).

The body too is a divine creation, and is in "sympathetic" relation to all parts of the universe, even if it is especially our minds as parts and portions of God's being, that are "so bound up with God that He perceives their very motion as being a motion of that which is His own and naturally united (συμφυοῦς) with Himself" (1.14.5-7). Epictetus is capable of downgrading the body in the interest of moral admonition, but he never loses sight of its relative worth and is at times even carried away by transports of enthusiasm on its behalf.[33]

The same nuanced complexity informs Epictetus' attitude towards marriage and parenthood. Questioning whether the ideal Cynic should marry and have children, Epictetus writes that, in a city of wise men, there should be nothing to prevent him from doing so:

> for his wife will be another person like himself, and so will his father-in-law, and his children will be brought up in the same fashion. But in such an order of things as the present, which is like that of a battlefield, it is a question, perhaps, if the Cynic ought not to be free from distraction, wholly devoted to the service of God ... How, then, will the Cynic still be able to keep society going? — In the name of God, Sir, who do humankind the greater service? Those who bring into the world some two or three ugly snouted children to take their place, or those who exercise oversight, to the best of their ability, over all humankind ...[34]

We are reminded of the words of Ben Azzai, "What shall I do? My soul longs for Torah. Let the world continue through the efforts of others!" (*t. Yebam.* 8.7, though the rabbi probably would not have referred to the

---

[33] Even when emphasizing the superiority of intelligence, knowledge, and righteousness, he is able simultaneously to give the bodily functions their due as inseparable parts of a human being who is endowed with both body and soul:

> Why do you not know the source from which you have sprung? Will you not bear in mind, whenever you eat, who you are that eat, and whom you are nourishing? Whenever you indulge in intercourse with women, who you are that do this? Whenever you mix in society, whenever you take physical exercise, whenever you converse, do you not know that you are nourishing God, exercising God? You are bearing God about with you, you poor wretch, and know it not! [*Diatr.* 2.8.12; cf. 2.8.21]

This passage verges on the later Hasidic conception of 'avodah be-gashmiyyut, the worship of God through corporeality. See, for example, Yaakov Yosef of Polonnoye, *Sefer Toledot Yaakov Yosef* (2 vols.; Jerusalem: Agudat Beit Wi'elifali, 1973), 1:312.

[34] Epictetus, *Diatr.* 3.22.67-69, 77. See D. Balch, "1 Corinthians 7 and Stoic Debate about Marriage," *JBL* 102 (1983): 429-39.

children as "ugly snouted"). In neither case, neither that of Epictetus nor of Ben Azzai, are their statements evidence of absolute denigration of the body. The same position is illustrated by Epictetus' emphasis on the importance of cleanliness (3.22.86; 4.11), which is reminiscent of the famous story told about the early sage Hillel (*Abot de-Rabbi Natan B* 30, end).

In summary, the Stoic attitude toward the body is basically positive, but demands what non-Stoics would undoubtedly consider a measure of asceticism, but which from their point of view followed necessarily from their radical reranking of human values in light of the school's cosmological and ethical theory.

It should now be evident that the radical devaluation of the body is not an automatic consequence of the body-soul dualism of Platonic metaphysics. As we have already seen, Plato himself displayed a dual view of the body-soul relationship, the *Phaedo* representing a considerably darker view of the body than that of the *Timaeus*. Moreover, although in the *Phaedrus* the incarnation of souls seems to be the result of an intellectual "fall", in the *Timaeus*, the soul seems to be destined from the beginning to give life to a body. Mortal creatures came into being so that the Heaven or universe not be imperfect, which would clearly be the case were it not to contain all the kinds of living beings (41B-C). This inconsistency in Plato's thought was already noted by Middle Platonists who attempted to remove it by emphasizing one or the other of these positions, the majority apparently opting for the pessimistic view. Plotinus sought to resolve the apparent contradiction between the idea of a "fall" and the idea of a "mission" of the soul by maintaining both.[35] As for Philo, he seems to vacillate, offering on various occasions different reasons for the soul's embodiment that reflect either the pessimistic or the optimistic view.[36] Furthermore, as our discussion has demonstrated, the Stoics, who had rejected the dualistic metaphysical schema of Plato, were just as capable of devaluing the body in their attempt to emphasize the supreme importance of keeping it under the control of intellect. For the specific purposes of our subject, ancient attitudes towards the body, it is essential to decide in each case whether the author's apparent devalorization of the body is largely rhetorical, for the sake of moral emphasis, or whether it reflects an inflexibly dark view of the body unredeemed by a joyous celebration of its proper role as a part of the larger divine harmony, as is clearly the case in certain Gnostic thinkers.[37]

---

[35] Armstrong, *Cambridge History of Later Greek and Early Medieval Philosophy*, 255.

[36] Winston, *The Wisdom of Solomon*, 27-28.

[37] The Neopythagorean Numenius of Apamea (2nd c. CE), for example, in whose dualist world view matter is a positively evil force, regarded all incarnations of the soul as an unqualified evil (fr. 48, Des Places). See Dillon, *The Middle Platonists*, 361-79.

Having said this, we may now determine the precise relationship between the rabbinic view of the body-soul compound and Philo's conception of it. Both would have agreed that the soul is superior, deriving as it does from the heavenly realm and therefore capable of recognizing its Creator. Philo, however, views its separation from the body as an act of final liberation, whereas the rabbis look forward to its eventual reunion with it as the culminating divine reward for its fidelity to the life of Torah. Yet even here, the tension between body and soul is ultimately relieved by the rabbinic image of a body utterly transformed, a body that in a sense is no longer really a body, but one in which the normal bodily functions of eating, drinking, and sexual relations have finally disappeared (b. Ber. 17a). Moreover, while both Philo and the rabbis see the soul as at the very least akin to the Deity, Philo is convinced that the soul is itself a divine entity, being an imprint (ἐκμαγεῖον), or fragment (ἀπόσπασμα), or effulgence (ἀπαύγασμα) of the divine Logos (Opif. 146).[38] The rabbis, however, who were not interested in speculative philosophy and made no attempt to penetrate the enigma of God's creative act or the logical relation of the created to its Creator, generally shunned any formulation that might lead the unwary to the notion of human deification.

In the case of the body-soul relationship, then, the rabbis and Philo, though differing in emphasis, are certainly not opposed in their view. We can now turn to the second area in which some scholars have recently attempted to find another point of opposition between Philo and the rabbis, namely, in their attitudes to marriage and to sexuality. Boyarin asserts that "for Philo and his congeners, the return to the original state of humankind involves a putting off of the body'and sexuality and returning to a purely spiritual androgyny." He assumes that it is Philo's view that the first Adam ("the man according to the image" [Philo, Opif. 134]) was an entirely spiritual being, whose non-corporeal existence can be defined as both male and female.[39] This assumption, however, is not shared by many students of Philo (myself included), who see in his so-called heavenly man only the "Idea" of humanity in its technical Platonic sense. Some have argued that Philo's description of "the man according to the image" as "an idea or type or seal" (ἰδέα τις ἢ γένος ἢ σφραγίς) involves a loose usage of terms that are often employed for the paradigmatic "Ideas", but the three-fold emphasis of these terms makes it, I think, unlikely that this is the case.

---

[38] For the term ἀπόσπασμα, cf. Plato Phileb. 29b6; Diogenes Laertius 7.143; Epictetus Diatr. 2.8.11.

[39] Boyarin, Carnal Israel, 37, 43.

A discussion of this knotty issue is beyond the scope of this paper, but the fact remains that Boyarin's assertion is at least questionable.[40]

Boyarin further claims that the feeling of intimacy produced by sexual intercourse is a notion foreign to Philo. Again, this generalization is questionable. In fact, Philo's position is not so different from that of the Stoics in general who believed that while the main aim of marriage was procreation, this did not exclude the making of a life in common with the concomitant intimacy and mutual love.[41] Thus, in *De specialibus legibus* 1.138, Philo writes that Moses

> shows his wish that marriages, the first produce of which is a fruit sacred to God's service, should be not only blameless but worthy of the highest praise. Reflection on this should lead both husbands and wives to cherish temperance and home-making (οἰκουρίας) and unanimity (ὁμοινοίας), and by being of one mind (συμπνέοντας ἀλλή-λοις) in word and deed to make the name of partnership (κοινωνίαν) securely founded on truth (trans. Colson, with modifications).

In *Quaestiones et solutiones in Genesin* 1.26 we read that

---

[40] See Runia, *Philo of Alexandria and the* Timaeus *of Plato*, 336-38. For Runia, the "man according to the image" is a human being as a human being should and can be when the cares of the body have entirely fallen away. It is best, he suggests, to regard this in eschato-logical terms, i.e., a person as he or she is when he or she has left the body and all earthly cares behind.

[41] Musonius Rufus, fr. 13a (C. A. Lutz, "Musonius Rufus: 'The Roman Socrates'," *Yale Classical Studies* 10 (1947): 89; fr. 14, p. 95). As A. C. Van Geytenbeek (*Musonius Rufus and Greek Diatribe* [Berlin: Georg Reimer, 1962] has noted, these sentiments were certainly not common. Aristotle regarded the spiritual side of marriage as valuable, but he would not have accepted Musonius' demand of complete mutual devotion, since "in all friendships that involve the superiority of one of the partners, the affection, too, must be proportion-ate: the better and more useful partner should receive more affection than he gives" (*Eth. nic.* 8.1158b). Antipater, however, like Musonius, in his *On Marriage* (Stobaeus 4.22.25; Von Arnim 3.255) calls married life a perfect mixture (ταῖς δι' ὅλον κράσεσιν), as of water and wine, the partners sharing everything. For Hierocles (Stobaeus 4.22.24), too, a marriage in which the partners share everything gives the greatest satisfaction (See D. L. Balch, *Let Wives Be Submissive: The Domestic Code in 1 Peter* [Atlanta: Scholars Press, 1981], 4-5). Similarly, Plutarch taught that the marriage of a couple in love with each other is an intimate union (ἐνώμενος καὶ συμφυῆ); that of those who marry for dowry or children is of persons joined together; and that of those who merely sleep in the same bed is of separate persons, who may be regarded as cohabiting (συνοικεῖν), but not really living together (συμβιοῦν). As the mixing of liquids, according to what men of science say, extends throughout their entire content (δι' ὅλον κράσιν), so also in the case of married people there ought to be a mutual amalgamation of their bodies, property, friends, and relations (*Conj. Praec.* 142f). See Van Geytenbeek, *Musonius Rufus and Greek Diatribe*, 62-71 and A. Bonhöffer, *Die Ethik des Stoikers Epictet* (Stuttgart: Ferdinand Enker, 1894), 86-89.

the harmonious coming together of man and woman and their consummation is figuratively a house.[42] And everything that is without a woman is imperfect and homeless. For to man are entrusted the public affairs of state; while to a woman the affairs of the home are proper. The lack of her is ruin, but her being near at hand constitutes household management.[43]

The latter statement is focused on material things, but a stronger assertion is found in *Quaestiones et solutiones in Genesin* 4.154: "It is necessary to receive enjoyment of love and affection from a wife and fulfill the law of the rearing of children." Finally, in *Quaestiones et solutiones in Genesin* 3.21 we have a touch of Plutarch's vision of Love that escorts the married couple to the pure realm of heavenly Beauty (*Amor. prol.* 764e). Giving the literal explanation of why in Genesis 16:3 Sarah is called "the wife of Abraham," he says: "For with the concubine the embrace was a bodily one for the sake of begetting children. But with the wife the union was one of the soul harmonized to heavenly love (ἕνωσις ψυχῆς ἁρμοζομένης ἔρωτι θείῳ). Philo's great appreciation of the importance of the love and affection between husband and wife is confirmed by his statement concerning those whose marriages turn out to be childless, that "they deserve our pardon, for they are vanquished by the imperious constraint of intimacy and are incapable of dissolving the ancient love charms imprinted in their souls through long companionship (*Spec.* 3.34-36). His attitude here is similar to that of R. Simeon b. Yohai in the story related in *Song Rabbah* 1.31.[44]

Moreover, Philo sees in the loving interdependence of all things in the physical universe a token of the all-pervading harmony that reveals its perfection:

> For God has given all created things to all on loan, and has made no particular thing perfect, that it should have no need at all of another. Thus in striving to obtain what it needs, it must necessarily approach that which is capable of furnishing it, and that in turn must approach it, and both one another. For through this interchange and

---

[42] *Debêta*, literally "of the house", is a rabbinic designation for "wife" (*b. Ber.* 27b; *Taan.* 23b).

[43] Cf. Xenophon, *Oec.* 7.17-32; Aristotle, *Eth. nic.* 8.1162a 15-25.

[44] This story apparently reflects a well-known folk-motif. See R. Minard, *Womenfolk and Fairy Tales* (Boston: Houghton Mifflin, 1975), 146-55 and the fine discussion in Boyarin, *Carnal Israel*, 54-55. Even the misogynistic Lucretius is aware of the power of extended intimacy between husband and wife to generate love (*De Rerum Natura* 4.1278-87: "It is habit that breeds love ... Do you not see that even drops of water falling upon a stone in the long run beat a way through the stone?"). It is a repeated truism in Roman love literature that continuous intimacy and mere lapse of time may promote affection. See R. Brown, *Lucretius on Love and Sex* (Leiden: E. J. Brill, 1987), 376.

intercourse, even as a lyre is tuned through unlike notes, they were meant to come to fellowship and concord and make harmony, submitting to a universal give and take with a view to the consummation of the entire cosmos. Thus does love attract inanimate to animate, irrational to rational, trees to men, men to plants, wild to tame, and tame to wild, male to female, female to male ... heaven to earth, earth to heaven ... each needs each ... so that the whole, of which these are the parts, might be a perfect work worthy of its creator, this world (*Cher.* 109-12, my trans.).

Both here and in *De opificio mundi* 9, where Philo says that the primordial matter is shaped by the divine mind "into this most perfect masterpiece, this world," he echoes God's highly positive evaluation of his own handiwork, and R. Isaac's comment with regard to the "generations of heaven," that "when their Creator praises them, who may disparage them ... but they are comely and praiseworthy" (*Gen. Rab.* 12.1 [Theodor and Albeck 99]).

Philo's view that marriage is more than merely a procreative necessity and that it can be the occasion for genuine love and mutuality is thus intimately connected to his positive evaluation of the material world. Not surprisingly, scholars who have not understood the latter feature of Philo's thought have also misundersood his evaluation of woman, a misunderstanding that is at the root of the contemporary view that Philo is a fountainhead of the Western tradition of misogyny. This is the position that has been taken by scholars like R. Howard Bloch, cited at the very beginning of this paper, and it is one that has been adopted by Boyarin as well. Writing about Philo's account of Adam's fall in *De opificio mundi* 151-52, he claims that the Philonic version

> combines two ingredients endemic to the discourse of misogyny. The first is woman as misfortune, not merely after the fact — contingently, as it were — but necessarily — essentially — misfortune. The second is the ontologically secondary status of the gendered human, and "woman" as the name for that entity which provides gender.[45]

The Fall, then, is merely the logical conclusion of what is implicit in Eve's creation. This interpretation of Philo is faulty on two counts. In the first case, Philo does not say that woman is man's misfortune. Let us look at the passage more closely:

> Since nothing in the sphere of becoming is constant and all mortal things necessarily admit change and vicissitude, the first man, too, had to experience some ill fortune (κακοπραγία). And woman becomes the occasion (ἀρχή, literally "beginning") for his blameworthy

---

45 Boyarin, *Carnal Israel*, 80.

life. For as long as he was single, he was like the world and God in his solitariness, and received in his soul the distinctive impresses of the nature of each, not all but as many as his mortal constitution could contain. But when woman too has been fashioned, beholding a sister figure and a kindred form, he found the sight satisfying and approached and greeted her. She, seeing no creature resembling herself more than he, shines with joy and coyly returns his greeting. Love supervenes, matches and joins into one the divided halves, as it were, of a single creature, and establishes in each a desire for fellowship with the other with a view to the production of their like. This desire begat also bodily pleasure, which is the source of wrongs and lawless deeds, and on which account men exchange the immortal and happy life for one that is mortal and miserable (*Opif.* 151-52, my trans.).

What Philo is saying is that it was impossible for a mortal creature such as man, in spite of his great bodily and mental endowments, to be insusceptible of change and thus of possible wrong-doing. As long as he was a contemplative solitary focused entirely on God and the universe, there was every likelihood that he would become entirely assimilated to the Divine, but when a kindred creature was fashioned for him to be his mate, she necessarily became the occasion for diversion from the ideal intellectual life that might have been his without undue strain. Philo's description of Adam's initial encounter with Eve is clearly idyllic and touchingly romantic. It highlights the feelings of love and fellowship and the couple's hope of future offspring. Moreover, it is explicitly stated that it was not their tender desire for one another in itself, but rather the bodily pleasure that it naturally begot that became the source of potential wrongs and lawless deeds.

Boyarin's second point was that for Philo "woman" bears a secondary ontological status. He thus argues that in Philo's Platonic thought, secondariness in time is a figure for lower ontological status. Although Philo's position in this matter is not entirely clear, I find it difficult to credit the notion that he understands the temporal sequence of Eve's creation literally, inasmuch as in *Legum allegoriae* 2.19, the Genesis account of her creation is rejected as myth in no uncertain terms.[46] It is therefore much more likely that in *De opificio mundi* 151-52, where Philo is doing his best to give the story of Adam's fall some sort of non-allegorical meaning, he sees in it an expression of the limited intellectual scope that God has in

---

[46] See Wolfson, *Philo,* 1:121-22. As for Philo's acceptance of the literal sense of the story of Eve's creation in *QG* 1.25, Wolfson suggests that the difference in attitude may be due to the difference in the type of reader to which that work was addressed. On this, compare my remarks below.

his mysterious wisdom imposed on the human creature. He thus envisages the perfect intellectuality that might have been Adam's if that indeed had been the divine will, and points out the more modest dimensions of what was in fact bestowed on him. It is a rationality that must constantly grapple with the irrational feelings that are inevitably generated in the human psyche as a result of various biological drives, among which the sexual looms very large. The apparent temporal sequence in Philo's analysis is thus only a product of the parabolic scriptural narrative that he is expounding in philosophical terms.

What, then, are we finally to say about this complicated man's attitude towards gender and sexual relationships? That Philo was thoroughly androcentric seems to me beyond dispute. Nor would I wish to deny that there appear to be traces of misogyny in some of his writings. There are indeed a number of passages, mostly concentrated in those *Quaestiones et solutiones in Genesin* that deal with the story of the Fall, but also some that are scattered elsewhere in his writings, where misogynist sentiments seem to shine through even on the level of Philo's literal exegesis.[47] I would nonetheless maintain that the claim that it was Philo who "set the scene for the production of the systematic misogyny that has plagued western cultures ever since,"[48] is considerably exaggerated.

Whether Philo is more or less misogynistic than the rabbis is a comparative question that we may refrain from answering. What can be said with certainty is that his views on sexuality are not identical with those of the rabbis, that in general his rulings are more severe. Consider, for example, Philo's insistence that husbands who do not mate with their wives in order to procreate and perpetuate the race are pleasure-lovers (φιλήδονοι), whose act resembles that of "pigs and goats in quest of the enjoyment that such intercourse gives" (*Spec.* 3.313; cf. *Q G* 4.86; and Musonius, fr. 12 [Lutz 87, line 35]). Elsewhere he says that "in their craze for sexual intercourse they behave unchastely with their own wives," although he hastens to point out that, unlike the act of adultery, which is driven by an incurably diseased soul, such action is due to a bodily disorder, in which an excess of fire and moisture produces "unceasing

---

[47] See Baer, *Philo's Use of the Categories Male and Female,* 42. To the passages there listed, add *Ios.* 56; *QG* 3.3; *Legat.* 319; *Congr.* 180. The fact that such a large number of these passages are in *QG* would seem to indicate that these views are not necessarily those of Philo himself, since his purpose in that work, as G. Sterling ("Philo's *Quaestiones*: Prolegomena or Afterthought?," in *Both Literal and Allegorical* [ed. D. Hay; Atlanta: Scholars Press, 1991], 123) has suggested, was probably "to present all the options, whereas in the Allegorical Commentary he wrote from a definite perspective."

[48] Boyarin, *Carnal Israel,* 81.

irritations, itchings, and titillations" (*Spec.* 3.9-10).[49] The rabbis, in contrast, permit any specific act of marital intercourse even when consciously nonprocreative.[50] Yet even among other of his contemporaries, Philo's position is unusually severe. Among the Stoics, Musonius (fr. 12 [Lutz 87]) appears to be the only one who explicitly prohibits nonprocreative intercourse even within marriage (κἂν ἐν γάμῳ ᾖ).[51] Philo similarly reproaches

---

[49] A similar notion is found in Plato's *Tim.* (86B-E), where sexual intemperance (ἀκολασία) is said to be a disorder of the soul arising from the marrow, or that part of it that forms the seed, which, owing to the porousness of the bones, floods the body with its moisture. According to Philo, the diseases of the body, provided the soul is healthy (i.e., that its three faculties are well-tempered), do very little harm (*Virt.* 13-14; cf. Seneca *Ep.* 74.2). For Philo's comment on those who "behave unchastely with their own wives," cf. the fragment from Seneca's *De matrimonio* that tells the story of a man who fell passionately in love with his own wife: "Nothing is more disgusting than to treat one's wife like an adulterer." See M. Nussbaum, *The Theory of Desire* (Princeton: Princeton University Press, 1994), 473, n. 48. Similarly, "in a celebrated passage, Nachmanides explains that the general command 'You shall be holy' was issued because the scope of the Torah's injunctions regarding personal conduct notwithstanding, a lustful sybarite could observe them to the letter [yet be lecherous with his wife, *yiheyeh shatuf bezimat 'ishto*], and [thus] be 'a scoundrel with Torah license' (*naval bireshut ha-Torah*)" (Nachmanides on Lev. 19:2 [A. Lichtenstein, "Does Jewish Tradition Recognize an Ethic Independent of Halakha?," in *Modern Jewish Ethics* {ed. M. Fox; Ohio State University Press, 1975}, 69; the bracketed words represent modifications of the quotation from Lichtenstein]).

[50] *b. Yebam.* 12b. See D. M. Feldman, *Birth Control in Jewish Law* (New York: New York University Press, 1968), 65-67.

[51] As Van Geytenbeek (*Musonius Rufus and Greek Diatribe*, 72-73) has correctly pointed out, "Plato (*Laws* 835D ff) speaks about a law that would regulate all sexual problems in an ideal manner and which contains a measure forbidding all intercourse that does not intend παιδαποιΐα. Later, however, it appears that he merely forbids extramarital intercourse (841D-E). Pseudo-Ocellos (*On the Nature of the Universe* 4 [R. Harder, *Ocellus Lucanus: Text und Kommentar* [Dublin/Zürich: Weidmans, 1966] 21) contrasts pleasure as an aim with procreation; but when he goes on to say that the children of those who have had intercourse for the sake not of procreation but of pleasure are despised by gods and men, it appears that he, too, thinks of extramarital intercourse only ... This seems to make it probable that other passages, too, should be interpreted in the same way (e.g. Charondas, in Stobaeus 4.2.24 [H. Thesleff, *The Pythagorean Texts of the Hellenistic Period* {Åbo: Åbo Akademie, 1965}, 62, lines 30-33]; Iamblichus, *On the Pythagorean Way of Life* 210 [J. Dillon and J. Hershbell, *Iamblichus, On the Pythagorean Way of Life* {Atlanta: Scholars Press, 1991}, 210-11]; *Sentences of Sextus* 231-32 [R. A. Edwards and R. A. Wild, *The Sentences of Sextus* {Chico: Scholars Press, 1981}, 43]). Limitation of sexual intercourse, as urged by Seneca (ap. Jerome *Against Jovinian* 1.49; J. T. Noonan, *Contraception* {Cambridge, MA: Belknap, 1986}, 47]) and Sextus (231) is a different matter, as there is no principle involved. Musonius' opinion is exceptional. Philo and Clement (*Paed.* 2.10.90-102; S. P. Wood, *Clement of Alexandria: Christ the Educator* [New York: Fathers of the Church, 1954], 169-78) are the only moralists who share it."

It should be noted that Musonius, far from being a misogynist, is sometimes cited by modern feminists with approval. He boldly advocated equal philosophical education for both sexes, and argued vigorously on its behalf (frs. 3 and 4, Lutz 38-49). "Whereas,"

those who mate with barren women with "being in quest of mere licentious pleasure and destroying the procreative germs with deliberate purpose" (*Spec.* 3.34). Likewise, he explains the biblical prohibition of sexual relations with a menstruating woman (Lev 18:19) as due to the fact that during her period the field of the woman's womb is flooded (*Spec.* 3.32-33), and he grounds the prohibition of male homoerotic acts (Lev 18:22) in the fact that only bad farmers would labor on sterile fields (*Spec.* 3.38-40). Moreover, unlike the rabbis, who insist on the husband's obligaton to provide for his wife's sexual gratification (even when pregnant or meno-pausal), based on the biblical injunction (Exod 21:10) not to withhold "her food, her clothing, or her conjugal rights" (ענתה, *'onatah*; LXX: ὁμιλίαν), Philo, who interprets this verse allegorically, knows of no such requirement (*Migr.* 105).[52]

Despite the severity of Philo's rulings in these cases, it would none-theless be a mistake to see their respective approaches to the subjects we have discussed in this paper as diverging radically. Both shared a funda-mentally positive evaluation of the sexual act; where they disagree it is mainly in the matter of nonprocreative sex, and even here, as David Biale has remarked, the rabbinic attitude is itself not without some ambiguity.[53] In any case, it should be now clear that all attempts to derive Philo's views on sex and the body from his adherence to the so-called Hellenistic body-soul dualism are misdirected. Similarly, it is equally wrong to claim, as the rabbinic scholar E. E. Urbach has done, that the rabbis' denial "that the evil inclination resides in the body and the good inclination in the soul" was directed against "a widespread view current in the Hellenistic world." Neither Plato nor Philo would have consented to such a formulation.[54]

---

writes Van Geytenbeek (*Musonius Rufus and Greek Diatribe*, 60), "in nearly all other Greek moralists men keep their leading role, no trace of this precedence can be found in Musonius. Only once does he speak of men as being superior (fr. 12 [Lutz 89]), but for Musonius this is merely a reason for demanding the greatest austerity from men ... After Xenophon most moralists expatiated on the duty of women to avoid cosmetics and the like, but Musonius ... directs his attack on luxuriousness (τρυφή) to both sexes alike." Unfortunately, although Philo's attitude toward nonprocreative sex is the same as that of Musonius, his views are quite different with regard to the position of women (See D. Winston, *Philo of Alexandria* [New York: Paulist, 1981], 280-82). A feminist Philo was not. For a detailed discussion, see Van Geytenbeek, *Musonius Rufus and Greek Diatribe*, 51-62; and for a contemporary feminist who cites Musonius, see Nussbaum, *The Theory of Desire*, 322-24.

[52] On this topic see the fine discussion in Boyarin, *Carnal Israel*, 107-33. According to Philo, "those who take wives past their prime are to be criticized for destroying the laws of nature" (*QG* 1.27).

[53] Biale, *Eros and the Jews*, 56.

[54] See R. Hackforth, *Plato's* Philebus (Cambridge: Cambridge University Press, 1972

To be sure, Philo's philosophical convictions carry him beyond the biblical horizon and the non-speculative perspective of rabbinic thought. This does not mean that the rabbis were wholly untouched by the philosophical currents that, in Philo's case, shaped him so decisively and profoundly. We have already seen how the rabbis were content to borrow some Stoic theories about the nature of the human embryo and the kind of soul that informed it. Other scholars like Immanuel Löw, Julius Preuss, and Saul Lieberman have uncovered many other parallels between rabbinic natural science and that of the Greeks and Romans of their period. To what extent the rabbis were familiar with Greek philosophy is a debated issue.[55] As Harry Wolfson pointed out long ago,[56] and as Saul Lieberman corroborated,[57] there is not a single technical Greek philosophical term to be found in all ancient rabbinic literature, nor the mention of any major Greek philosopher (with the exception of Epicurus whose name was a common emblem for heresy). The single exception to this rule is Greek ethical teaching, especially that of the Stoa, which caught the attention of the rabbis and left its mark on their writings. Yet even in the case of ethics, it was not so much its theoretical aspect that attracted their interest as its practical side. If it behooves us to formulate the difference between Philo and the rabbis, perhaps, at least in part, this is where it lies: the difference between the theoretical and the practical.

[1945]), 61; and D. Winston, "Theodicy and the Creation of Man in Philo of Alexandria," in *Hellenica et Judaica: Hommage à V. Nikiprowetzky* (ed. A. Caquot; Leuven/Paris: Peeters, 1986).

[55] W. Harvey, "Rabbinic Attitudes Toward Philosophy," in *"Open Thou Mine Eyes"* (ed. H. J. Blumberg et al.; Hoboken: Ktav, 1992), 83-101.

[56] Wolfson, *Philo,* 1:92.

[57] Lieberman, "How Much Greek in Jewish Palestine?," 124, 130.

Index of Ancient Authors and Texts

1. Ancient Near Eastern Authors and Texts

2. Classical Authors and Texts

3. Hebrew Bible/LXX

4. New Testament

5. Philo

6. Hellenistic Jewish Authors and Texts

11:25	22
14:2	22
15:11	22

15:14	22
17:12-19	22
18:23	22

7. Pseudepigrapha

Ahiqar Slavonic no. 73   110n

Ahiqar Syriac Berlin 165 no. 55   110n

Apocalypse of Abraham
7	159n
22:14	55
23	45

2 Baruch
42:7	53n, 55
48:40	90n

1 Enoch
4:3	56
5:7	56
5:8	101
10:9	55n
18	101
19:3	102
33-36	101
41:8	48n
60:10 ff	102
67:1	47n
69:11	56n
72-82	101
91-93	101
91:10	101
92:1	101
93:2	101
93:10	101
93:11-14	104n
103:2-4	101
104:12	101
106:19	101

2 Enoch
49:2	53n

4 Ezra
3:8	45n
3:20-22	45n
3:22	48n
4	104n
4:10-11	56n
4:21	56n
4:30	48n

7:20-24	90n
7:47-48	45n
7:116	45
8:42-44	45n
8:60	56n
10:57	56n

Jubilees
1:23	46n
5:12	46n
22:20-21	56n

Liber antiquitatum biblicarum (Pseudo-Philo)
11:1-2	90n
12:3	46n
21:2	46n
22:7	46n
25:5	48n
51:3	90n

Psalms of Solomon
5:4	53n
5:6	47n
9:4	53n

Pseudo-Orpheus
3	90n

Testament of Asher
1.4-5	17n, 37n, 48n

Testament of Job
36.8	56n
38.3-4	104n

Testament of Levi
14.4	90n

Testament of Naphtali
2.2-7	48n
2.7	17n, 37n, 48n

Testaments of the Twelve Patriarchs   109n

10. Early Christian

11. Arabic Literature

12. Iranian Literature

13. Medieval and Renaisance Literature

Index of Modern Authors

Titles Available from Brown Judaic Studies

Brown Studies on Jews and Their Societies

Brown Studies in Religion